JUSTICE IN THE CHURCH

The 1992 Michael J. McGivney Lectures
of the John Paul II Institute for Studies
on Marriage and Family

JUSTICE IN THE CHURCH

Gender and Participation

Benedict M. Ashley, O.P.

The Catholic University of America Press
Washington, D.C.

The paper used in this publication meets the minimum requirements of
American National Standards for Information Science—Permanence
of Paper for Printed Library materials, ANSI Z39.48–1984.
∞

LIBRARY OF CONGRESS CATALOGING-IN-PUBLICATION DATA
Ashley, Benedict M.
    Justice in the church: Gender and participation/ by Benedict
M. Ashley.
        p. cm.—(The McGivney lectures of the John Paul II Institute
for Studies on Marriage and Family: 1992)
    Includes bibliographical references and index.
        1. Women in the Catholic Church. 2. Women in church work—
Catholic Church. 3. Ordination of women—Catholic Church.
4. Catholic Church—Doctrines. 5. Catholic Church—Clergy.
I. Title. II. Series.
BX2347.8.W6A74 1996
282'.082—dc20
96-5379
ISBN 0–8132–0857–2 (cloth: alk. paper).—ISBN 0–8132–0858–0 (pbk.:
alk. paper)

To the Knights of Columbus,
Carl Anderson, and Romanus Cessario, O.P.

Contents

Foreword

These lectures and my teaching at the Pontifical John Paul II Institute for Studies in Marriage and Family were made possible by the Knights of Columbus, by Carl A. Anderson, Dean of the Institute, and by my brother in St. Dominic, Romanus Cessario. I am deeply grateful to them for those pleasant years of teaching and fellowship. I want also to thank the Archbishop Carlo Caffarra, former president of the Institute, for his warm encouragement. My love and thanks go out to Donald Goergen, O.P., former Provincial of the Chicago Province of the Order of Preachers, and to the friars of St. Louis Bertrand Priory, St. Louis, of which I am a member and who make my life happy. Special thanks also to Prior John A. Farren, O.P., and the priests and student brothers of the Priory of the Immaculate Conception, Washington, D.C., for their gracious hospitality during my residence there. I learned much from Fr. Francis Martin, Fr. William Virtue, and Sister Paula Jean Miller, F.S.E., on the topics discussed in these lectures, and from Fr. Victor La Motte, O.P., Professor Mark Johnson, and Fr. Avery Dulles, S.J., who read the draft and made very helpful suggestions for this book. Its shortcomings remain my own. Fr. J. Raymond Vandegrift, O.P., James P. Riley, and Gloria Falcão Dodd were of great bibliographical assistance in preparing the lectures.

A version of Chapter III with a summary of Chapter IV has appeared in *The Thomist* 57 (July 1993): 343–80; like all the lectures it has been revised for inclusion in this book. Three appendices have been added here which were not part of the original lecture series.

I realize that my conclusions about the role of women in the church may seem sexist to some of my sisters in St. Dominic and sister friends in other religious communities to whom I owe so much. I would have dedicated this book to my sisters in the Order of Preachers if I had been sure that they would have felt honored by it. I also recognize that what I have written about sexual orientation will seem outrageous to some, but there is no greater sign of respect and concern than to try to speak to others the truth as one sees it. I sincerely ask forgiveness of anyone who may be offended by what I have written as a result of my failure to comprehend the whole truth or my lack of sensitivity in expressing my understanding of it. Only honest dialogue about justice in the church will eventually lead to peace and reconciliation in the "war of the sexes" waged so long in this fallen world, whose redemption, nevertheless, is assured in Christ and in Mary. I have confidence that as time passes it is the women of the Christian community who will show us most truly what Christ calls them to be in his church.

JUSTICE IN THE CHURCH

CHAPTER I

Equal and Unequal Disciples

Introduction: Justice in a Pluralistic Society

Today the Catholic church in the United States is often accused both from within and from without of preaching justice to the world, while itself practicing injustice. Is not the church unjust to its employees by underpayment? To its clergy by imposing celibacy on them? To its laity by neglecting to respond to their complaints of clerical sexual abuses, ignoring their concerns in the election of bishops, and failing to account for church finances? Is not the church unjust to its theologians by suppressing their free speech? To its ethnic minority members by imposing the traditions of white, Western culture? To gays and lesbians by its homophobic attitudes?

Yet no accusation of injustice in a church called "catholic," i.e., inclusive, is so embarrassing as that raised by its exclusion of women—an exclusion recently declared by Pope John Paul II to be "definitive"—from ordination to its priesthood.[1] This seems

1. The Sacred Congregation for the Doctrine of the Faith first took up the question in "Declaration on the Question of the "Admission of Women to the Ministerial Priesthood," *Inter Insigniores* (Oct. 15, 1976; *Origins* 6 [Feb. 3, 1977]), which was issued with the approval of Pope Paul VI. But since the precise authority of this declaration was questioned, John Paul II issued in his own name the "Apostolic Letter on Ordination and Women" (*Ordinatio Sacerdotalis*, May 22, 1994; *Origins* 24 [June 9, 1994]: 50–52). Both documents had been proceeded by National Conference of Catholic Bishops, *Theological Reflections on the Ordination of Women* (Washington, DC: National Conference of Catholic Bishops, 1973). For analyses of American reaction see Daniel J. Trapp, *The Discussion of the Ordination of Women to the Priesthood Among Roman Catholics in the United States, 1977–1987* (Rome: Pontificio Athenaeo S. Anselmi, 1989), and Terrance A. Sweeney, *A Church Divided: The Vatican versus American Catholics* (Buffalo: NY: Prometheus Books, 1992), who links it with other divisive issues.

especially unjust when it excludes members of the sisterhoods whose selfless and tireless devotion has done so much to build up the Catholic church in the United States. It is to this urgent question that the following reflections are principally addressed, but in the wider context of what "justice in the Catholic church" really ought to mean.

Our country is a pluralistic society in which many world views and value systems are supposed to compete in a free market of opinion. Among so many concepts of justice, by which one ought the Catholic church to be judged? In a pluralistic society who dares to claim that *their* concept of justice is self-evident? To make such a claim is to make reasonable dialogue impossible. The fair question is whether the Catholic church in the United States is honestly striving to abide by its own conception of justice, the very same that it proposes to others.

Too often what is just in the church is judged on the model of what is just in the state—in particular the democratic state—without sufficient attention to the merely analogical character of this comparison. Since different institutions have different missions, it would seem obvious that it is risky to presume that what is just in a democratic state is just for every human community without taking account of what is unique to each.

Therefore, in the first two chapters of what follows, I will deal in a general way with the principles of *equality, functional differentiation,* and *participation,* which are valid for just relations in the church as they are for most human communities. In the last two chapters I will use these principles to clarify the problem of justice in the special case of the relation of women and men in the Catholic church. I hope that this analysis will also be useful for those interested in ecumenical issues, since the question of gender roles is fundamental for the reunion of the Christian churches and their dialogic relations with other faiths and value systems.

Relations of Equality

Equality in Community

The major accusation of injustice in the church, accepted by many Catholics as grounds to demand reform, is that the church inconsistently teaches the *equality* of all human persons while treating them unequally. In her well-known book, *In Memory of Her*, Elisabeth Schüssler Fiorenza, claims that the "discipleship of equals" is at the very heart of the Gospel, and that to exclude women from priesthood contradicts the Gospel message.[2] This argument implies that gender discrimination is as unjust as religious or racial discrimination. Others extend this same argument to sexual orientation. Some even proclaim the equality of animals with humans and decry the "sin of speciesism"!

But is all inequality unjust? In a Christian perspective, an altogether just God has created a world of unequal beings, a hierarchy of creatures that ranges from angels to atoms. St. Thomas Aquinas argued that God was much too wise ever to create mere duplicates (we can leave that to Xerox!) since multiplicity as such adds no perfection to the cosmos. Every created spirit differs from every other specifically; among material things, though there are many individuals in a species, each is unique. Thus every being in the universe reflects the glory of God in some way possible to no other. As for human beings, who by our material bodies and spiritual minds are midway between atoms and angels, we are many individuals in a single species, yet each of us is so unique in our

2. "Only when we place the Jesus stories about women into the overall story of Jesus and his movement in Palestine are we able to recognize their subversive character. In the discipleship of equals the 'role' of women is not peripheral or trivial, but at the center, and thus of utmost importance to the praxis of 'solidarity from below'" (*In Memory of Her: A Feminist Theological Reconstruction of Christian Origins* [New York: Crossroad, 1984], 152). "The woman-identified man, Jesus called forth a discipleship of equals that still needs to be discovered and realized by women and men today" (ibid., 154). See also the section headed "The Basileia Vision of Jesus as the Praxis of Inclusive Wholeness" (ibid., 118–30). For a feminist who questions the notion of woman's freedom as understood by radical feminists, see Ronda Chervin, *Feminine, Free, and Faithful* (San Francisco: Ignatius Press, 1986).

person as to be a "quasi-species."[3] We often like to avoid the struggle for precedence by admitting that we are "different" without raising the question whether we are "superior" or "inferior" to one another. But if you are different from me, it must mean that you have what I lack or lack what I have, and are, at least *in that respect*, my superior or inferior. Is it, then, a shame to be inferior to another in some respects if one is first of all a unique and irreplaceable reflection of the infinite God?

Nothing, therefore, would be more unjust than to reduce this rich variety of creation to the sameness of equality (like so many units in a number), unless at the same time the differences, and hence the inequalities, of things were in some way reconciled with their equalities. To do justice in any human society, we must do justice to the similarities and the differences, the equalities and inequalities, and the superiorities and inferiorities of its interrelated members.

Personal Equality

Empirically it is not obvious that all members of the species *homo sapiens* are equal. In fact the modern doctrine of human equality is largely an abstract, essentialist notion popularized by eighteenth-century theorists. Experience, both historical and contemporary, does not directly manifest this equality, but rather the vast inequalities of the human condition.[4] The relations between human beings are largely relations of inequality: parent to child, teacher to pupil, employer to employee, bureaucrat to helpless citizen, male to female. Even in the peer relations of siblings, gang members, team members, and club members, a "pecking-order" is quickly established. Government has its familiar levels of township, county, state, and national authority, and every corporate organization its levels of authority and responsibility. Also, it seems that every ethnic group has at some point in its history con-

---

3. *Summa Theologiae* (Turin/Rome: Marietti, 1952) I, q. 47, a. 1–2. Cited hereafter as *ST*.

4. On economic and social inequality in the United States today, see Mickey Kaus, *The End of Equality* (New York: Basic Books, 1992), 25–57.

sidered its members the only true human beings and looked down on all outsiders as subhuman. Feminists complain that many American white males still despise women, children, and persons of color as inferiors. Slavery and caste- or class-distinctions exist, or existed not long ago, in America and in most cultures.

Yet in our national history other experiences have led us to acknowledge the commonality of human nature and to recognize that the differences among us are more superficial than the likenesses. In our great slavery crisis, it was religious conviction based on the Bible that led the abolitionists to point out the glaring but long-denied contradiction between our Constitution, which at that time supported chattel slavery, and our Declaration of Independence, which asserted our right to be a free nation based on the "self-evident" principle that "all men are created equal."

While the Jews, like every nation, were convinced that they were the Chosen People, the first page of their Scriptures declares that "God created man in his own image; in the divine image he created man, male and female he created them" (Gn 1:27), and from these first parents all the nations are descended (Gn 9:19, 10:5, 11:8). Jesus confirmed this teaching of Genesis by saying, "See that you do not despise one of these little ones, for I say to you that their angels in heaven always look upon the face of my heavenly Father" (Mt 18:10), meaning by "little ones" not just children, but all those least in the world's estimation.

Thus for the Christian, human equality is not rooted in some abstract theory nor only in the experience of our common humanity, but in God's revealed purpose in creating us as members of one family. We are created in God's "image and likeness" (Gn 1:27, 5:1–3) to cooperate with God in his work, "to cultivate and care" for the earth and all its creatures (Gn 2:15). This participation in God's care for the world indicates that, at the most profound level, the divine image consists in our participation in the intelligence and freedom of a God who is Three Divine Persons. Thus our personhood enables us to transcend the material world and share in the life of a God who is Spirit and Truth (Jn 4: 23–24).

This does not guarantee, of course, that all of us are equally intelligent or equally free, nor even that we are actually intelligent and free, since an infant, a sleeper, or a comatose person is neither. It simply means that God has given each member of the human species the radical capacity for intelligence and freedom. I will call this fundamental and radical equality *personal equality* because it constitutes us human persons.[5]

Of course, Americans today generally agree that we are all equal as human persons. Yet many deny that the unborn child is a human being, or they admit that the embryo or the fetus is human but claim that it is not a person, or they admit that at least the fetus (or the fetus near to term) is a human person but deny that it has human rights or, at any rate, rights equal to its mother's human rights.[6] They can take such stands without self-contradiction because they differ from Christians in their notion of personhood and the rights that flow from it.

For such Americans, values are not determined primarily by the objective order of creation, but are constructed freely by the individual or at most by social agreement. For them the objective scientific term "member of the human species" has no value implications. On the other hand, for them the term "person" *is* a value word referring not to objective, but to subjective reality. Hence a "person" has rights, but a mere "human" or a "potential human" does not.[7]

For many Americans, the minimal criterion of personhood is

5. In the terms of a distinction much used in Catholic theology at present, we might speak of the *transcendental* equality of human beings, as distinguished from their *categorial* inequalities in actual, historical social structures.

6. Thus Judith Jarvis Thomson in her often anthologized article, "A Defense of Abortion," *Philosophy and Public Affairs*, Fall 1971: 47–66, argued that a woman has no moral obligation to lend her body to sustain an unwanted child, in spite of the fact that, except in the case of rape, she is responsible for its being there.

7. For further discussion and bibliography see my paper, "Contemporary Understandings of Personhood," in *The Twenty-Fifth Anniversary of Vatican II, A Look Back and A Look Forward: Proceedings of the Ninth Bishops' Workshop, Dallas, Texas*, Russell E. Smith, ed. (Braintree, MA: The Pope John Center, 1990), 35–48.

the capacity actually to feel pleasure or suffer pain.[8] By that criterion the pregnant woman is certainly a person, and hence American society reasonably attributes human rights to her; but, since it is doubtful that the unborn child—at least in the early stages of development—has sentient and conscious life, our society thinks it reasonable to leave freedom of choice to the mother to decide whether to treat it as a person with rights equal to her own or as subhuman. Of course, this understanding makes it logically difficult to refuse equal rights to animals who certainly suffer pain—but society can draw the line however it decrees.[9]

If Christians are to have a dialogue with those who sincerely hold such views, they must recognize that humanists have sometimes been more sensitive to human suffering than Christians and have often been ahead of us in fighting for the rights of such victims. At the same time we must raise the troubling question, How secure is a doctrine of human rights that rests on purely subjective grounds and is subject to arbitrary social construction? What if some begin to maintain, as slave-owners used to do, that a certain class of human beings is after all not so sensitive to suffering as their more fully human masters? Animal suffering seems to be of a different order than human suffering; why not maintain, then, that some human beings suffer only as animals do and therefore need not be regarded as persons?

Basic Rights

Thus it is necessary to speak of *basic rights* which follow from *personal equality*, and to distinguish these from other rights which are less fundamental. It is necessary, for example, to distinguish my right, dependent on man-made laws, to a particular piece of property from my right to sustenance and shelter, which does not

8. See Joseph Fletcher, "Four Indicators of Humanhood: The Enquiry Matures," *Hastings Center Report* 4 (1974):4–7.

9. See H. Tristram Engelhardt, Jr., "Some Persons Are Humans, Some Humans Are Persons, and the World Is What We Persons Make It," in Stuart C. Spiker and H. Tristram Engelhardt, Jr., eds., *Philosophical Medical Ethics* (Boston: Reidel, 1977), 183–94.

depend on man-made laws but on the simple fact that I am human, i.e., on natural law.

It is true that the very existence of a "natural law" is questioned by some. Positivism has so deeply penetrated the legal system of the United States that even "conservative" legal scholars can dismiss the natural law as irrelevant to interpreting our Constitution.[10] Of course, it must be recognized that the law of the state differs from the natural moral law, and this for two reasons: first, civil law is concerned with maintaining public order and cannot regulate the details of private life without doing violence to the individual conscience, and second, civil law cannot maintain its authority if its rules cannot be effectively enforced—this means that civil law must be supported by public opinion, which often falls far short of the moral law. Hence, our judiciary cannot be blamed for seeking always to ground its decisions in the written law of the state rather than in some "higher law." This is the element of truth in the prevailing doctrine of legal positivism.[11]

Nevertheless, if we do not also admit the existence of human rights independent of and prior to the laws of the state, public opinion, and even the values of our culture, we have no grounds on which to criticize those laws or customs as unjust. In a racist or sexist culture there can be no claim to human personal equality if there is not a "higher law" by which to judge this state of affairs to be wrong and demanding remedy. Hence, it is generally admitted today that "civil disobedience" is sometimes entirely justified. We must not, therefore, fall into the error of the *Dred Scott* de-

10. Laurence H. Tribe writes in "'Natural Law' and the Nominee," (*New York Times*, July 15, 1992, p. A15): "Many conservatives criticize the judiciary for expanding its powers by 'creating' rights rather than 'interpreting' the Constitution. These critics talk of returning issues like abortion to democratically elected and politically accountable bodies. Clarence Thomas, judging from his speeches and scholarly writings, seems instead to believe judges should enforce the Founders' natural law philosophy—the inalienable rights 'given man by his Creator'—which he maintains is revealed most completely in the Declaration of Independence. He is the first Supreme Court nominee in 50 years to maintain that natural law should be readily consulted in constitutional interpretation."

11. For a criticism of legal positivism see John Finnis, "Natural Law and Legal Reasoning," in Robert P. George, ed., *Natural Law Theory: Contemporary Essays* (Oxford: Oxford University Press, 1992), 134–57.

cision, which on the basis of our Constitution denied the natural right of freedom to slaves. Nor can it be claimed that abortion is justified simply by *Roe v. Wade.*

Thus the notion of *personal equality* ultimately stands or falls with the natural law, that is, an order of things determined by the Creator and built by him into our very nature, not imposed on us by human legislators. This doctrine is a matter of philosophy based on human experience, but it is confirmed and supported by Christian revelation.

Any Christian view of justice must maintain that all members of the human species, whatever their age or condition or social status, possess natural personal equality.[12] It is on this basis that abortion, racism, and sexism must be declared to be grave sins against justice, because they violate personal equality. Other claims of injustice must be judged by the same criterion.

Relations of Inequality

Hierarchy and Functional Inequality

Does this personal equality of all human beings, then, exclude all types of just inequality between them? Our American public discourse often seems to take as axiomatic that to admit either natural or cultural inequalities somehow implies the denial of equal rights.[13] This is bad and very dangerous logic. Even if, for example, Asiatics were proven to have on the average higher IQs than Anglo-Saxons, that would in no way alter the personal equality of members of the two groups nor their basic rights. Similarly it is obvious that the unborn child is inferior to the mother in most

---

12. Vatican II, "Pastoral Constitution on the Church in the Modern World" *(Gaudium et Spes)*, no. 12. I have throughout used Walter M. Abbott, S.J., *The Documents of Vatican II* (Baltimore: The America Press, 1966), for all of the Council's work.

13. I recently heard the head of an organization for the deaf deplore the use of surgery to restore partial hearing to some deaf children on the grounds that this stigmatizes the deaf as inferior to those who can hear! Also statements about how unfortunate it is that so many children today are raised by only one parent are denounced as unfair and stigmatizing.

respects, including self-consciousness, moral agency, and the capacity to feel pain and pleasure, yet this in no way alters the fact that both are members of the human species endowed with personal equality and the same basic rights.

We must, therefore, distinguish *functional* from *personal* equality and inequality. Functional inequality requires an order or "hierarchy" of functions if these functions are to be coordinated in a unified action, yet some are outraged by the very notion of hierarchy. Thus a leading Catholic feminist theologian Sandra Schneiders writes,

It is not simply that those in authority are exercising authority badly or that those who should be obeying lack faith, humility, or some other virtue (although both are sometimes true). It is that the principle of hierarchy, which is the nerve of both secular and religious obedience as they have been traditionally understood, is being radically questioned and the principle of participation is supplanting it in more and more sectors of life.[14]

Why does Schneiders sees an opposition between what she calls "the principle of hierarchy" and "the principle of participation"? The term "hierarchy" literally means "sacred order" but today is also used in a very general sense of "a graded or ranked series," as for example "a hierarchy of values." It entered into theological usage in the fifth century in the writings of the famous Pseudo-Dionysius the Areopagite, a Christian Neo-Platonist who conceived the universe as a *linear* order of entities emanating from the Divine One in which each entity totally contains all its inferiors

14. *New Wineskins: Re-Imagining Religious Life Today* (New York: Paulist Press, 1986), 106. Speaking of the "crisis of obedience," she defines "hierarchy" as follows: "A hierarchical organization of society is one in which some members are thought to be really, intrinsically, personally, and relatively permanently superior to others" (p. 107). This seems to me a confusion between "office" (function) and "office-holder" (person). A hierarchy of offices does not as such imply a hierarchy of intrinsic, personal worth. Schneiders is then forced by this definition of "hierarchy" and consequent rejection of all "hierarchical" organization into the odd notion that members of religious orders vow to obey God and their community but not the persons who are officers of the community except when they express community consensus. I will try to show in Chapter II, in the section entitled "Participation in Decision," that the principles of hierarchy, as traditionally understood, and of participation are not opposed but that the latter presupposes the former.

and is totally contained by its superiors.[15] Pseudo-Dionysius applied this linear conception to the celestial hierarchy of angelic spirits and the ecclesiastical hierarchy of church offices. In such an ecclesiology the laity are totally dependent on their priests for all graces, the priests totally dependent on the bishops, the bishops on the pope, the pope on Christ, and Christ on God.[16] Another model of hierarchy, Aristotelian however rather than Platonic, was developed by St. Thomas Aquinas, who did not accept this linear conception of the order of being. For Aquinas the "great chain of being" is generically but not specifically or individually hierarchical.[17] Any entity in the chain of being is generically subordinated to its superiors but not totally so, since it also has unique specific or individual characteristics not contained in any of its superiors except the Creator. It likewise contains its inferiors only generically and not totally, so they are in some respects superior to it.

This Thomistic notion of nonlinear "hierarchy" implies an ecclesiology according to which the hierarchy of offices in the church does, of course, constitute its members as functionally unequal, yet because each member functions to make a unique contribution

15. Pseudo-Dionysius, *The Complete Works*, trans. Colum Luibheid, The Classics of Western Spirituality (New York: Paulist Press, 1987), 197 n. 11; see also Ronald F. Hathaway, *Hierarchy and the Definition of Order in the Letters of Pseudo-Dionysius* (The Hague: Martinus Nijhoff, 1969), xxi. For Pseudo-Dionysius this ordering is not one of "domination" but of "sanctification" through the three processes of "purification, illumination, and unification." For him, "a hierarchy is a sacred order, a state of understanding and an activity approximating as closely as possible to the divine. And it is uplifted to the imitation of God in proportion to the enlightenments divinely given it. The beauty of God—so simple, so good, so beautiful, so much the source of perfection—is completely uncontaminated by dissimilarity. It reaches out to grant every being, according to merit, a share of light and then through a divine sacrament, in harmony and in peace, it bestows on each of those being perfected its own form. The goal of hierarchy, then, is to enable beings to be as like as possible to God to be at one with him" (*The Celestial Hierarchy*, 3.1-2, in *Complete Works*, 153–54).

16. Pseudo-Dionysius divides the "celestial hierarchy" into the three orders and nine ranks of angels, and the "ecclesiastical hierarchy" into three sacraments (baptism, chrismatian, Eucharist), three clerical orders (bishop, priest, deacon), and three lay orders (monk, people, catechumens). Pseudo-Dionysius does not mention the successor of St. Peter, but for Latin theology this was an obvious application of the schema.

17. *ST* I, q. 105, a. 1; q. 45, a. 5, c.

to the common good, all members equally have a right to participate in the common good. Thus the "principle of hierarchy" and
"the principle of participation" need not stand in opposition, but
can complement each other in an ecclesiology based on a nonlinear
model. In such an ecclesiology, while the laity receives the broad
range of graces through the church's official hierarchy, this general
subordination of the laity to the hierarchy does not render the laity
more distant from God since each Christian has unique graces directly from God, mediated only through Christ, his Divine Son,
by Christ's Holy Spirit.

It would seem, therefore, that the demand of some liberation
and radical feminist theologians for the abolition of "hierarchy"
in the church is predicated on a linear conception of hierarchy and
a consequent identification of functional inequality with personal
inequality. Hence, for these theologians, the explicit Gospel teaching that all human persons participate in society with the same
basic rights and all the baptized participate in the church with the
same access to God in the "equality of discipleship" seems to make
hierarchical structures in the church a contradiction of the Gospel.

Anarchy and Consensus

The extreme opposite of "hierarchy" is "anarchy." While anarchism is associated in many minds with communism and ter-
rorism, as a political theory it has taken many forms.[18] What all
have in common is the rejection of the hierarchical organization
of decision-making power in society and hence the promotion of
a radical egalitarianism. For the anarchist, justice is based on the
principle of "one person one vote" so that power of decision is
equally distributed. This of course runs into the difficulty that the
majority can oppress minorities. Hence consistent anarchists believe not in majority rule, but in rule by *consensus*. They call for

---

18. On the varieties of anarchism see George Woodcock, *Anarchism: A History of Libertarian Ideas and Movements* (Cleveland: Meridian Books, 1962). On
the rise of egalitarianism in the United States and Europe, see Paul Johnson, "The
Coming of the *Demos*," chap. 12 in *The Birth of the Modern: World Society 1815–
1830* (New York: Harper Collins, 1991), 904–1000.

a utopian society grounded in total individualism, with no one having authority over anyone, but with everyone living in complete freedom from external coercion and acting together only by unanimous vote.

What has made anarchism as a theory plausible to so many has been the ugly historical experience that social and political superiority has always tended to tyranny and exploitation. But its utopian implausibility is also exposed by experience—the fact that no community has managed to live very long simply by consensus and cooperation. Yet many Christians, often under the influence of St. Augustine, who attributed the necessity of government to original sin, have accepted anarchism as an ideal.[19] Again and again, radical-minded Christians, have drawn, logically enough, from this faulty premise the conclusion that baptism abolishes all social hierarchy in a "discipleship of equals." Anarchism has also taken on secular form, not only in Marxist political theory with its prophecy of "the withering away of the state," but even, in somewhat tempered guise, in American conservatism—with its libertarianism and individualism expressed by the groundless conviction that "the best government is the least government."

Anarchists should reread that great utopianist, Plato, who in his *Republic,* came in the end to realize that true justice, far from producing functional equality among the members of a community, depends on a hierarchical division of offices. Since individuals cannot live satisfactorily by themselves, they need community; but community living would be of no advantage if each member still had to perform all the tasks of life. Hence these tasks must be divided up among the members. Plato concluded that, "Justice is one man, one task."[20] Thus functional inequality, a hierarchy of jobs, is what makes communal life possible and profitable for all.

A great political realist, Aristotle, carried this argument still further in his *Politics,* which convinced St. Thomas Aquinas of its truth and inspired him to add some finishing touches. My revered

---

19. Augustine, *De civitate Dei,* bk. 19, chap. 15; cf. book 4, chap. 4.
20. Plato, *Republic,* trans. I.A. Richards (Cambridge: Cambridge University Press, 1966), 4.433a4.

teacher, the philosopher and defender of democracy, Yves Simon,[21] demonstrated on Thomistic principles that it is a fallacy to suppose that authority and obedience are necessary only between persons of unequal wisdom or virtue, as for example, between parent and child, expert and layman, teacher and pupil. In fact, even in an ideal society of mature persons entirely equal in ability and virtue, effective unity of action for the common good is impossible without a hierarchy of authority and obedience and the functional inequality it generates.

The reason, pointed out by St. Thomas Aquinas,[22] that such authority is necessary even in a community of equals is that the judgment of human practical reason is essentially indeterminate, that is, in practical decisions it is seldom the case that there is one way to achieve a goal that is clearly superior to every other way. Usually each of the various means to the same end has its own advantages and disadvantages, so that no single, absolute reason can be given to choose one rather than another. If that were not so, there would be no rational human freedom of choice. Thus the very fact that human beings are free necessitates that if they are to live in community and agree on certain common actions necessary for their communal life, they must obey someone in authority who has final free and determinative judgment.

This authority need not always be vested in a single person, but perhaps in a representative body, or in the vote of the majority. It does always require obedience on the part of the members of the community, even those whose own free personal judgment disagrees with the authority's judgment—provided, of course, that authority does not transgress the limits on its power set by the natural and divine law on which its own justification rests. Therefore, contrary to St. Augustine and the anarchists, the existence of government is not the result of sin but of the finitude, freedom,

21. *A General Theory of Authority* (Notre Dame, IN: University of Notre Dame Press, 1962).

22. *ST* II–II, q. 47, a. 3, ad 3, citing Aristotle, *Nicomachean Ethics* 3.5–6. Cf., Aquinas's commentary, *In X libros Ethicorum Aristotelis ad Nicomachum*, ed. R. M. Spiazzi (Turin/Rome: Marietti, 1949), lect. 8–10, and *ST* I–II, q. 13, a. 6; q. 14, a. 4; q. 17, a. 1, ad 2; a. 7 c.

and sociability of human beings as originally created through God's goodness.

Role and Status

The distinction I have made between the just personal equality of members of a community endowed with equal basic rights and their functional inequality based on the different contributions they make to the common good is complicated by a further distinction between what sociologists term "role" and what they term "status." In a community some roles, i.e., functions, are easily transferred from one person to another. For example, in an athletic team, a particular position may be played by different members of the team. But other functions more or less permanently determine the position of the functionaries in the organization, i.e., give them a "status." This distinction between role and status does not invalidate that between the equality of persons as members of the society and their inequality in functions or roles, but it helps to explain why so often the two distinctions become confused, and those who have subordinate roles are thought to be inferior also as persons.

That the notion of "status" is not irrelevant to the Christian community is clear from the theology of the "rites of initiation," namely, baptism, confirmation, and Holy Communion. Catechumens do not have the same status in the Christian community as the baptized, although they may be already performing some of the same functions of witness and service.[23] They are not yet fully members of the community, although the community welcomes them as persons. Moreover baptism and confirmation are not merely an external legal act of admission to the community. These sacraments "seal" the person with sacramental "characters" which

23. Thus Pseudo-Dionysius recognizes a threefold status for the laity in the church, namely, catechumens, the baptized, and monks, as he recognizes the same for the clergy: the deacons, priests, and bishops (*The Ecclesiastical Hierarchy*, chap. 6). In the ancient church this was expressed by the location of each status in the sacred space of the church. The post-Vatican II urge to remove the altar rail and gather everybody together around the altar would probably have seemed to Dionysius a violation of cosmic order.

are genuine, permanent transformations of persons, giving them the status of an adopted and Spirit-anointed daughter or son of God for eternal life. Indeed, the term "adopted" is too weak since legal adoption cannot cause a child to be reborn or recreated as baptism really does.

Furthermore, within the community of the baptized, the confirmed have a different status than the merely baptized,[24] and the ordained still another status, since each of these sacraments impresses a permanent sacramental character. An ordained priest, according to the traditional citation of Psalm 110, is "a priest forever" (cf. Heb 5:6) even if the church for a good reason dispenses him from exercising his ministry. The merely "functional" concept of priesthood, accepted by some Protestants as regards their own ministers—according to which any member of the congregation when necessary can perform all the functions of the ordained minister—is not acceptable in Catholic or Orthodox tradition because some functions require not only functional competency but also the status of priest as effected by the character of ordination, especially the administration of the sacraments of the Eucharist, anointing, reconciliation, and (for holy orders) episcopal consecration.[25]

This does not mean, of course, that the confirmed or ordained person is any more a member of the church than are those simply

24. The exact nature of the sacrament of confirmation and its relation to that of baptism is still much debated among theologians faced with the very different practices in the Eastern and Western churches. On the present understanding of the Latin church see *The Catechism of the Catholic Church*, no. 1303.

25. In cases of necessity, the church recognizes "extraordinary" ministers for certain sacraments. Anyone intending to baptize as the church does baptizes validly. Deacons can witness marriages. Priests can confirm. In the Middle Ages confession—probably not sacramental—was sometimes made to laypersons and, just as again today, laypersons distributed Holy Communion. Could the church in necessity recognize laymen and women as extraordinary celebrants of the sacraments of the Eucharist, reconciliation, and anointing of the sick? On this basis some have argued that Anglican and even other Protestant ministers are validly ordained. Of course, this would not solve the problem of justice, since the "extraordinary" woman minister would still lack a status equal to that of the ordained priest. It would seem that the same apostolic tradition appealed to in *Ordinatio Sacerdotalis* would apply here also: the church has never recognized extraordinary ministers for those three sacraments.

baptized. Baptism is the rebirth into eternal life and no difference can equal the difference in status between the dead and the living. But within the life of the Christian community there can be an inequality of status as there is an inequality of the functions which flow from these differences in status.

Although the sacrament of matrimony and consecration by religious vows do not produce special "characters" such as those imprinted by baptism, confirmation, and ordination, they do establish persons in a special status in the church. Although religious consecration transcends death it adds no character to the baptismal one, but rather is a "second baptism," i.e., not a repetition of baptism but its renewal by a more profound commitment. Matrimony produces no permanent character because it ends with the death of the partner. "When they rise from the dead, they neither marry nor are given in marriage, but are like the angels in heaven" (Mk 12:25). Yet a marriage is sacramentally sealed by the union of the couple "in one flesh" (Gn 2:24, Mk 10:8), creating a status until the death of a partner. Thus within the Christian community, while all members are reborn persons who are equally children of God by baptism, there is also a variety of functions and the gifts to perform them. Moreover, though some of these functions are common to all, others are distributed to different members, and of the latter, some can be exchanged, while others require a permanent commitment to service and hence produce differences of status. Thus any conception of the Christian community that identifies "justice" with egalitarianism or on principle rules out "hierarchy" is wholly inadequate to describe its complex, organic, and dynamic unity.

Equal Opportunity and Exclusion

Does this deny the principle, so dear in our American tradition, of "equality of opportunity"? In the United States we readily grant that there has to be a range of functions from the president to the lowliest citizen, and from the CEO of a corporation to the janitor, but we proudly maintain that every boy and girl should have the opportunity to be president of a corporation and of the nation. Is not this the real question about the church's refusal to ordain women? Is it not obviously unjust to refuse to at least fifty percent of the baptized members of the church the opportunity to function as bishops and priests or, what is perhaps even more serious, to attain to a status whose dignity makes clear that women are not second-class citizens?

To answer this question will require the rest of this book, but let us first be sure that we understand what this notion of "equal opportunity" really means. Obviously it does *not* mean that everyone will actually become president or priest. While no women become priests in the Catholic church, very few men do either. Nor does it mean that anyone who wants to be president will actually be elected. What it means is that all whom the community judges qualified can become president. The question, therefore, is whether the Christian community judges that gender is a qualification for priesthood. Moreover, this must be a judgment based not on purely human criteria, but on what the Christian faith tells us Christian priesthood must be.[26] Therefore, we can grant that there should be equal opportunity in the church, and still not have settled whether this requires the ordination of women.

It follows from this analysis, that the text of St. Paul, so often cited as decisive in ecclesiological questions, "There is neither Jew nor Greek, there is neither slave nor free person, there is not male and female; for you are all one in Christ Jesus" (Gal 3:28), cannot be used to prove that in the church there ought to be no hierarchy of status.[27] Paul is here preaching against those who claimed a

26. Although polls have varied, it would seem that in the United States a majority of Catholics queried have replied that they would accept women priests. So would I, if the church through its magisterium came to a definitive decision that according to Scripture and Tradition the church has the authority from Christ to ordain women to priesthood; but without such a decision we would have no way of knowing how to receive the authentic sacraments of the Eucharist, reconciliation, or anointing of the sick.

27. In Col 3:11, the parallel to Gal 5:8, "male and female" is omitted. Since many biblicists consider *Colossians* deuteropauline and hence late, a feminist exegete might well cite this omission as evidence of the early church's alleged retreat from Jesus' radical teaching on "discipleship of equals" back to Jewish or Hellenistic sexism. But it is also possible that Paul's statement in Gal 5:28 about the equality of male and female was mistakenly interpreted by some women in the

different status in the church for the Jews who practiced the Law compared with the Gentiles who did not. All the baptized, he says, are by baptism "one in Christ Jesus." To convert this specific statement into a general principle ruling out all hierarchy of status within the church is arbitrary and contradictory to Paul's own conception of the church as an organism having a diversity of "organs" and "functions" (1 Cor 13).

We cannot leave this topic without also considering the case of those persons who are excluded from the community and hence, it would seem, are deprived of the basic rights common to its members. At one time it was almost universally the case, and is still so today in some places, that a considerable part of the human family were in the status of slaves (or later of serfs), who, as Aristotle said, are valuable to the community for their services but not as persons, and who share only in the "trickle down" of the common good. Even in our modern democracies we find it necessary to deport aliens and to imprison many of our own citizens as criminals and even to execute them.

The Christian church has never claimed the right to execute capital punishment; however, for centuries it tolerated the institution of slavery, and it has always enforced sanctions for sins and for violations of church law, and has, often very freely, excommunicated members for heresy and other offenses. It has defended such actions on the basis of the Old Law which prescribed not only monetary punishments, but also corporal punishments, the death penalty, and holy war. It has also appealed to the teachings of St. Paul (Rom 13:4) and of St. Peter (or attributed to him, 1 Pt 3:13–14) justifying the use of the "sword" by the state, and of excommunication by the church (1 Cor 5:4–5).

Some have seen in the teachings of Jesus on nonviolence (Mt 5:38–48) a rejection of all coercion either by state or church. Carried to its extreme, philosophical anarchism comes to the same

---

Corinthian church to favor the enthusiastic behavior that he refers to in 1 Cor 11:12–13 as needing to be moderated for the sake of avoiding scandal, and that Paul or his pseudonymous follower had this in mind when writing Col 3:11.

conclusion. If all decision is by consensus, then no one who disagrees with the majority can be coerced to obey their will. This is not the place to discuss the complicated question of Christian nonviolence in any detail,[28] but only to make the point that the very concept of justice and of basic human rights becomes meaningless if the violation of justice and human rights is ignored and not effectively opposed. Jesus taught that the ultimately most effective opposition to injustice is the Cross, i.e., the willingness to give up one's own life rather than to do what is unjust. We must understand Jesus' teaching on nonviolence in the context of the whole New Testament, which authorizes the moderate and merciful use of coercion in the cause of justice, even to the point of just war and capital punishment by the state, and excommunication by the church. When lesser penalties can maintain justice, we are obliged to refrain from greater ones, and this raises grave doubts whether capital punishment, war, or excommunication can do more good than harm under our present conditions.

Moreover, the necessity of maintaining justice does not altogether exclude the criminal from society or the heretic from the church. Exclusion from the human and divine community is what we mean by "hell." Those destined for hell exclude themselves by willingly and deliberately rejecting God's company in favor of their own autonomy. This self-exclusion is known only to themselves and to God.[29] Therefore, in this life the state must always be concerned for the basic human rights and human dignity even of the alien and the criminal, and its punishment of the criminal must be limited to the maintenance of public standards of justice and must aim at their rehabilitation. The church must likewise have no other motives in excommunication than the spiritual welfare of the other

28. See *The Catechism of the Catholic Church*, nos. 2266–68 on capital punishment; nos. 2307–17 on just war; and no. 1463 on excommunication. The frequent statements of the U.S. bishops deploring capital punishment are not contradictory to the traditional Catholic teaching on this subject, but are a prudential judgment on its necessity, efficacy, and justice in the concrete situation of today's society.

29. Ibid., nos. 1034–41.

members of the church and of the public, and the conversion and reconciliation of the excommunicated.

Primacy of Service

Christian Service

How then are we to reconcile relations of personal equality and basic human rights with the relations of functional inequality necessary for communal life? Some might think that the apparent contradiction between these two kinds of relations demonstrates the paradoxical, dialectical character of the human person. Certainly the struggle between individual freedom and the demands of social order is one of the principal facts of human historical experience, and the context of our American lives. Its actual resolution is the aim of most of the decisions of our lives, and a perfect solution is only an eschatological hope. Nevertheless, we must be able to give at least a theoretical resolution to this question or be forced to admit that "justice" is an empty word.

Fortunately, the Gospel does give a profound answer to this problem, an answer which can be philosophically confirmed. St. Paul was confronted by a "crisis of authority" in the Corinthian church. Some of the Corinthians, no doubt reasoning pretty much as St. Augustine was to do, had concluded that human authority was made necessary only by sin. If Christians were now freed by Christ from sin to live in the Holy Spirit, all these social structures resulting from sin must have ceased to oblige, and perfect equality must prevail among all the baptized. Paul gave a straight answer to the Corinthians:[30]

There are different kinds of gifts but one Spirit; there are different forms of service but the same Lord. . . . As a body is one though it has many

30. I am well aware that any author today who quotes the Bible without exegetical and hermeneutical discussion is open to the common charge of "proof-texting." The texts I cite are ones that, after study and reflection, seem to me pertinent and instructive, but that I have no room here to defend. Readers may evaluate the relevance of the texts for themselves.

parts, and all the parts of body, though many, are one body, so also Christ. For in one Spirit we were all baptized into one body. . . . If they were all one part, where would the body be? But as it is, there are many parts but one body. . . . God has so constructed the body as to give greater honor to a part that is without [honor]. . . . If one part is honored, all the parts share its joy." (1 Cor 12:4–26)

Thus Paul is saying that while all members of the Christian community are equal in that all have the right to the same truth of the Gospel, the same sacraments, and the same life of holiness, this is not contradictory to the existence of authority and of a diversity of services within the community. Moreover, Paul faces the fact that this means a hierarchy or scale of superior and inferior offices. As long as these are exercised for the common good of the church, this inequality does not contradict the more fundamental equality of membership, but *is in its service.*

In order to defend this teaching rhetorically, Paul makes use of the analogy, familiar to the Greek and Roman philosophers, between a community and the human body.[31] He gives this a specifically Christian interpretation when he says that the members of highest dignity must serve those of lowest dignity. Since, for Paul, Christ is the Head of the "mystical Body" of the church, this is an allusion to Christ's humble service of the "little ones." Did not Jesus say at the Last Supper, "If, I, therefore, the master and teacher, have washed your feet, you ought to wash one another's feet" (Jn 13:14)?

This teaching seems to go back to the answer given by Jesus himself to James and John when they were quarreling about which one should be highest in his kingdom. If Jesus had been an anarchist he would have corrected them by declaring that in his kingdom all will be equal. But he promised the apostles that in the kingdom they would "sit on twelve thrones judging the twelve

31. See Hans Conzelmann, *1 Corinthians,* Hermeneia Commentaries, (Philadelphia: Fortress Press, 1975), 210–15, and Christophe Senft, *La première épître de Saint Paul aux Corinthiens,* (Delachaux and Nestlé, 1979), 161–62, on the use of this body-society analogy in Hellenistic, especially Stoic, thought.

tribes of Israel" (Mt 19:28, Lk 22:30).[32] Moreover, in the Johannine literature, Jesus clearly claims to be the head of the church and demands absolute obedience from its members: "You call me 'teacher' and 'master,' and rightly so, for indeed I am" (Jn 13:13). So the answer Jesus gave James and John about who should be first in the kingdom was not that of anarchism: "You know that those who are recognized as rulers over the Gentiles lord it over them, and their great ones make their authority over them felt. But it shall not be so among you. Rather, whoever wishes to be great among you will be their servant; whoever wishes to be first among you will be the slave of all. For the Son of Man did not come to be served but to serve and to give his life as a ransom for many (Mk 10:42–45)."

Thus Jesus' evangelical reconciliation of personal equality with functional inequality correlates with the philosophical reconciliation, which is to say that functional inequality is *subordinate* to personal equality when it is exercised for the common good, which consists precisely in the interrelated personal good of all the members of the community. Jesus did not call for the anarchic abolition of the power structures of family, state, and organized religion, but rather for their employment in service of the community.

Yet the Christian answer transcends the philosophical answer, since it recognizes, as the Corinthians and St. Augustine did, how deeply rooted in the sin of the world is the abuse of authority, and it therefore commands those invested with authority in the church to imitate Christ's total sacrifice of himself for the least member of the community. Christian authority, therefore, must be not only a servant authority but a sacrificial authority. Christ is Lord as suffering servant. Only if authority imitates Jesus in this emptying (*kenosis*, Phil 2:7) of himself of all mere self-seeking and acts out

32. A text from the early hypothetical source Q, but questioned as authentically dominical by the hypercritical "Jesus Seminar" because it reflects the theme of apocalyptic judgment which they believe could not have been spoken by Jesus. See Robert W. Funk, Roy W. Hoover, and the Jesus Seminar, *The Five Gospels: The Search for the Authentic Words of Jesus* (New York: Macmillan, 1993), 223, 389.

of true love for its subjects can the sinful tendency to tyranny be overcome. The church teaches this lesson liturgically by the Holy Thursday reenactment of the foot-washing.

Persons and the Common Good

In our democratic experience and in the world history of our century it has always been difficult to reconcile not only authority and freedom, but also the notion of the good of the individual and the good of society. Our liberal society seems to swing always between individualism and totalitarianism—the totalitarianism of Hitler and that of Lenin and Stalin were the disastrous reaction to the breakdown of social solidarity. Marxist theory itself aimed ultimately at anarchism, "the withering away of the state," but Lenin converted it into a totalitarianism in which the individual was completely sacrificed to state interests.[33] Hitler and Mussolini fought Marxism only by adopting a similar totalitarianism.

We must avoid two extremes in ecclesiology both of which risk ending as a kind of religious totalitarianism. One extreme is so to stress the church's responsibility to work for social justice in earthly life as to forget that Jesus' kingdom is "not of this world" (Jn 18:36).[34] The other extreme is so to emphasize the unity and authority of the church as to forget that it exists primarily to enable its members to fulfill the spiritual gifts each has received from God.

In the 1940s an important controversy took place in the United States and Canada among Catholic philosophers attempting, in the context of World War II, to answer the challenge of Marxist

33. On this topic see Tom Rockmore, et al., *Marxism and Alternatives: Towards the Conceptual Interaction Among Soviet Philosophy, Neo-Thomism, Pragmatism, and Phenomenology*, Sovietica (Boston/Dordrecht: D. Reidel, 1981), 3–27.

34. "There is a tendency [among some theologians of liberation] to identify the kingdom of God and its growth with the human liberation movement, and to make history the subject of its own development, as a process of the redemption of man by means of the class struggle" (Congregation for the Doctrine of the Faith, *Instruction on Certain Aspects of "The Theology of Liberation"* [Boston: St. Paul Editions, 1984], no. 3). The positive aspects of these theologies is further developed in the same Congregation's *Instruction on Christian Freedom and Liberation*, (Boston: St. Paul Editions, 1986).

and Nazi totalitarianism. Jacques Maritain, the leader in this discussion, put forward a theory—for which he claimed a Thomistic basis—according to which human beings are subordinate to the common good of the state by reason of their *individuality,* but not as *persons* whose destiny altogether transcends earthly society.[35] Charles DeKoninck of Laval University criticized, correctly I believe, this solution as contrary to St. Thomas's thought, and dangerous because it tends to confuse "personalism" with "libertarianism"—the very confusion which in the name of "freedom" has so often spawned totalitarianism.

What, according to DeKoninck, was Aquinas's solution to the problem of the relation of the person to the common good? Human persons are essentially social and can achieve their personal good only by participation in the common good of society. Hence Maritain was mistaken in claiming that Aquinas taught that the human person as such *transcends* the common good. In fact Aquinas explicitly taught that the good of the human person is always subordinate to the common good, first to that of earthly secular society and of the church, and then to that of the eternal Kingdom of God.

For Aquinas the good of a human person is twofold. Some personal goods are "private," as in the "right of private property." These are chiefly *material* goods because material things to be used must be divided and consumed privately, so that their enjoyment is *exclusive.* This is the truth in Maritain's position, since he ascribes the term "individual" to the human person in its materiality. But there are other personal goods that are "common," such as friendship, truth, love, the exercise of the higher virtues. These are chiefly *spiritual* goods because spiritual goods such as truth are not divided or consumed but actually enhanced when they are

---

35. Jacques Maritain, *The Person and the Common Good* (New York: Charles Scribner's Sons, 1947). Charles De Koninck, *De la primauté du bien commun contre les personalistes* (Laval: University of Laval, 1943), had already taken a contrary position which was seen as an attack on Maritain and refuted by I. Th. Eschmann, O.P., "In Defense of Jacques Maritain," *Modern Schoolman* 22 (May 1945): 182–208, which was in turn rebutted by De Koninck, "In Defense of St. Thomas," *Laval théologique et philosophique* 1 (1945): 1–103.

shared with others. Hence, spiritual goods can be *common* in a strict sense, while material goods can be so only in a broad sense of the term. Our spiritual goods, therefore, are not to be hoarded but shared: "Nor do they light a lamp and put it under a bushel basket" (Mt 5:15). By such sharing these gifts are multiplied: "Give and gifts will be given to you: a good measure, packed together, shaken down, and overflowing" (Lk 6:38).

Therefore, the common good of society does not consist principally in material things such as economic prosperity or military power, but in the exercise of the higher virtues of social service, the pursuit of truth, and the worship of God. At this level of spiritual goods there can be no conflict between the personal and the common good since they are identical. The conflict between person and community, with its swinging back and forth between individualism and totalitarianism, results from the fact that modern societies, whether democracies or dictatorships, are directed not to spiritual but to material goods, to wealth and military power. In democracies this orientation generates consumerism and "privatism" to the neglect of the common good. In dictatorships it produces the brutal sacrifice of the masses to the pursuit of power by an elite for their own private interests.

Definition of Ecclesial Justice

We are interested here in justice in the church, and our analysis has led us to the following conclusions:

1. The church is just only when it is faithful to its mission, namely, the formation of a community of persons each of whom has equal access to the spiritual goods with which the church is entrusted by God. By this effective pursuit of the common good the church teaches secular society that political justice has as its goal not merely the material but the spiritual good of its citizens. Church and state by fidelity to their missions establish the personal equality of their members.

2. Injustices arise in the church when the hierarchy of offices is not subordinated to the common good of the members, but be-

comes a means to power for individual persons or groups, or is directed to materialistic ends rather than the true, spiritual common good, or when it so neglects the common good that the members no longer have full access to their rightful heritage.

3. The church is not unjust but truly just when it is faithful to the hierarchical structure of diverse and unequal offices and states of life established by Christ its founder,[36] and develops these in ways suited to its situation in our time and culture and to the conditions of its members and its ministry.

4. Justice in the church, however, demands that persons having authority over others, including majorities over minorities, exercise their authority not only for the true common good, but also in the sacrificial spirit of Jesus, the suffering servant.

Right of Free Speech

Free Speech in the Church

Underlying the charge that the church is unjust to women is a still more fundamental accusation that I must consider before going on to the question of gender roles. Is it not true that after Vatican II opened the church to dialogue with the modern world, the Vatican curia, and especially the Congregation for the Doctrine of the Faith, reverted to the policies of the bad old days of the Index of Forbidden Books and the hysterical suppression of Modernism?[37] Is not this refusal of the magisterium to enter a dialogue with the many "mainstream" theologians who defend the possibility of women's ordination, or even to open up the question to debate among theologians, the root injustice that makes impossible what would otherwise be a quick and satisfactory solu-

---

36. Vatican II, "Dogmatic Constitution on the Church" *(Lumen Gentium)*, no. 8: "Christ, the one Mediator established and ceaselessly sustains here on earth, his Holy Church, the community of faith, hope, and charity, as a visible structure"; thus reaffirming Trent, DS nos. 3050, 3056.

37. For this view see Richard A. McCormick, S.J., "The Chill Factor in Contemporary Moral Theology," chap. 4 in *The Critical Calling: Reflections on Moral Dilemmas Since Vatican II* (Washington, DC: Georgetown University Press, 1989), 71–94.

tion? Is not one of the basic rights of the person (without which the others, including women's rights, can never be adequately defended in either state or church) the right of free speech? To answer that question today, it is essential to recognize that in the elusive entity often referred to as "the mind of modern man" the possibility of revealed truth transcending human intelligence is ruled out, but two kinds of truth are admitted: the objective truth achieved by the methods of modern science, and the subjective "creative truth" of aesthetic and ethical preference. Since the current scientific method claims no more than probability and since subjective truth is not liable to conclusive debate, our culture is dominated by the notion that the human intellect cannot attain infallibly certain truth; so that even the Christian faith becomes "a leap in the dark."[38] This puts the Catholic church in a countercultural position in the modern world since the church claims both that reason can attain certainty on such matters as the existence of God and the principles of the natural law and also that faith attains to the truth of infallible dogmas.[39]

Nevertheless, the church agrees with "modern man" that human beings have a basic right to seek the truth, to communicate it to others, and to engage in dialogue in the pursuit of truth. It would, therefore, be an injustice upon the part of the officials of the church to prevent or punish free discussion aimed at truth, even when this concerns the infallible truths of the Gospel. Vatican II spoke plainly of the rights of conscience, which demand that no one should be compelled to believe the teachings of the church or punished for accepting other religious teachings.

38. Hans Küng succumbs to this current tendency in *Infallible? An Inquiry,* rev. ed., trans. Edward Quinn (Garden City, NY: Doubleday, 1983), when he claims that the certitude of faith rests on fidelity to Jesus Christ, but that no proposition (including, it would seem, propositions about Jesus Christ!) can be certain (pp. 197–99). Küng is correct, of course, in denying that dogmatic propositions can have Cartesian clarity, but if such propositions as "Jesus exists" and "Jesus is truly God" are not factually certain, why should we put our faith in Him? We see here the influence of Kant who had recourse to practical reason for the certitude that he denied to theoretical reason beyond its empirical application.

39. Vatican I, Session III (DS 3004), and Vatican II, "Dogmatic Constitution on Divine Revelation," *(Dei Verbum),* nos. 3 and 6.

Abuse of Free Speech

The term "freedom of speech," however, is a very ambiguous one. The right of free speech is grounded in the more basic right of access to the truth. The axiom, "The truth is mighty and will prevail," holds only under conditions where the truth can have a fair hearing. Yet we have extended the economic theory of the "magic of the market" to the market of ideas. That today the media or social means of communication do not provide a fair hearing for the Christian view of things is a frequent, and I believe amply justified, complaint of the Vatican. While the Gospel message is not suppressed in our culture, it is jammed by the incessant blare of propaganda and disinformation. Nor can it be heard in the apparently calmer milieu of academia where it is put on mute as not "politically correct" or at least as a subjective, private matter not appropriate to rational debate.

There is great hypocrisy in the demand of many liberals that speech should be totally free of all "previous censorship" when it is obvious that in every culture the communication of certain kinds of "truth" is favored and that of others silently restricted.[40] Moreover, some form of censorship is a necessity for any community, since if a society did not favor certain views by its mode of education, entertainment, and publication, the members would soon be lost in a chaos of misinformation and prejudicial myths.

If the common good of a society consists first of all in the access to truth, as I have maintained, then its authorities must be concerned to promote what is objectively true in preference to what is objectively false. We have only to consider the restrictions in favor of well-tested drugs and proper food labeling, or the refusal

40. Hence Supreme Court Justice Hugo Black's claim that the First Amendment is absolute, and the explanation of constitutional law professor Charles Black that this means that although freedom of speech is in fact limited in our country we should not say so in plain English lest it tempt people to infringe this right; see Mary Ann Glendon, *Rights Talk: The Impoverishment of Political Discourse* (New York: The Free Press/Macmillan, 1991), 42–43. See also Stephen L. Clark, *The Culture of Disbelief: How American Law and Politics Trivialize Religious Devotion* (New York: Basic Books, 1993).

to permit "creationism" to be presented in our schools on a par with warranted scientific theories on evolution, to realize that in fact the right of free speech is not absolute but requires a just regulation in order to promote constructive rather than destructive debate.

Yet today it is easy to find distinguished intellectuals who will shamelessly testify in court that gross commercial pornography is an exercise of free speech necessary to the progress of truth and morals! Is it not much more honest to face the responsibility to draw some line between reasoned debate and appeals to base passion and prejudice than to look to unrestricted license of speech to achieve truth?

Episcopal Discernment

The Catholic church, therefore, has never taken and can never take the naive position that Catholics have a right to say or write anything they please under the label of Catholicism. It has always been a duty of the bishops of the Catholic church to urge responsibility to truth in thought and speech as a supreme moral value. To Pilate's question, "What is truth?" (Jn 18:38), the church has to proclaim that the Gospel with which it has been entrusted is indeed the truth and that whatever contradicts it is the work of the "father of lies" (Jn 8:22).

This infallibility in fidelity to the Gospel pertains first of all to the church as a whole. All believing members of the church share in this ecclesial infallibility through their "sense of the faith" *(sensus fidei)*,[41] i.e., their witness to the faith that has been transmitted to them at baptism or in post-baptismal catechesis by the official teachers of the church or their delegates, and which they have ex-

---

41. "The body of the faithful as a whole, anointed as they are by the Holy One (cf. Jn 2:20, 27), cannot err in matters of belief. Thanks to a supernatural sense of the faith which characterizes the People as a whole, it manifests this unerring quality when, 'from the bishops down to the last member of the laity,' it shows universal agreement in matters of faith and morals" (*Lumen Gentium*, no. 12). See also the Congregation for the Doctrine of the Faith, *Instruction on the Ecclesial Vocation of the Theologian* (Vatican City: Libreria Editrice Vaticana, 1990), no. 25, citing John Paul II, *Familaris Consortio*, no. 5.

perienced by living in accordance with the direction of their pastors. Note that this is not a tradition independent of the pastors of the church but precisely that tradition which the pastors have confirmed.

Although, as I have indicated in discussing the nonlinear character of hierarchy in the church, the laity makes a unique contribution to the development of the faith, it does so by adding specific insights within the generic truths taught by the church, not by contradicting them. Thus some of the Marian doctrines arose from popular piety, but they only added details *within* the more general truths taught by the magisterium, i.e., by the *analogia fidei*.

The faith lived and transmitted by the church as a community needs, however, to be confirmed and officially expressed by the legitimate pastors of the church who have been ordained by predecessors endowed with apostolic authority. This apostolic authority going back to the Twelve and to Jesus himself, unlike the authority of the state, is not derived from the people but from Jesus and his Holy Spirit through the sacrament of orders.[42] While it is true that the authority of the state is also ultimately from God through the natural law, the form of constitution by which it is invested in certain persons is a matter of human invention and communal agreement. Moreover, election to state office does not confer charisms of authority in teaching and efficacy *ex opere operato* in administering the sacraments as does ordination.

Thus there is a functional inequality and difference of status in the church between the bishops, headed as a college by the bishop of Rome, who are endowed with the plenitude of apostolic authority, and the other members of the church. Only to the bishops belongs the power of definitive doctrinal and pastoral judgment, not only as regards infallible judgments, but as regards lesser acts of "binding and losing" (Mt 16:19 and 18:18; cf. Jn 20:23) in their ordinary teaching and pastoral direction.

42. *Lumen Gentium*, nos. 20–21. Many of the criticisms of the Vatican documents on the exclusion of women from priestly ordination have centered on the claim of these documents that the bishops of the Catholic church are "successors of the Twelve Apostles." For a discussion of this criticism see Appendix 1.

It follows, therefore, that the freedom of inquiry, writing, and speaking of theologians is subordinate to the authority of the bishops in teaching and pastoral direction, and may not used to "dissent" from it.[43] Yet it is for the common good of the church that theologians, within the limits set by this subordination, enjoy the freedom of theological speculation and discussion necessary to advance the understanding of the faith and defend it.[44] The less theologically expert members of the church share in this same right of inquiry and discussion and under similar limitations, but do not carry the same responsibility of teaching as the theologians.

Remedies of Abuses

Formerly, almost all theologians were priests who taught in seminaries, and their identification with the concerns of the bishops or of the religious orders was very strong. Today, the theologian is often a layperson, a member of a university faculty, whose career is dependent on the standards of the academy. In this changed situation theologians are not likely to think of themselves as "speaking in the name of the church," but rather in the name of a body of academic peers who especially value originality of ideas, backed up of course with solid scholarship.

Consequently, a theologian can be tempted to forget that Catholic theology, as a discipline, differs from other academic disci-

---

43. The term "dissent" has become very ambiguous. I think it is most properly used to mean giving one's own theological opinion an authority superior or equal in certitude and practical value to that of the church's magisterium, especially if this is made public and used to discredit and promote resistance to the theoretical or practical force of the magisterial pronouncement. Hence, it is *not* dissent for a theologian to point out defects or suggest corrections or improved formulations in fact or argumentation in magisterial documents with a view to sound doctrinal development, nor to debate the exact authoritative weight of a document, provided this is done prudently in a forum where a genuine search for truth can be reasonably expected and faith and objectively good consciences fostered.

44. Congregation for the Doctrine of the Faith, *Instruction on the Ecclesial Vocation of the Theologian*, nos. 9–12. For a nuanced discussion, see Avery Dulles, "The Magisterium and Theological Dissent," and "The Teaching Mission of the Church and Academic Freedom," chaps. in *The Craft of Theology* (New York: Crossroad, 1992), 105–18 and 165–78. See also Ladislas M. Orsy, S.J., *The Church: Learning and Teaching: Magisterium, Assent, Dissent, Academic Freedom* (Wilmington, DE: Michael Glazier, 1987).

plines in that it is based on the Christian faith transmitted in the church and authoritatively proclaimed by the bishops. The theories proposed in other disciplines must answer to the type of evidence appropriate to a given discipline, but in the case of theology that evidence is primarily the faith of the church. Hence Catholic theologians cannot responsibly ignore the fact that what they teach and write is received by the members of the church and the public as witnessing to the faith of the church.

We theologians, like other academicians, can be tempted to abuse our institutional office or our access to publishers and the media to make a name for ourselves by speculations that are stimulating but nevertheless insecurely founded or even objectively erroneous, and to promote these opinions in ways that undermine or confuse the faith of those who are less informed, or lead them into moral errors or contempt for ecclesial authority. Such abuses are further exaggerated by the sensationalism of the media and the academic premium on "creativity" and the prestige of publication.

The opposite mistake, of course, is the adamant refusal of some Catholics to acknowledge the very real intellectual and moral problems in the church and our culture with which theologians have to struggle in responsibility to their function in the church. Christianity in the face of the modern world cannot merely condemn error, it must strive—as in the days of the transition from Jewish to Hellenistic culture, and during the influx of Greek thought into the universities of the Middle Ages and Renaissance—to recognize and assimilate all that is true and good and hence of the Holy Spirit, in our times. This is an enormous task for theologians, who cannot succeed without the support and encouragement of the whole church. How then are these contrary kinds of unjust abuse to be avoided? I would suggest that it is necessary for the bishops actively to promote theological discussion under conditions really favorable to a fair hearing of all informed and reasoned opinions, while keeping clearly before all the responsibility of theologians not to usurp the role of the bishops, but to abide by their pastoral judgment in matters of faith and morals promulgated either in extraordinary or ordinary modes. In this way, the just inequality of functions in the church will be reconciled with the just and still more basic personal equality of all its members. As Adrian Edwards, C.S.Sp., has said, "The imposing of equality has, however, often gone with the view of society as being composed of so many atomic individuals. But, as one of the characters of Malraux's *L'Espoir* remarks the real opposite of oppression is not equality but fraternity. Life is enriched when it is experienced as the interplay of differences, rather than the juxtaposition of equivalences."[45]

Naturally such justice in the church will not come about without some contention, but the Holy Spirit can achieve this holy justice if due order and charity are observed. Did not St. Paul ask, "Do you not know that we will judge angels? . . . Can it be that there is not one among you wise enough to be able to settle a case between brothers?" (1 Cor 6:3, 5).

45. "Gender and Sacrifice," *New Blackfriars* 67 (1986): 376. He makes the unusual suggestion that to give women a liturgical role, they might appropriately be made the ordinary ministers of baptism, the sacrament of rebirth.

CHAPTER II

Passive and Active Laity

Nature-Culture Interaction

Nature and Human Nature

Peter Gay in a well-known work, *The Enlightenment,* vigorously defends the cause of a secular humanism.[1] He argues that modern democracy and its advocacy of human rights required the elimination of the tragic history of Christian religious fanaticism by a return to the rational Greco-Roman approach to life. The historical fallacy in Gay's thesis is that the heart of Enlightenment political theory was *individual freedom* but the heart of Greco-Roman political theory was *nature.* For classical thinkers, action "according to nature" was the standard of morality and good government.

Our American political tradition is based on the deism of the Enlightenment rather than on Judaic theism.[2] Nor is it securely based on that of the Christian tradition, as some have tried to

1. *The Enlightenment,* 2 vols. (New York: Alfred Knopf, 1967). Immanuel Kant gives the following definition in his "An Answer to the Question: What Is Enlightenment?" in *Perpetual Peace and Other Essays on Politics, History and Morals,* trans. Ted Humphrey (Indianapolis, IN: Hackett, 1983), 41: "Enlightenment is man's emergence from his self-imposed immaturity. Immaturity is the inability to use only one's understanding without guidance from another. This immaturity is self-imposed when its cause lies not in lack of understanding, but in lack of resolve and courage to use it without guidance from another. *Sapere Aude!.* Have courage to use your own understanding!—that is the motto of enlightenment." This vaunted "freedom to think for oneself" excludes religious faith which is the willingness to be guided by God's wisdom—see Kant's *Religion Within the Limits of Reason Alone,* trans. T. M. Greene and H. H. Hudson, with an essay by John R. Silber, "The Ethical Significance of Kant's Religion" (New York: Harper Torchbooks, 1960).

2. See Adolf G. Koch, *Religion of the American Enlightenment* (1933; reprint New York: Thomas Y. Crowell, 1968).

prove.[3] For the Christian tradition, which assimilated but transformed classical thought, to be free is to be released from the evil powers holding us back from joining our already redeemed brothers and sisters in God's kingdom. We need to be free in order to surrender ourselves to the Creator who made us. But for the Enlightenment, *my* freedom is the only goal, the supreme value.

Modernity, climax of the Enlightenment, admires the classical ideal of living by reason, but it has long since abandoned the ideal of living according to nature because to ground reason in nature restricts individual freedom. *Natura,* as the scholastics said, *est determinata ad unum* (nature is intrinsically determined to act in one way only),[4] and thus it would seem that nature eliminates the very possibility of freedom.

One escape is to say that our freedom is a necessary illusion. Another has been to invoke the fact that modern physics knows only statistical not absolute laws of nature, leaving some small room for freedom. That solution, however, reduces freedom to chance. A better way out is, with Aristotle, to distinguish natural, chance, and free events.[5] To do this, however, requires us to specify the relations among these three sorts of events; in other words, to propose a theory of natural law—physical and moral.

Natural Law

Without such a theory of natural law, we cannot fruitfully discuss justice in the church. We need to ask: Is justice a matter of obeying laws decreed by human government or constructed by social consent or proposed by a creative elite, or is justice a matter

3. The Declaration of Independence was closer to Christian tradition than the Constitution, yet as Gary Wills, *Inventing America: Jefferson's Declaration of Independence* (Garden City, NY: Doubleday, 1981), has shown, even this document rests on the "common sense philosophy" of the Scottish School which tended to deism. The notion of natural law and of "nature" proposed by this school leads directly to an individualism destructive of medieval communitarianism. See also Goetz A. Briefs, "The Ethos Problem in the Present Pluralistic Society" in *The Solidarist Economics of Goetz A. Briefs,* special number of *Review of Social Economy* 41 (1983): 275–76.

4. *ST* I q. 41, a. 2, c. and many other places.

5. *Physics* 2.6.197b.

of being accountable to a natural order revealed to us by our reason reflecting on our experience?

This is the difference between an ethics that is legalistic, positivistic, voluntaristic, and relativist and an ethics that is based on "the nature of the human person and its acts."[6] It amounts to the difference between saying that an act is good because social authority approves it and saying that authority is legitimate because it seeks to approve only what is good according to the nature of things.

Yet, the courts of the United States, to preserve our American idea of individual freedom, have been compelled to adopt a positivist theory of laws and human rights.[7] To say that one *ought* to respect the rights of others, such positivism declares, means only that the majority of citizens or some group of social activists are ready to defend those rights. Since it is a matter of my own choice to join in this consensus, my decent behavior is not coerced by anyone and my freedom is maintained.

Certainly, it is true that the civil law is not identical with the moral law, and that it cannot be effectively enforced without the support of public opinion and the customs of a culture. Conse-

6. Vatican II, *Gaudium et Spes*, no. 51. Oddly this phrase is used by some proportionalists to claim that to hold for exceptionless concrete moral norms is to consider only acts and not the person who performs them. But according to virtue theory the moral character of the person is formed by his or her acts. Good persons can perform bad acts and thus begin to become bad and vice versa. Bishop Dr. Walter Kasper, in an excellent article, "Theological Foundation of Human Rights," *The Jurist* 50 (1990): 148–66, shows the "ascending" defense of human rights by reason and natural law is complemented by the "descending" theological defense in terms of our participation in the Divine Nature and of the Incarnation. He also explains why the church so long resisted the notion of "human rights" as propounded by the Enlightenment, and points out that human rights have validity within the church only in an *analogical* way. "The analogy is based on the fact that the Church's fundamental rights, in contrast to general human rights, do not precede the Church. For while men exist before the State, Christians do not exist before, or independent, of the Church. The Church is the given sphere of salvation for the individual Christian. The human right of religious freedom can therefore not hold good in the Church, which is a community of the faithful and hence the community in one faith. Nonetheless the human right of religious freedom is necessarily relevant for the Church, insofar that admission to the Church must be free from any kind of compulsion" (p. 165 n. 49).

7. See Chapter I n. 10 above.

quently, our judges cannot be faulted for seeking always to ground their decisions in written law and precedent as the valued heritage of social experience. Nevertheless, they ought to recognize that if their judicial authority has no other grounds than custom and public opinion, they are not promoting justice but merely a power that may equally well violate as protect basic human rights.

Nor can *justice* be defined on the basis of what is only another form of positivism, namely, an "emotive theory" of ethics as proposed with a straight face by some of our analytic philosophers. Emotive ethics originated with Jean Jacques Rousseau, who thought that once freed from the absurd moral rules imposed on us by a decadent society we would all discover that we have the same free "natural" sentiments which can constitute the "general will" of a reformed society.[8] We hear Rousseau's notion echoed in the confident appeal of our politicians to opinion polls and the "common sense of the American people."

Immanuel Kant attempted to make this Rousseauean theory a little more plausible by admitting that human feelings without the correction of reason tend to evil. But he thought that we would all be able to agree on the moral law without submitting ourselves to any higher authority than our own rational consciences if we remain self-consistent, stay true to our better selves, and do not do to others what we do not want them to do to us.[9] Thus in its popular American version, "freedom" becomes permission to do what I please if I do not encroach on others doing what they please. As

8. Arthur M. Melzer, *The Natural Goodness of Man: On the System of Rousseau's Thought* (Chicago: University of Chicago Press, 1990), 45: "Man has a positive self and existence, for Rousseau, but it is not as a rational animal. On the contrary, reason, which understands only 'objects,' projects us out into the external world—the world of things, comparisons, means, interests—and thus positively alienates us from our true self. 'To exist, for us, is to sense'; to exist more is to feel more; and he 'has lived the most . . . who has most felt life.' (*Lettres morale* in *Oeuvres completes*, vol. 4, 1109; and *Emile* I, 42, cf. IV, 290). Rousseau begins, or at least greatly extends, the cult of feeling: the view that through feeling as such, regardless of content—and not through knowledge—one exists more and moves closer to being." See also ibid., chaps. 9 and 10 on the notion of "the general will."

9. See "Concerning the Indwelling of the Evil Principle with the Good, or the Radical Evil in Human Nature," book 1 of *Religion Within the Limits of Reason Alone*, 15–39.

Alasdair MacIntyre has shown, history has exposed the incoherence of such "modern" ethical systems not based on natural law—we are now stranded high on the rocks of "post-modernity."[10]

Nature and Culture

Closely related to these debates about meta-ethics are the often boring controversies over "nature versus culture." The new science of sociobiology strives to explain human behavior by reducing it to determinate evolutionary processes. Its claims have outraged social scientists whose expertise is in explaining human behavior by "culture," which rests ultimately on nondeterminate human invention.[11]

Feminist scholars, in particular, are trying to show that the historical phenomenon of male dominance is merely a cultural product and therefore can be radically changed by those who have the will to change it.[12] The ethical inference is that the subordination of woman to man is an injustice. Not only *can* it be changed, it *ought* to be changed. Does not this argument commit "the naturalistic fallacy" of deducing the "ought" from the "is" without

10. See Alasdair MacIntyre, *After Virtue: A Study in Moral Theory* (Notre Dame, IN: University of Notre Dame Press, 1982), which thoroughly documents this dead-end in modern ethics. Thus Richard Rorty, *Contingency, Irony, and Solidarity* (Cambridge: Cambridge University Press, 1992), 192, rests his ethics on a feeling of solidarity. He admits his view is "incompatible with the idea that there is a 'natural' cut in the spectrum of similarities and differences which span the difference between you and a dog, or you and one of Asimov's robots." But his position is not, he says, "incompatible with urging that we try to extend our sense of 'we' to people whom we have previously thought of as 'they.' This claim, characteristic of liberals—people who are more afraid of being cruel than of anything else—rests on nothing deeper than the historical contingencies to which I referred." He argues that "there is such a thing as moral progress and this progress is indeed in the direction of greater human solidarity. But that solidarity is not thought of as recognition of a core self, the human essence, in all human beings. Rather, it is thought of as the ability to see more and more traditional differences (of tribe, religion, race, customs, and the like) as unimportant; compared with the similarities with respect to pain and humiliation—the ability to think of people wildly different from ourselves as included in the range of 'we'."

11. See Arthur L. Caplan, ed., *The Sociobiology Debate* (New York: Colophon Books, 1978).

12. See Cynthia Fuchs Epstein, *Deceptive Distinctions: Sex, Gender, and the Social Order,* (New Haven: Yale University Press for Russell Sage Foundation, 1988), especially chap. 3, "The Bio-Social Debate."

sufficient warrant? Yet it seems valid in a culture where individual freedom is the ultimate standard of morality, since woman's subordination to man certainly limits her freedom.

Nevertheless, nature has its claims, and science will never be content to say that human behavior, any more than disease, is purely a product of culture. Consequently many try to resolve the debate by saying that neither nature nor culture entirely determines human behavior, but only their mutual "interaction." But the question remains, What are the respective effects of nature and culture as they interact?[13] Therefore, to define justice in society and in the church, we must try to specify exactly how nature and culture, nature and freedom, interact to establish a social order in the context of which the word "justice" can have objective meaning.

Human Nature and Society

The Greek notion of "living according to nature" is ambiguous. The Cynics, somewhat like Rousseau, took this to mean that one ought to "live naturally," following one's natural instincts without regard to the imposition of man-made laws or cultural patterns.[14] St. Thomas Aquinas has been much criticized for quoting the Roman legalist Ulpian who said that the natural law is "the law common to men and animals."[15] What these critics fail to notice is

13. This dialectic is well summed up by an anthropologist, who is a leading proponent of culture theory. "The disagreement between sociobiologists and cultural materialists on the issue of human nature is a matter of the contraction versus the expansion of human nature. Cultural materialists pursue a strategy that seeks to reduce the list of hypothetical drives, instincts, and genetically determined response alternatives to the smallest possible number of items compatible with the construction of an effective corpus of sociocultural theory. Sociobiologists, on the other hand, show far less restraint and actively seek to expand the list of genetically determined traits whenever a plausible opportunity to do so presents itself" (Marvin Harris, *Cultural Materialism: The Struggle for a Science of Culture* [New York: Random House, 1979], 128).

14. On Cynic ethics, which is closely related to that of the Stoics, see Diogenes Laertius, *Lives of Eminent Philosophers,* trans. R.D. Hicks, Loeb Library (Cambridge, MA: Harvard University Press, 1958), vol. 2, bk. 6, 2–109.

15. Justinian I, *Digesta corpus juris civilis,* I, tit. 1, leg. 1, quoted in *ST* I-II, q. 94, a. 2 c.

that Aquinas integrates this formula with another: "Morality is living according to reason."[16]

What is the relation of nature to reason? First, our reason enables us to analyze our experience so as to come to know our own human nature, its limitations and potentialities. We do not know our nature by some metaphysical intuition of essences, but by observing the *relations* between ourselves and others and our environment, and then sorting out stable from unstable relationships.[17] We will err about our nature if, like adolescents, we lack the necessary experience, or ignore it, or reason badly about it. But in good reason we cannot ignore our nature in making ethical decisions, since it is unethical to injure our nature or to injure that same nature in others, without whom our own social nature cannot be fulfilled.

Second, unlike the Cynics, Aristotle and Aquinas did not mean by "living according to nature" simply following instinctually determined patterns of human behavior. For them the term "human nature" was only *analogous* to the term "nature" as that was distinguished from "chance" and "freedom" since human nature is essentially *free*. *Human* nature is only partially *determinatum ad unum* and chiefly according to its animal aspect, which is generic, not specifying.[18] Our specific nature is to be persons having intelligence and freedom, and we are only generically animal and material. As the Psalmist says, we are "only a little less than the angels" (Ps 8:6); we are the least of all created intelligences, so weak that we require a body to think and to will, but we are intelligences first and foremost. Nevertheless, Ulpian was not wrong, nor is it an error of "physicalism" or "biologism" as some theologians today are claiming,[19] to make the physical, animal char-

---

16. *ST* I-II, q. 18, a. 5 c.

17. On the primacy of relations in human knowledge see Ralph A. Powell, *Freely Chosen Reality* (Washington, DC: University Press of America, 1983), and his summary quoted by John N. Deely, in the bilingual edition of *Tractatus De Signis: The Semiotic of John Poinsot* (Berkeley: University of California Press, 1985), 468–71.

18. *ST* I, q. 75, a. 3 c.

19. On the notion of "physicalism" or "biologism" in ethics, see my book co-

acter of human acts a decisive determinant of morality, although it is not the sole determinant.

To live according to reason is to live according to human "nature," but not "nature" in the univocal sense that brute animals and rocks have natures or that nature is distinguished from freedom and chance. Hence to understand and evaluate human behavior demands that we take into account both our nature as determinant and our culture as relatively free, along with their interactions, in the context of history, that is, of a world in which natural and free order are liable to disruption by chance. To reduce our behavior to either pole of nature or culture, or to ignore the role of historical chance, makes ethics impossible.

When Aristotle said that "Man is by nature a political animal," i.e., a "city animal" (polis is Greek for a city-state),[20] he implied that our nature as rational animals requires us to be inventors of civilizations (civis is a Latin equivalent for polis). It is obvious from the vast range of forms of government and other social organizations among existing and historic societies that much of the structure of any community is a free human invention. For instance, language is species specific for homo sapiens as a social animal, but we have invented many, many languages and are constantly modifying them. And yet the linguist, Noam Chomsky, has maintained that all known human languages exhibit a common "deep structure," which probably has a genetic foundation.[21]

No matter what resistance we meet from social scientists, however, we need to acknowledge a certain subordination of culture to nature because the survival of a social construct depends on its ability to meet natural requirements. For example, a society that attempts to live by an economic system that cannot produce

---

authored with Kevin O'Rourke, *Healthcare Ethics: A Theological Analysis,* 3rd ed. (St. Louis: Catholic Health Association, 1989), 168–69, and my *Theologies of the Body: Humanist and Christian* (St. Louis: Pope John Center, 1985), 369–70, 415–22.

20. *Politics* 1.2.1253a2.

21. *Cartesian Linguistics: A Chapter in the History of Rationalist Thought* (New York: Harper and Row, 1966), 31–50, 72–73; and *Language and Mind,* rev. ed. (New York: Harcourt Brace Jovanovich, 1972).

enough food (like the former Soviet Union), or with a military system that provokes great alliances against it (like the former Nazis), or is unable to protect itself from aggressors (like France under Petain), or has a family system that fails to reproduce sufficiently (like Imperial Rome), cannot long endure.[22]

I will not attempt here to expound a theory of the natural requirements for a truly adequate human culture, but certainly one major requirement is justice.[23] In my first chapter I argued that such justice demands that all members of the community be *personally equal*, but that, by reason of the necessary division within the community of offices serving the common good, they must also be *functionally unequal*.

Nature and the Family

Natural Family Structure

We can go a step further, however, when we consider a specific human community, namely the family. Anthropologists generally agree that the family is a feature of all known historic societies, although it has had countless variations. Yet in the midst of these variations, the nuclear family of man, woman, and children overwhelmingly prevails, so that the variations are essentially permutations of a basic structure.[24]

22. Anthropologists sometimes argue that the wide variation in behavior in long-surviving cultures proves that human nature is so indeterminant that it contributes minimally to the nature versus culture interaction. Hence, they support cultural and moral relativism. But since chance plays so large a role in history, we cannot judge simply from its survival that a society is *well* conformed to nature, nor that it will not ultimately self-destruct, any more than we can always conclude that a failed society was self-destructive. To evaluate the adequacy of a culture to the needs of nature we must proceed critically and discriminately.

23. See "Ethics of Co-Creative Stewardship," chap. 10 in my *Theologies of the Body*, for a sketch of the requirements of a just society. See also Germain Grisez, et al., *Living a Christian Life*, vol. 2 of *The Way of the Lord Jesus* (Quincy, IL: Franciscan Press, 1993), 320–32. Contemporary theories of justice tend to be Kantian, e.g., John Rawls, *A Theory of Justice* (Cambridge, MA: Harvard University Press, 1971); or libertarian, e.g., Robert Nozick, *Anarchy, State, and Utopia* (New York: Basic Books, 1974).

24. This point was much debated in the 1950s by anthropologists, but the conclusion reached by Clifford Kilpatrick in *The Family: Its Process and Institu-*

Nevertheless, from Plato's *Republic*, to Marx, to the Israeli kibbutzim, and finally to today's radical feminists, utopians have proposed to abolish the nuclear family as a necessary means to social reform.[25] These prophecies of the death of the "traditional" family seem fulfilled today in the proliferation of single-parent households and same-sex parenthood, so that the very term "family" seems no longer to have a fixed definition.[26] In nature the foundation of the family is first of all the mother-child relationship. The child needs a mother to bear it, to nurse it, to give it an intimate kind of care at least in its first years. Yet even the mother-child bond is being undermined today by artificial reproduction. Some radical feminists argue that until all children are not only conceived *in vitro* but gestated in artificial wombs, women will not be truly emancipated.[27] To date, however, artificial

---

tion (New York: Ronald Press, 1963), stands: "The familial group known as the biological or nuclear family exists and is recognized in practically all the cultures of the world. . . . Occasionally only a blurred glimpse of the nuclear family is obtained, imbedded as it may be in the polygamous family structure or perhaps in a kinship or household structure; yet the vast majority of all the children in the world grow up experiencing distinctively intimate contact with their biological parents" (p. 47). William N. Stephens, *The Family in Cross-Cultural Perspective* (New York: Holt, Rinehart and Winston, 1963), similarly concludes "It is probably too much to say that the [nuclear] family . . . is universal. However, if it is not universal, it is probably almost universal" (p. 29). He discusses some alleged "exceptions," such as the polyandrous Nayars of Malibar, but shows they are marginal.
    25. The Israeli *kibbutz* is an example of utopian socialism that has gradually reverted to the nuclear family. See Yonina Garber-Talmon, *Family and Community in the Kibbutz* (Cambridge, MA: Harvard University Press, 1972), 42–50. For a socialist feminist discussion see Ann Ferguson, *Blood at the Roots: Motherhood, Sexuality and Male Domination* (London: Pandora, 1989).
    26. On the rise of "nontraditional" families see Jay D. Teachman, Karen A. Polenko, and John Scanzoni, "Demography of the Family," in *Handbook of Marriage and the Family*, ed. Marvin B. Sussman and Suzanne K. Steinmetz, (New York: Plenum Press, 1987). Also in the same volume, see Patricia A. Gongola and Edward H. Thompson, Jr., "Single-Parent Families"; and Barbara H. Settles, "A Perspective on Tomorrow's Families."
    27. Ann Ferguson, *Blood at the Roots* argues that "Full reproductive rights also have to include the right to homosexual sex with no social penalties, and the development of full rights to artificial reproduction techniques for gays and lesbians and non-coupled heterosexuals" (p. 240). "Sex can be used for pleasure, or for committed couple relationships. However, heterosexual intercourse can also be used to produce children. Thus, where a committed couple relationship and raising children are valued, heterosexuality will probably continue to be the preferred sexual identity of the majority of individuals, even where artificial reproductive tech-

reproduction cannot dispense with the pregnant mother and it seems unlikely that the child's psychological and developmental needs can ever be adequately satisfied without maternal care.[28] Of course, the way this mother-child bonding is expressed is modified by various cultural contexts.

Less evidently but yet surely children need a father. A father is not simply an impregnator, but an integral member of the community in which the child grows up and with whom the child and its mother are intimately bonded.[29] It should be evident that the pregnancy of the mother and her protracted intimate care of the child demands that at least during the period of child-raising she can count on someone to protect her and her brood and provide for their physical needs.

In our technological culture we are experimenting with arrangements by which a woman bears only a child or two, supports herself by her own work (provided she has leave time for the most demanding period of pregnancy and child care), sends the children early to day care, and does without a man in the home. But widespread complaints about the great strain this puts on women are already to be heard, and it is a safe bet that in the long run the single-parent household will come to be regarded a failure or at best a poor substitute. No doubt a culture where women work

---

niques are available on demand regardless of sexual preference" (p. 244). On the other hand, Gena Corea, argues that artificial reproduction is really a form of male oppression, since by it males finally take over from women the one gift of women which males have always envied, the power to give birth! (*The Mother Machine* [New York: Harper and Row, 1985]; abridged in Kenneth D. Alpern, ed., *The Ethics of Reproductive Technology* [New York: Oxford University Press, 1992], 220–31).

28. This dependence of the offspring on their female parent is of course characteristic of all mammals and reaches its climax in *homo sapiens* where the child, because of the long time its large brain requires to develop needs an especially long period of maternal care. See Irene Elia, *The Female Animal* (New York: Henry Holt, 1988), 167–68.

29. While among primates the males protect their mates and young, and occasionally substitute for the female in holding the young, they have little parenting function beyond impregnating the female. They do not seem to be "fathers" in the human sense of sharing in the education of the young. See Irene Elia, *The Female Animal,* 199–200.

outside the home is viable, but only if difficult adjustments are made.[30]

Bible and Family

For Christians the doctrine of original sin implies that human nature as we experience it historically is obscured and wounded. To recover human nature as the Creator intended it to be we must turn to God in whose "image and likeness" (Gn 1:27) we were formed. The Bible confirms the divine origin and natural character of the family structure, especially in those passages of the New Testament that contain admonitions for the conduct of family life (1 Cor 7:1–7; 11:1–16; 14:33–38; Eph 5:21–33; Col 3:18–21; 1 Tm 2:8–15; Ti 2:1–10; 1 Pt 3:1–7).[31]

Many women have great problems with these texts, because they speak of the father as "head" of the family, and exhort the wife to be "submissive" to him.[32] Even male exegetes struggle with these texts and tend to compare them to the similar admonitions to slaves to obey their masters (1 Cor 7:21–24; Phl 7–20; Eph 6:5–9; Col 3:22–4:1; 1 Tm 6:1–2; Ti 2:9; 1 Pt 2:18–25). If we now admit that the New Testament acceptance of slavery was a reflection of the social conditioning of the inspired writers and is no longer normative for Christians, should we not say the same thing for these passages about the relations of husband and wife? The answer, I believe, is yes and no.

Certainly these passages do reflect the social structures of New

30. See Teachman, et al., "Demography of the Family," on the problematic adjustments now being made in American society as a result of the increase of women working outside the home.

31. For the New Testament teaching on the family see the syntheses in Rudolf Schnackenburg, *The Moral Teaching of the New Testament* (New York: Seabury Press, 1973), 244–60, and Wolfgang Schrage, *The Ethics of the New Testament,* (Philadelphia: Fortress Press, 1988), 222–28.

32. In a remarkable, and very detailed study, a French woman exegete, Lucile Villey, *Soumission: Thème et variations aux temps apostoliques: La fonction d'une préposition 'hypo'* (Paris: Beauchense, 1992), has shown that "submission" is a specifically Christian theme developed from the paradigm of Jesus' "submission" to God the Father. Far from derogating the human dignity of male or female, it elevates it.

Testament times, which were deeply conditioned by the sinful injustices of sexism and also by the pastoral gradualism of St. Paul and others. As such they are no longer literally normative for us. It is always wrong, however, to dismiss any biblical text as a mere relic of the past. All Scripture is "inspired by God and is useful for teaching, for refutation, for correction, and for training in righteousness, so that one who belongs to God may be competent, equipped for every good work" (2 Tm: 16–17). Thus the doctrine of biblical inspiration, gives us good reason for assuming that even very time-bound biblical texts, since they have God for their principal author, have some timeless, universal significance which it is the duty of theological exegesis to free from its cultural or literary particularity.

The texts about family relations in the New Testament are all related to the fundamental teaching of Genesis 1–3 about the personal equality and functional difference of humanity created in God's image. They tell us that humanity was created sexual for the sake of the family community and that this community has a basic structure ordained by the Creator.

Man and woman were created such in order that they might be bound to each other in an indissoluble covenant of love on which the survival of humanity depends (Mk 10:1–12 and parallels). The principle of the division of offices requires that the roles of male and female be distinguished so that each will contribute something special to the family. The theory of evolution requires that the human species has survived because it is able to reproduce and to care for its offspring until they can reproduce. How could this be if the female and male of the species were not physically and psychologically adapted to effective child care? Since it is clear that the mother has a special role in child care, it would be very inefficient for survival if the father were not also adapted to some special role in caring for mother and child, a role different from but complementary to that of the mother. Although this natural relationship is obvious, it remains difficult to define the psychological and spiritual gifts of the human female and male with precision.[33] Certainly there are great cultural variations in exactly how these gender differences should be understood and expressed, but no culture has failed to recognize that such differences are somehow natural and require to be culturally supported and stylized.

The New Testament contents itself with using the analogy of the family community to the human body that I have already discussed, and defines the male role simply to be "head" of the body and the role of the woman to be the "body" as a whole. It gives this commonplace analogy a theological note by the more specific analogy between Christ as Head of the church and the church as his Bride (1 Cor 11:3–16; Eph 5:21–33). This latter analogy is deeply rooted in the Old Testament as the metaphor of a marriage covenant between Yahweh and Israel (Hos 1–3; Is 1:21–26, 50:1, 54:6–7, 62:4–5; Jr 2:2, 3:1–12; Ez 16; Ps 45; Sg *passim*).

The function of this analogy in the biblical texts is to stress four themes that are applications of the principles that I described in Chapter I as governing all human communities: (1) husband and wife are "one flesh" (Gn 2:24; Mk 10:7), one body with one life, so that they have personal equality; (2) they have different and complementary roles for the sake of the family community, i.e., functional inequality; (3) in this hierarchy or functional system the wife's role is hierarchically subordinate to the husband's; and (4) the husband is to exercise his subordinating role not only for the good of the family, but *sacrificially* as Christ does for the church,

---

33. The results of the vast literature of research on gender differences is summed up in Lea P. Stewart, Pamela J. Cooper, and Sheryl A. Friedley, *Communication Between the Sexes: Sex Differences and Sex-Role Stereotypes* (Scottsdale, AZ: Gorsuch Scarisbrick, 1986), 24–27. See also Cynthia Fuchs Epstein, *Deceptive Distinctions;* Bruno Leone and M. Teresa O'Neill, *Male/Female Roles: Opposing Viewpoints* (St. Paul, MN: Greenhaven Press, 1983); Malkah T. Notman and Carol C. Nadelson, eds., *Women and Men: New Perspectives on Gender Differences* (Washington, DC: American Psychiatric Press, 1991); and Robert Pool, *Eve's Rib* (New York: Crown Press, 1994). Many feminists credit women in contrast to men with numerous positive traits. For example, Sally P. Purvis, "Christian Feminist Spirituality," in *Post Reformation and Modern Spirituality*, vol. 3 of *Christian Spirituality*, ed. Louis Dupré and Don E. Saliers, vol. 18 of *An Encyclopedia of World Spirituality* (New York: Crossroad, 1989), lists characteristics of feminine spirituality as "Inclusivity, Connectedness, Embodiment, Liberation," qualities often mentioned by feminist writers (pp. 500–519).

i.e., as they are subordinated to him by nature he must voluntarily subordinate himself to his wife and children in mutuality.

Why must one of the marriage partners be subordinate to the other? And why must it be the woman who is first of all subordinate to the husband, since in fact she is even more directly related to the children who are the pledge of species survival? As a community, a family must make practical decisions that affect all the members. Each should be free to do this in regard to matters in which she or he is most competent (the principle of subsidiarity).

Yet, as I have already argued,[34] because in practical matters rational consensus is seldom possible, in every community there must be a designated authority to make ultimate decisions, whether this be the majority or a special representative group or a single leader. In a family young children are too immature to have a determinative vote in such matters, and a representative group or a majority vote would be impractical since there are only two adults to vote.

Consequently, in the family either the husband or the wife must have the right of ultimate decision no matter how equal in personal dignity and in functional capacities the couple may be. Hence authority ("headship") is either vested in one or the other by reason of intelligence, virtue, etc., or by some natural designation. But who is to decide which of the couple is more intelligent or virtuous? Therefore, headship must be based on a *natural,* not a free, designation. Because the male is physically stronger, less occupied by pregnancy and nursing, and more concerned with the family's external relations he seems the naturally designated head. Thus the explanation of the almost universal fact of male dominance in family structures in all known historic cultures, and the weak evidence for genuine matriarchy, cannot simply be cultural but must have genetic roots, i.e., it must derive from human nature.[35]

34. See the subsection "Role and Status" in the "Relations of Inequality" section of Chapter I.

35. Steven Goldberg, *The Inevitability of Patriarchy* (New York: Morrow, 1974), tried to demonstrate that male dominance has been universal in all known human societies. The criticisms of his thesis have been: (1) "dominance" is not

Nor are these roots really obscure. Feminist scholars generally admit that historical experience shows that males are more aggressive than females. They have not been able to provide any plausible yet purely cultural explanation why this should be so.[36] Can we really doubt that male aggressiveness is an evolutionary adaptation to the need of the woman for someone to protect and gather food for her during pregnancy and child care, as well as to the need of the man to compete for her with other males for this privilege?

If this is the case it becomes theologically plausible that male dominance, by nature designed for the common good of the family, would in a sinful world degenerate into violent competition with other males and the oppression of women. This sinful injustice of sexism will never be remedied, therefore, unless males become not just impregnators and masters, but husbands and *fathers*

---

easily definable; (2) male dominance varies in degree in different societies; and (3) the factors that have led to male dominance up to now are changing, or could be changed if women organize to change them. Goldberg's point, however, was that the universality of a recognizable phenomenon, namely the "patriarchy" which feminists denounce and propose to change, makes it highly probable that male dominance is somehow rooted not in historical circumstance but in human nature.

36. Elizabeth Dodson Gray, *Patriarchy as a Conceptual Trap* (Wellesley, MA: Roundtable Press, 1982), 31–36, thinks males produced civilization out of envy of women's ability to bear children. Marilyn French in *Beyond Power: On Women, Men, and Morals* (New York: Ballantine Books, 1985), claims patriarchy overcame an original matriarchy (pp. 1–64) not because men were stronger but because "men believed they had the controlling role in procreation, and because the gods of their hunting cults were in some sense already controlling gods." Hence, "men began to worship a transcendent deity, a god who was not part of nature, like the old immanent goddess, but who had power over nature without being part of it." As men's "deity had power over the earth, men had power over the creatures of the earth, animals and women" (pp. 68–69). French advocates a morality of freedom and equality aimed at the maximum of pleasure, above all of sexual pleasure freed from all domination or power (pp. 500–46), and questions whether this is possible through heterosexual relationships (pp. 521–27). Other similar theories are proposed by Peggy Reeves Sunday, *Female Power and Male Dominance: On the Origins of Sexual Inequality* (Cambridge: Cambridge University Press, 1981), and Gerda Lerner, *The Creation of Patriarchy* (New York: Oxford University Press, 1986). For a refutation of the "original matriarchy theory," see Susanne Heine, "Matriarchy—The Lost Paradise," chap. 3 in *Matriarchs, Goddesses and Images of God: A Critique of a Feminist Theology*, trans. John Bowden (Minneapolis, MN: Augsburg, 1989).

in the sense that Jesus uses "Father" of God to mean a Creative-Power-that-loves-and-cares (Mt 6:23–32).

Feminist writers have coopted the word "patriarchy" to give it the technical sense of "oppressive, tyrannical domination," when in ordinary usage the word "father" connotes the very opposite, namely a loving, caring, tender use of power to defend and foster.[37] It is paradoxical that these writers so often denigrate the family, since it has often been said that marriage is not a male but a female invention—he can reproduce himself easily enough by promiscuous contacts, but she requires a stable relationship to help her throughout her pregnancy and nursing.[38]

In the biblical view the human male, however, need not be judged to be an oppressor by nature, but rather by nature a human person who tends to fatherhood in the favorable sense. His present inclination to sexism is the result of original and personal sin that has distorted his male "aggressiveness" so that it results in destructive rather than constructive expression. Thus we can conclude that the family has a specific structure, although one capable of great variation, which is rooted in human nature because of our specific mode of reproduction.

Societies have long survived in which social organization re-

37. On what feminists mean by "patriarchy," which in their usage has a much broader meaning than its original use by anthropologists or in relation to the biblical "patriarchs," see Elizabeth Moltmann-Wendel, "What is Patriarchy?" chap. 2 in *A Land Flowing with Milk and Honey: A Perspective on Feminist Theology* (New York: Crossroad, 1986). See also Elisabeth Schüssler Fiorenza, "To Console or Challenge" in *New Women, New Church, New Ministry: Proceedings of the Second Conference on the Ordination of Roman Catholic Women, Nov. 10–12, 1978, Baltimore, Maryland* (Rochester, NY: Kirk-Wood Press, 1980), 43–60. She writes, "I understand *patriarchalism* in the sense of a social system maintaining male dominance and privilege based on female submission and marginality" (p. 43 n. 1).

38. This integration of the male into child-rearing, however, had deep roots in evolutionary adaptation; see Irene Elia, *The Female Animal*, 168–69. She also argues that the gradual development of the proto-nuclear family made human evolution possible: "Having hit upon ways to incorporate males into the nuclear family, female primates entered new habitats—grasslands; semideserts; colder snowy regions; and caves. They became tough and gregarious ground dwellers, giving rise to the physically, socially, and symbolically most manipulative organisms on earth [i.e., *homo sapiens*]" (p. 200).

mained at the family level, but such communities were never able to meet any but the most basic human needs.[39] A richer and more viable culture demands a society transcending the family unit and thereby able to provide a greater division of offices. Yet such larger societies remain rooted in family groups, and sometimes the larger society seems merely an extended family. Thus the chief of a tribe tends to be thought of as the patriarch of the community, even when in fact he is not their physical father. Because of the analogy between family and state, it seems to have taken a long time historically for the state to become clearly differentiated from the family in its organization, and even today in many parts of the world the largest effective community is not the state but the clan or tribe based theoretically on blood relationships.

Creativity and the State

Patriarchy

This analogy between family and state, however, is only an analogy. The state meets needs that the family cannot provide, not only needs for a richer economy and a stronger military defense, but above all for progress in knowledge and moral sensitivity. Advance in science and technology are social projects, and the full range of human virtue can be achieved and exercised only in a complex society. Hence Aquinas noted that justice in the strict sense is not possible within the family because the members are too identified with each other to achieve that objectivity of relationship on which justice is based.[40] Justice is exercised toward someone we perceive

39. Ronald Cohen, in his introduction to *Origins of the State: The Anthropology of Political Evolution,* ed. Ronald Cohen and Elman R. Service (Philadelphia: Institute for the Study of Human Issues, 1978), writes, "To be a 'true' state the system should exhibit some stable or permanent hierarchy that can withstand the disruptive effects of succession struggles" (p. 4). He explains that social organization prior to the evolution of the state produces communities that tend to divide into smaller communities in which the family is the only ultimately stable unit. See also in the same volume Wolfgang Weissleder, "Aristotle's Concept of Political Structure and the State," on the importance of the household or *oikia.*

40. *ST* II-II, q. 58, a. 7, ad 3.

as *other* than ourselves, and we cannot easily view our family members in that objective way.

The analogy between family and state led many cultures to conclude that as the father is often regarded as "head" of the family, so the state is best organized as a monarchy with a single "father" at the head. Can we say then that nature determines the basic structure of the state as it does that of the family?

Best Form of Government

Aristotle in his *Politics* tackled the problem of whether by nature one form of government is better than the others.[41] Since, as we have already seen, anarchy or cooperation by consensus is unworkable, a community cannot achieve the common good without a government, which can be of three basic types: rule by one, by a few, or by a majority. Each of these types has both advantages and disadvantages.

The rule of one (as the father in the family) provides unity and efficiency of decision and action, but depends entirely on the mere possibility that the king will be of superior virtue and wisdom. Even so, his experience and knowledge of the problems of the society he rules will necessarily be limited. The rule of a representative few has the advantage that the defects in virtue and knowledge of one can be supplemented by the others. Yet it has less unity than the rule of one and is open to rivalries and factions among the several equal rulers. The rule of the majority has the advantage of the freedom and participation of most of the community who complement each others' deficiencies. Yet in such a rule unity of decision and action is difficult, and the minority is likely to be discontent.

Aristotle concluded that the rule of one virtuous and wise person is best when achieved, but that is rare; while rule by the majority is likely to be so inefficient as to end in the tyranny of a demagogue.[42] Consequently, in practice a republic or mixed government in which a strong executive leads but is controlled by an

41. *Politics* 3.6–13; 4.1.
42. *Politics* 3.16–17; 4.4–5.

elite body representing the people is the best. Our Founding Fathers built this classic theory into our United States Constitution, with the result that our republic has proved remarkably stable and been widely imitated.[43]

We often today call our government a "democracy" and claim that it is, in the words of Lincoln, "government of the people, by the people, and for the people." We claim also, on the basis of the American experience, that it is the best form of government for all societies. Some philosophers such as Mortimer Adler have even attempted to prove it is best by an analysis of human nature.[44] Is that really true?

Participation in Decision

Participation and Subsidiarity

It is possible of course to argue that democracy is the best form of government because it maximizes individual freedom.[45] Also it

43. At the federal level, the Presidency supplies a monarchical principle, Congress (especially the Senate) and the Supreme Court an aristocratic principle, and universal suffrage a democratic principle. This structure is replicated (with some modifications) at the state level. The strength of our federal executive, the President, independent of Congress, gives our government a strong monarchical character, balanced however, by the Congress and the Supreme Court, and by the fact that it is an elective monarchy.

44. Mortimer Adler and Walter Farrell, O.P., "The Theory of Democracy," *The Thomist* 3 (1941): 397–449, 588–652; 4 (1942): 121–81, 286–354, 446–522, 692–761; 6 (1943): 49–118, 251–77, 367–407; 7 (1944): 80–131. I was told by colleagues of Farrell that he finally decided that the argument was inconclusive; consequently, the treatise was never completed.

45. Maritain in *Christianity and Democracy* (originally published in French in 1943; republished with *The Rights of Man and Natural Law*, trans. Doris C. Anson [San Francisco: Ignatius Press, 1986]), argues that "The word democracy, as used by modern peoples, has a wider meaning than in the classical treatises on the science of government. It designates first and foremost a general philosophy of human and political life and a state of mind. This philosophy and the state of mind do not exclude a priori any of the 'regimes' or 'forms of government' which were recognized as legitimate by classical tradition, that is, recognized as compatible with human dignity" (p. 25). "Are we called upon now to define that form of government to which the principles of the humanist political philosophy naturally tend? This philosophy maintains that the human person as such is called up to participate in political life and that the political rights of a community of free men must be firmly secured. That is why it claims the right of suffrage for all adult

would seem, as the anarchists argue, that all other forms of government, since they require obedience to an authoritative elite and thus further restrict the freedom to do what one pleases, are in a measure tyrannical.

The trouble with this argument is that it reduces the notion of the common good to the right for everyone to do what he or she pleases as long as it does not unduly interfere with others doing what they please. We are familiar with this libertarian view in current politics.[46] Has it ever proved practicable? We have only to look at our American society, the exemplar of democracy, to see that in fact we have not survived on pure libertarian principles but have been forced to expand vastly the role of government in daily life.

Moreover, in our culture the so-called private sphere consists of ever-larger corporate organizations for business, education, and other purposes, which greatly restrict the freedom of individuals to do what they please. The most that the libertarian can really hope for is to diminish a few regulations here or there, but there is no prospect of reducing the authority structures of our culture very much without a total revolution.

Another way to approach the problem, more consistent with the Christian world view, is to attempt to define more exactly what the "freedom" for which democracy is valued consists in, other than simply "doing what one pleases." The argument of Adler, Maritain, and others turns out to be that since *participation in social decision* is a need rooted in human nature, and democracy more than any other form of government favors such participation,

---

citizens, of whatever race and social condition, and demands also that a juridically formulated constitution determine the basic laws of the regime under which the people deliberately resolve to place their political life" (p. 59). But he also says, "Not only does the democratic state of mind stem from the inspiration of the Gospel, but it cannot exist without it" (p. 49). He claims that democracy in the United States, had "never lost sight of its Christian origins" as it had done in Europe (p. 23).

46. For expositions of the libertarian position see Tibor R. Machan, ed., *The Libertarian Reader* (Totowa, NJ: Rowman and Littlefield, 1982), and David G. Green, *The New Conservatism: The Counter-Revolution in Political, Economic, and Social Thought* (New York: St. Martin's Press, 1987), especially the conclusion, pp. 210–20.

democracy is the form of government that best meets the needs of human nature.

The major premise of this argument is established by reference to what the papal encyclicals have called "the principle of subsidiarity," which states that in a community decisions should be made if possible by those whom they immediately affect rather than by higher authority, whose role is to correct or supplement but not to replace such decisions made closer to home.[47] This principle in turn rests on the fact that practical decisions require not only the knowledge of general principles but of concrete circumstances better known by those immediately affected than by higher authorities often limited to more general knowledge.

Thus it seems to be true that participation in decision by all adult members of a community is necessary for the best social decisions and hence for the full achievement of its common good. Moreover, since the common good of a community is not something other than the personal good of each and all its members mutually shared, and since the virtue of prudence required to participate well in social decisions is a perfection of each of these members, they have a right to participate in order to acquire and exercise such a virtue. Ideally, therefore, a community consists of virtuous persons who have achieved maturity by participation in the responsible decisions of the community to which they belong.

Participation and Democracy

Therefore, if democracy is the best form of government it ought to maximize participation by the citizenry. If, however, the United

47. "Authorities must beware of hindering family, social, or cultural groups, as well as intermediate bodies and institutions. They must not deprive them of their own lawful and effective activity, but should rather strive to promote them willingly and in orderly fashion. For their part, citizens both as individuals in association should be on guard against granting government too much authority and inappropriately seeking from it excessive conveniences and advantages, with a consequent weakening of the sense of responsibility on the part of individuals, families, and groups" (Vatican II, *Gaudium et Spes*, no. 75). *Gaudium et Spes* uses the term "participation" *(actuosa participatio)* both of economic (no. 68) and political participation (no. 75).

States is our exemplar, it must be admitted that ours is hardly a "participatory democracy," as its young critics during the 1960s forcefully pointed out. Ours is in fact a country where the majority of citizens do not bother to vote even in major elections, let alone actively participate in the political process.[48] Increasingly Americans view "politics" as somebody else's business.

Furthermore, a government need not take the form of a democracy to have excellent participation by its citizens in the political process. One can at least imagine a hereditary monarchy in which ultimate decision rests with the king (as it tends to rest with our president), yet through a system of consultations beginning at the local level and rising up to the level of the king's council, genuine participation by all citizens would be achieved so that the monarch in having the last word would have the benefit of the experience of all her or his subjects. The same might be true of any of the forms of government, except tyrannies.

One may argue of course that only in a democracy, where the power of majority vote always remains a possibility, can the participatory process be protected from tyrannical manipulation. But it must be remembered that unless the people do in fact participate actively in the political process the majority vote may not really represent the people's real experience of their true interests but only demagogic manipulation. Indeed, it must be admitted that even in a tyranny, the dictator governing for his own interests and not for the common good usually finds it expedient to promote the appearance of very wide consultative participation in order to better control his victims. Some say that this is the case in Libya, where Gadaffi encourages much grass-roots participation.

48. "Although it is seldom openly admitted, many members of both the liberal and conservative camps are wary of fuller popular participation in American politics. Conservatives fear blacks, while liberals often have disdain for working- and lower-middle-class whites" (Benjamin Ginsberg and Martin Shelter, "Electoral Decay and the Power of the American State," in *Do Elections Matter?* 2nd ed., ed. Benjamin Ginsberg and Alan Stone [Armonk, NY: M. E. Sharpe, 1991], 76). The federal election of 1992 was a happy surprise since the percentage of registrations and of registered voters was unprecedentedly high. It remains to be seen if this marks a trend in public attitudes.

Obstacles to Participation

The truth is, I believe, that those with political power, even when truly seeking justice, find it very difficult not merely to permit but to arouse in those they govern a real will to participate in government decisions. Anyone who has been an executive in any organization has experienced the tendency of many in the organization to shirk responsibility even when freedom to exercise it is open to them.[49] They hate to go to meetings. They dislike being bothered with information necessary to make decisions. They hate to accept responsibility and would prefer to leave it to others to take credit or blame. They would prefer to criticize those in authority rather than to share in it. They are aroused only when their private interests are endangered.

The greatest skill in political leadership is required not simply to get unity of action (that can be done by various forms of coercion), but to get everyone involved as a team of persons not merely carrying out decisions but sharing in the making of them in view of common goals.[50] Thus talk about "freedom" as if all our political ills are due to oppression by tyrannical authorities promotes an illusion. It masks the fact that if all the people were to use the

49. Joseph Dunne, *Back to the Rough Ground: 'Phronesis' and 'Techne' in Modern Philosophy and in Aristotle* (Notre Dame, IN: University of Notre Dame Press, 1993), shows the tendency in modern thought to reduce moral and political decision (*phronēsis*, prudence) to technique (*tekhnē*, art), so that the problem of participation becomes a matter of teaching the members of a society a set of subordinated *skills*. Yet, a great authority on the art of management, Peter Drucker, argues in an essay "Management as a Social Function and a Liberal Art," in *The New Realities in Government and Politics, in Economics and Business, in Society and World View* (New York: Harper and Row, 1990), that "Management is thus what tradition used to call a liberal art—'liberal' because it deals with the fundamentals of knowledge, self-knowledge, wisdom and leadership, 'art' because it is practice and application" (p. 231). If that is the case "management" which seeks to obtain the maximum of active participation by all members of a corporate body, is more than a technique, but includes *phronēsis*, the virtue of free, rational decision proper to free persons.

50. See Drucker, *New Realities*, 94–97. On the special problem of restriction of women to the private sphere see Jean Bethke Elshtain, *Public Man, Private Woman: Woman in Social and Political Thought* (Princeton, NJ: Princeton University Press, 1981).

freedom they actually have to participate in the political process in a real and not a specious way tyranny would hardly be possible. In fact, history illustrates that commonly people in authority initially dream of using their power for the common good, but when authorities meet the resistance of the masses to active participation, in desperation to get something done they begin to use unjust methods of coercion, and finally are corrupted by their pragmatic authoritarianism. Thus, ceasing to work for the common good in the face of the passivity of their followers, leaders begin cynically to pursue their own interests. Lord Acton's saying, "Absolute power corrupts absolutely," holds, but even limited power tends to absolutism and corruption when it fails to obtain participation by its subjects in the pursuit of the common good.

Economic Participation

What does this analysis say for participation in the church? The minimal form of participation in the church by an active member is financial support of its mission. Such participation incarnates, as it were, our spiritual participation in earthly reality. No one participated more in the early Gospel mission than St. Paul, but he had to busy himself in the midst of his preaching not only with making a living for himself (Acts 18:3; 1 Cor 9:1–18) but with the financial support of the struggling church. Defending his apostleship he writes, "James and Kephas and John, who were reputed to be pillars [of the church at Jerusalem], gave me and Barnabas their right hand in partnership, that we should go to the Gentiles and they to the circumcised. Only, we were to be mindful of the poor, which is the very thing I was eager to do" (Gal 2:9–10; cf. Rom 15:25–28; 1 Cor 16:1–4; 2 Cor 8–9; Acts 11:27–30).

Correlative to participation by contributing to the collection, of course, is the responsibility of stewardship in use of the resources. The church is often accused of violating justice by underpaying her personnel, especially women, since it seems unreasonable to expect gifted people to participate actively in the church's mission if they have to impoverish themselves or their families to do so.

The social doctrine of Vatican II, the papal encyclicals, and the pastoral letters of the United States Bishops on the forms of economy are too well known to need discussion here.[51] The church supports any form of economy that is sufficiently productive to meet basic human needs and that distributes its abundance fairly to all. Distributive justice, therefore, requires that workers receive equal pay for equal work, and that all receive a "living wage" or, if they are the support of a household, a "family wage."[52]

The investments of the Catholic church in the United States, however, are far from sufficient to maintain its ordinary operational expenses. It exists principally by the voluntary contributions of its members, and for various historical and sociological reasons the level of these contributions is well below what is expected by most Protestant churches.[53] Consequently, the work of the church depends largely on freely contributed services by its priests, religious, and lay auxiliaries.

Thus if the church is to maintain and perhaps expand its mission, it has only two resources: more generous money contributions from the laity, or an increase in contributed services. No doubt in the past the clergy too easily accepted the voluntary sacrifices of religious women, without just consideration of their needs, especially for education and retirement.[54] The principle of equal pay for equal work should be applied—as it is in many

51. A brief introduction can be found in David Bohr, "Catholic Social Teaching," chap. 11 in *Catholic Moral Tradition: In Christ, A New Creation* (Huntington, IN: Our Sunday Visitor Publishing Division, 1990).

52. Vatican II, *Gaudium et Spes*, no. 67.

53. See Peter Steinfels, "Churches Are Caught in Economy's Grip," *New York Times*, June 20, 1991, sec. A, p. 1, final edition; and Andrew Greeley and William McManus, *Catholic Contributions: Sociology and Polity* (Chicago: St. Thomas Moore Press, 1987). Greeley argues that the decline in financial contributions by U.S. Catholics is due to anger with the church's insistence on the intrinsic immorality of contraception. For a discussion of the problem of Vatican finances see Corrado Pallenberg, *Vatican Finances* (London: Peter Owen, 1971), Nino Lo Bello, *The Vatican Empire* (New York: Trident, 1968), and Malachy Martin, *Rich Church, Poor Church* (New York: Putnam, 1984).

54. The U.S. Bishops collected $25.4 million from parishes through their December, 1988, "Campaign for a Retirement Fund for Religious"; see *Origins* 19 (Sept. 28, 1989): 274.

dioceses today. Most Catholic clergy today live very moderately,[55] but we need seriously to consider how efficiently the resources of the church are employed according to the real priorities of the Gospel.

Less recognized is the fact that the church will in the future have to support more trained lay people in functions once performed by clergy and religious, not only because of declining clerical and religious vocations, but also to achieve greater lay participation in the church's life and mission. No matter how dedicated, these lay workers must still be educated, and provision made for their families, health, and retirement.

Decisional Participation

The participation of all members of the church in caring for those in need and supporting its ministry economically implies that they ought also to participate somehow in decisions about how this ministry should be conducted, lest their contributions be squandered by a negligent bureaucracy. Of course there must be a degree of trust in the officers of the community, but this trust cannot be unlimited in the face of abuse.

This active participation of all members of the church must, however, be conditioned by the special nature of the church community and its unique mission. While the church as a community is analogous to both state and family and has certain features in common with them, it differs greatly from both. The essential structure of the church, according to the Council of Trent and reconfirmed by Vatican I and II, was instituted by historical acts of Christ.

Jesus structured his church when he chose the Twelve, gave them special instructions, conferred on them authority over his other disciples not merely as individuals but as a convoked assem-

55. In a typical diocese known to me, a priest receives a stipend of about seven hundred dollars a month (with a small yearly bonus up to twenty-five years of active service) from which he must pay all expenses except room, board, and health and accident insurance. He must save for his own vacations and retirement, although he may receive care in a common residence for retired priests if necessary. While formerly bishops had large mansions, many are now living in modest apartments.

bly *(ecclesia)*, and commissioned them to baptize, to absolve from
sin, and to celebrate the Eucharist. This *ecclesia* was then empowered to continue until the end of history by Jesus' promise to send
his Holy Spirit as its animating and directing principle. No doubt
this structure was conditioned by Jewish customs and the situation
of Jesus' times. Its historical development through the ages was left
to the creative action of the church under the guidance of the Holy
Spirit. Although the paucity of historical data does not permit us
to trace the exact steps of this evolution, the church's essential
structure was manifested by the second century in the three-fold
hierarchy of bishop, priest, and deacon, with the college of bishops
recognizing a certain primacy in the Bishop of Rome as a successor
of St. Peter and claiming their own authority to be founded in that
of the Twelve Apostles.[56]

The structure of the church is analogous to the structure of
other human societies, so classical ecclesiology could speak of it
of it as "a perfect society."[57] It is similar both to a family and to
a secular state. Just as the state and the family are corporations
with a hierarchical structure, so is the church. How then does the
church differ radically from family and state? On the one hand,

56. At least this is the picture given by Ignatius of Antioch (circa 110) as regards the threefold hierarchy, and of St. Irenaeus (circa 180) as regards the Roman
primacy. Current scholarship holds that Ignatius's insistence on the authority of
the bishop in the primitive church shows that the institution of a single bishop in
each church was "recent"; but, how could Ignatius without further argument appeal so confidently to it if it was not already traditional (at least in the Pauline-
Johannine churches of Asia Minor to which he wrote)? On the Petrine office see
Raymond E. Brown, et al., eds., *Peter in the New Testament: A Collaborative Assessment by Protestant and Roman Catholic Scholars* (Minneapolis: Augsburg
Publishing House, 1973); J. M. R. Tillard, O.P., *The Bishop of Rome*, trans. John
de Satge (Wilmington, DE: Michael Glazier, 1983): 68–120; J. Michael Miller,
C.S.B., *What Are They Saying About Papal Primacy?* (New York/Ramsey: Paulist
Press, 1983), 86–92; and Karl-Heinz Ohlig, *Why We Need the Pope: The Necessity
and Limits of Papal Primacy*, trans. Robert C. Ware (St. Meinrad, IN: Abbey Press,
1975), 86–92. In my opinion, Ohlig exaggerates the historical flexibility of the
form of the papal office. On the development of ministries in the church see the
magisterial article of Raymond E. Brown, S.S., "*Episkopē* and *Episkopos:* The New
Testament Evidence," *Theological Studies* (June 1980): 322–38; and, from a different point of view, Manuel Miguens, O.F.M., *Church Ministries in New Testament Times* (Arlington, VA: Westminster Press, 1976).

57. See Avery Dulles, "Church as Institution," in *Models of the Church*, rev.
ed. (Garden City, NY: Doubleday Image Books, 1987).

the church's structure, unlike that of the family, is not determined by human nature but is more like that of the state in that it is the creation of a human founder—the historical human Jesus—who freely chose its form. On the other hand, unlike the state, this essential church structure fixed by Christ cannot be changed by any human agency, although in nonessentials it can be modified by those authorized within the church to do so.

Furthermore, the church's mission as a community is quite different from the purposes of the family or the state and transcends any determination by human nature as such. Even to call it a "papal monarchy," as some have done, does not accurately describe its structure. The church is not a state, and many of the most serious ecclesial problems of the past have been the result of undue influence of secular forms of government (such as the Constantinian Establishment) on the church. Nor indeed, is the church a family in any literal sense. Jesus was insistent that the Christian must transcend familial relations in the church in favor of relations based on its mission (Mk 3:31–35).

According to Vatican II the unique purpose of the church is above all to offer a worthy worship of God and, so that this can be effected, to call a community to faith by preaching and unify it in the bonds of the Holy Spirit of love—purposes unattainable by any natural institution. In the church the kingdom of God is already seminally present.[58]

Yet the analogy of ecclesial structure to that of human societies does hold as regards the ideal of participation. Vatican II emphasizes that the church's fundamental tasks of worship, community formation, and preaching the Gospel are shared in by *all* the members of the church who are made participants of this mission by

58. See Vatican II, "The Mystery of the Church," chap. 1 of *Lumen Gentium* (nos. 1–8). The Council teaches that while the earthly church is not simply identical with the Kingdom of God initiated in Jesus Christ, yet "The Church, . . . equipped with the gifts of her Founder and faithfully guarding His precepts of charity, humility, and self-sacrifice, receives the mission to proclaim and to establish among all peoples the kingdom of Christ and God. She becomes on earth the initial budding forth of that kingdom. While she slowly grows, the Church strains toward the consummation of the kingdom and, with all her strength, hopes and desires to be united in glory with her King" (no. 5). See also *Gaudium et Spes*, nos. 39–43.

baptism and empowered to actively engage in it by confirmation. A principal point of Vatican II's liturgical reforms was to insist on the "active participation" of the faithful in the liturgy, paradigmatic of their mission in all the works of the church.[59] History and contemporary experience, however, show us how far the church, just as the state, has fallen short of achieving this activation of its members. Even in the earliest days of the church, as the New Testament epistles and the book of Revelation witness, there were not a few lethargic and merely passive members of the Christian communities (see, e.g., Rv 2–3). Today it would appear that the great majority of those baptized as Christians, even as Catholics, share in the life of the church only in a minimal, or even nominal way.[60]

Justice in the church, therefore, is not to be defined by asking how "democratic" is the church, if by "democracy" is meant some particular form of government. Jesus' authorization of the Twelve was not in this sense "democratic." Nor do the apostolic writings seem to "engage in dialogue" with the churches, but rather make authoritative demands, although with great charity and sensitivity.[61] Some of these early church leaders may have been elected, but

59. "In the restoration and promotion of the sacred liturgy, this full and active participation by all the people is the aim to be considered above all else; for it is the primary and indispensable source from which the faithful are to derive the Christian spirit. Therefore, through the needed program of instruction, pastors of souls must zealously strive to achieve it in all their pastoral work" ("Constitution on the Sacred Liturgy" [Sacrosanctum Concilium], no. 14).
60. Opinion research seems to show that the United States remains statistically much more "religious" than Europe. Thus according to Religion in America: 50 Years: 1935–1985, The Gallup Report, no. 236 (May 1985), 71 percent of Americans "believe in life after death" compared to 45 percent in Great Britain (p. 53). Yet, according to the same survey, while the church or synagogue membership rate in 1937 was 73 percent and the church attendance rate in a typical week was 41 percent, by 1984 these numbers had dropped to 68 percent and 40 percent, and this decline has so far not been reversed. Wade Clark Roof and William McKinney, American Mainline Religion (New Brunswick, NJ: Rutgers University Press, 1987), conclude, after a detailed analysis, that "Whether these communities of memory have the requisite resources—the symbols, the language, the conviction—to restore a broadly based public faith appears unlikely, at least in the manner we knew it prior to the 1960s. The forces of modern individualism have become far too powerful, and the dislocations in religion and culture far too great" (p. 250).
61. For example, Paul's excommunication of the incestuous man in 1 Cor 5:1–

others were authoritatively appointed, no doubt with concurrence of the local church.[62] Nor did they make decisions by a consensus process, but ruled their communities as pastors over a flock. It is anachronistic to reconstruct an early church that is supposed to be "democratic" in the modern manner, a "Jesus Movement" based on "equality of discipleship."[63]

On the other hand, if by "democratic" we mean participatory,

---

13 and his advice on reconciling the sinner in 2 Cor 2:5–11. Jerome Murphy-O'Connor, O.P., commenting on 1 Cor 5:3–4 in *The New Jerome Biblical Commentary*, ed. Raymond E. Brown, Joseph A. Fitzmyer, S.J., and Roland E. Murphy, O. Carm. (Englewood Cliffs, NJ: Prentice-Hall, 1990), claims that "The decision is to be made by the whole assembly . . . Paul is indicating the decision he wants, not imposing it" (p. 803). But Paul says, "I, for my part, although absent in body but present in spirit, have already, as if present, pronounced judgment on the one who has committed this deed" (1 Cor 5:3). Thus the man is excommunicated by Paul's own *independent*, apostolic authority even if the local church fails to do so (*pace* Murphy-O'Connor, who sees in this only Paul's claim to be heard as if he were a member of the council of the local church!). Current commentators, influenced by contemporary anti-authoritarian attitudes, are uncomfortable with Paul's insistence on his apostolic power "to bind and to loose" (Mt 16:19).

62. According to Acts, the place of Judas among the Twelve was filled by lot (1:15–24), but the Seven were elected by the community (6:5). Yet in the Pauline epistles it would seem that Paul appoints, although presumably with the consent of the community. Thus Miguens writes, "It is obvious that Paul, even as an 'apostle,' felt that he had authority over his communities and that he, in factual reality, ruled and organized his communities, and was the judiciary officer of these communities as well. The most obvious alternative [to the hypothesis of elections], therefore, is that he appointed the officers of these communities and delegated part of his authority to them, while he remained the undisputed leader of his communities. This is the view of the Pastoral Letters which cannot be proven to run against an historical fact. On the other hand, there is strong evidence that Paul himself was 'sent' by the leaders of the Church, he himself being an officer of the Church—first, as a teacher (Acts 11:26; 13:1) and then as an apostle. This renders unnecessary any other link between Paul and Twelve" (*Church Ministries*, 103).

63. Wayne A. Meeks at the end of his *The First Urban Christians: The Social World of the Apostle Paul* (New Haven, CT: Yale University Press, 1983) writes, "The churches, too, were mixtures of social statuses. The kinds of relationships that the members had previously had to one another, and still had in other settings—between master and slave, rich and poor, freedman and patron, male and female, and the like—stood in tension with the *communitas* celebrated in the rituals of baptism and the Lord's Supper. There was tension, too, between the familiar hierarchy of those roles and the freedom of the Spirit to confer distinction, by means of some charisma, upon a person of inferior status. So, too we find in the letters a stress on symbols of unity, equality, and love, but also correlative symbols of fluidity, diversity, individuation" (pp. 191–92). Couldn't this also be said of the church today? A charismatic figure like the monk Thomas Merton has had more influence than most bishops.

then it is clear that the early church strove to get all its members actively involved in the church's mission and to make use of all their individual gifts and their experience as Christians. St. Paul in trying to bring order into the Corinthian church was insistent that the gifts of the spirit in each member not be stifled (as he also wrote to the Thessalonians, 1 Th 5:19).

How these two values of authority and participation are to be reconciled in practice is something that necessarily varies from place to place, time to time, situation to situation. What we can lay down as a principal conclusion of this whole discussion is that justice in the church is not to be judged by attempting to reduce the church to some secular model, even of an ideal democracy. On the contrary, *justice in the church must be judged by how the church in its governance succeeds in bringing about full participation of all its members in the church's life and mission.* Considering how great are the obstacles to participation in our democratic state, should we be surprised that living in this same culture we must move mountains to obtain full participation in the church? Our hope is that, in the words of St. Peter, we the baptized although "rejected by human beings, . . . [are] chosen and precious in the sight of God, and like living stones [are to] be built into a spiritual house to be a holy priesthood to offer spiritual sacrifices acceptable to God through Jesus Christ" (1 Pt 2:4–5).

CHAPTER III

Men and Hierarchy

Men and Priesthood

Participation and the Restriction of Priesthood to Men

I have tried to show in Chapter I that the violations of legitimate free speech in the church can be best remedied by balancing the right of the bishops to doctrinal decision against the bishops' active promotion of fair theological debate. In Chapter II, I have tried to show that justice in church government should be judged not by whether the forms of church organization are "democratic" but by the degree to which all members of the church actively participate in the church's life and mission. I turn now to the problem of ordination as a form of participation in that life and mission.

The problem of women's ordination might be approached in two ways. One would be to criticize the Vatican documents, the *Declaration on the Question of the Admission of Women to the Ministerial Priesthood (Inter Insigniores)* of the Sacred Congregation for the Doctrine of the Faith of 1976 and John Paul II's subsequent, more authoritative declaration, "Apostolic Letter on Ordination and Women," *(Ordinatio Sacerdotalis)* of 1994,[1] in order to show that they are not conclusive and the question is still open. But the authority of decisions of the magisterium do not

1. References in Chapter I note 1 above. This tradition is also witnessed by the Eastern churches. For essays by various authors on the Orthodox point of view, see Thomas Hopko, ed., *Woman and the Priesthood* (Crestwood, NY: St. Vladimir's Seminary Press, 1983). Nevertheless, the Orthodox theologian, Elisabeth Behr-Siegel, *Le Ministère de la femme dans l'Église* (Paris: Ed. du Cerf, 1987), a work praised by Hopko, makes a plea for a more open stance on the question in her church.

depend on the arguments with which they are presented, and *Ordinatio Sacerdotalis* is clearly a very serious act of the ordinary magisterium, as is evident from its conclusion in which John Paul II declares:

> In order that all doubt may be removed regarding a matter of great importance, a matter which pertains to the Church's divine constitution itself, in virtue of my ministry of confirming the brethren (cf. Lk 22:32) I declare that the Church has no authority whatsoever to confer priestly ordination on women and that this judgment is to be definitively held by all the Church's faithful.

That this definitive declaration is not merely disciplinary but doctrinal and pertinent to the *depositum fidei* has recently been affirmed by a response of the Congregation of the Doctrine of the Faith to inquiries, and has been published with John Paul II's approval.[2]

Evidently this decision is intended to stop agitation for a change in the church's traditional practice and to restrict theological debate to the strictly theoretical plane in view of a deeper understanding of the issues. Hence, continued theological study of the matter, provided it is sincerely respectful of the authoritative steps already taken by the magisterium, can greatly assist in this development.

Hence it seems more constructive to pursue a second way and to deal directly with the question, stating the reasons that have been proposed for a change in the church's practice, criticizing these arguments, and then seeking a theoretical theological solution. Naturally, the solution I will propose will try to take faithfully into account the authoritative position of the magisterium in its full weight, since I believe that this is required by any sound theological method. Rather than confuse this constructive argumentation I have relegated my analysis of the criticisms made of the Vatican documents to Appendices 1 and 3.

What, then, are the principal arguments that favor the possi-

2. See Appendix 3.

bility of women's ordination?[3] They seem to be seven. First of all, is it not a fact that the Scriptures do not explicitly reserve ordination to men, and even contain traces of a time in the early church when women played important ministerial roles that must have required ordination or its equivalent?[4]

3. For a general bibliography on women's studies see Patricia K. Ballou, *Women: A Bibliography of Bibliographies*, 2nd ed. (Boston: G. K. Hall, 1986). On women's ordination see John H. Morgan and Teri Wall, eds., *The Ordination of Women: a Comprehesnive Bibliography* (Wichita, KS: Institute on Ministry and the Elderly, 1977). For a select bibliography pro and con on the present topic see my *Theologies of the Body: Humanist and Christian*, 560 n. 92, and Wendell E. Langley, S.J., and Rosemary Jermann, "Women and the Ministerial Priesthood: An Annotated Bibliography," *Theology Digest* 29 (1981): 329–42. Strong cases against ordination are made by Ida F. Görres, "Women as Priests," *Herder Correspondence* 3 (1966): 205–11; *The Order of Priesthood: Nine Commentaries on the Vatican Decree Inter Insigniores*, from *L'Osservatore Romano* (Huntington, IN: Our Sunday Visitor Press, 1978); L. Ligier, "Women and the Ministerial Priesthood," *Origins* 7 (Apr. 20, 1978): 694–702; Louis Bouyer, *Woman in the Church*, trans. Marilyn Techert (San Francisco: Ignatius Press, 1979), with an epilogue by Hans Urs von Balthasar and essay by C. S. Lewis; Hans Urs von Balthasar, "Frauenpriestertum," *Neue Klarstellungen* (Einsiedeln: Johannes Verlag, 1979); Janine Hourcade, *La Femme dans l'Église* (Paris: Téqui, 1986); Manfred Hauke, *Women in the Priesthood? A Systematic Analysis in the Light of the Order of Creation and Redemption*, trans. David Kipp (San Francisco: Ignatius Press, 1988); Helmut Moll, ed., *The Church and Women: A Compendium* (San Francisco: Ignatius Press, 1988), including essays by Hans Urs von Balthasar, Walter Kasper, and Joseph Cardinal Ratzinger; and Patrick Dunn, *Priesthood: A Re-Examination of the Roman Catholic Theology of the Presbyterate* (Staten Island, NH: Alba House, 1990), 173–96. Strong cases for ordination are made by Ida Raming, *The Exclusion of Women from Priesthood: Divine Law or Sex Discrimination?* trans. Norman R. Adams (Meutchen, NJ: Scarecrow Press, 1976); Haye van der Meer, *Women Priests in the Catholic Church: A Theological-Historical Investigation*, trans. Arlene and Leonard Swidler (Philadelphia: Temple University Press, 1973), and the authors in the volume the Swidlers edited, *Women Priests: A Catholic Commentary on the Vatican Declaration* (New York: Paulist Press, 1977), with a helpful survey of literature by Ann E. Patrick, "Studies in Women Priests" (pp. 70–75); George Tavard, *Woman in Christian Tradition* (Notre Dame: University of Notre Dame, 1973); Karl Rahner, "Priestertum der Frau?" *Stimmen der Zeit* 195 (1977): 291–301; Joseph Komonchak, "Theological Questions on the Ordination of Women" *Catholic Mind* 75 (Jan. 1977): 13–28; Carroll Stuhlmueller, C.P., ed., *Women and Priesthood: Future Directions* (Collegville, MN: Liturgical Press, 1978); and Elisabeth Schüssler Fiorenza, *In Memory of Her*. See also *Women and the Catholic Priesthood: The Detroit Ordination Conference, 1975* (New York: Paulist Press, 1976).

4. The best case for this seems to be Elisabeth Schüssler Fiorenza, *In Memory of Her*, but this was severely criticized by a number of reviewers; see the reviews

The difficulty with this line of argument is that most Catholic biblical scholars seem to have concluded that the New Testament, when subjected to historical-critical methods, does not supply us with sufficient data on priesthood in the early church to answer our question on purely historical grounds.[5] Instead, keeping in mind the teachings of Trent of and Vatican II on the intimate relation of Scripture and tradition,[6] we must interpret the biblical data on ministry in the early church, not only by historical-critical methods but in the light of that tradition of living faith.

Second, it seems to many obvious that the real source of this "tradition" is the "patriarchalism" of the Jewish and pagan milieu of the early church, and that its subsequent theological history is

---

by Ross S. Kraemer, *Journal of Biblical Literature* 104 (1985): 722–25, and Robert M. Grant, *Journal of Religion* 65 (1985): 83–88. Her conclusions are determined by her hermeneutical stance, which she has clearly stated elsewhere: "In conclusion, what leads us to perceive biblical texts as providing resources in the struggle for liberation from patriarchal oppression as well as models for the transformation of the patriarchal church, is not some special canon of texts that can claim divine authority. Rather it is the experience of women themselves in their struggles for liberation" ("The Will to Choose or to Reject," in *Feminist Interpretations of the Bible*, ed. Letty M. Russell [Philadelphia: Westminister Press, 1985], 133–35 n. 11). Can this be squared with the nature of biblical inspiration as stated by Vatican II, *Dei Verbum*? For an evaluation of the evidence not determined by a feminine liberationist hermeneutic see Ben Witherington III, *Women in the Ministry of Jesus: A Study of Jesus' Attitudes to Women and Their Roles as Reflected in His Earthly life* and *Women in the Earliest Churches*, Society for New Testament Studies Monograph Series, nos. 51 and 59 (Cambridge: Cambridge University Press, 1984 and 1988).

5. "It belongs therefore to exegetes to try to situate geographically as well as historically these various ministerial forms and to outline their evolution. This is a difficult task because of the occasional character of the apostolic letters and also on account of the varied historical evaluation of the work of the evangelists and the author of Acts" (André Lemaire, "The Ministries in the New Testament," *Biblical Theology Bulletin* 3 (June 1973): 139–40. The Catholic Biblical Association Task Force on "The Role of Women in Early Christianity," *Catholic Biblical Quarterly* 41 (1979), claimed "Women did in fact exercise roles and functions later associated with priestly ministry" (p. 612), and that the "NT evidence, while not decisive by itself, points to the admission of women to priestly ministry" (pp. 612–13). To say it "points to" in the face of the Pauline statements about women's role in the church assemblies goes beyond the evidence.

6. "Hence there exists a close connection and communication between sacred tradition and sacred Scripture. For both of them, flowing from the same divine wellspring, in a certain way merge into a unity and tend toward the same end" (Vatican II, *Dei Verbum*, no. 9).

based on the notion of woman's natural inferiority and subordination to man. Moreover, they call attention to certain events in later church history that seem to show that this tradition has not been absolutely consistent.[7]

Inter Insigniores, countered this objection by pointing out that Jesus was countercultural in many respects, especially in his attitude toward women. If "equality of discipleship" is really so central to the Gospel as Christian feminists are arguing, is it really credible that Jesus himself would have compromised it by such an act of injustice to women?[8] As for the alleged historical exceptions, the intensive search for these in the course of this controversy has confirmed rather than weakened the evidence for the universality of the church's practice in ordaining only males. The "exceptions to the rule" are ambiguous, and even if valid, have been so rare they can better be explained as abuses than validating precedents.[9]

7. Giorgio Otranto, "Priesthood, Precedent, and Prejudice," trans. Mary Ann Rossi's, *Journal of Feminist Studies in Religion* 7, 1 (Spring 1991): 73–94, has called attention to the *protest* of Pope Gelasius I (492–96) against the *abuse* of permitting women to perform "all" offices "at the sacred altars" in certain churches of Southern Italy and Sicily. Otranto tries to support this document with ambiguous epigraphic data and thus to interpret these practices as valid ordinations, not to the diaconate as other scholars have done, but to the priesthood. Therefore, Mary O'Collins, O.S.B., of the Catholic University of America in the same symposium, commenting favorably on Otranto's theory, raised the question whether a local bishop can validly ordain a woman even if the Bishop of Rome condemns the action (!). Other supposed exceptions will be found in van der Meer, *Women Priests in the Catholic Church;* Joan Morris, *The Lady Was a Bishop* (New York: Macmillan, 1973); Ida Raming, *The Exclusion of Women from Priesthood;* and Robert J Heyer, ed., *Women and Orders* (New York: Paulist Press, 1974).

8. On the theological weight of *Ordinatio Sacerdotalis,* see the discussion in Appendices 1 and 3, below. On the supposed novelty of the question, see Hauke, "A Historically Conditioned Undervaluation of Women as the Reason for Their Exclusion from Priesthood?" chap. 8 in *Women in the Priesthood?* where he says, "Testimonies favoring both a low evaluation and a high evaluation of women run through the whole of human history without any recognizable sign of essential historical progress. The present-day situation, too, is not as new as many contemporaries like to suppose. For instance, the social position of women in the second century, A.D., . . . is in many respects a veritable showcase of 'modern' conditions" (p. 471).

9. We know of these cases usually because of documents showing their suppression as abuses by church authorities. See note 7, above, on the action of Gelasius I against abuses in Southern Italy; and Hauke, *Women in the Priesthood?* on the actions of the patristic church against the Montanists (pp. 404–25) and of Honorius III against conferring jurisdiction on abbesses (p. 464).

Therefore, those who believe in the possibility of women's ordination now generally bypass argumentation from the Bible and tradition as too time-conditioned to be any longer relevant, and rely rather on arguments based on the needs of the church in the modern world. The third argument, therefore, is that in our times it seems impossible for the church to satisfy the faithful's right to the Eucharist by male vocations alone, at least in Europe and the United States.[10]

This argument, however, seems to beg the question, since the people's need for the Eucharist can hardly of itself qualify an unqualified candidate for priesthood. Moreover, does not the faithful's "right to the Eucharist" imply a correlative obligation on their part to provide sufficient and suitable candidates for the priesthood?[11] In the past the laity supplied themselves with priests

10. On the problem of the shortage of priests and measures to remedy the situation see "Norms for Cooperation Among Local Churches and for a Better Distribution of the Clergy," (Postquam apostoli), Sacred Congregation for the Clergy, March 25, 1980, in Austin Flannery, ed., Vatican Council II: More Postconciliar Documents (Northport, NY: Costello Publishing Co., 1982), no. 99. At the same time some religious sisters resent and even refuse to attend the Eucharist if it is celebrated (and especially if concelebrated) by male priests, see Sister Mary Collins, O.S.B., address to the Leadership Conference of Women Religious, "Is the Eucharist Still a Source of Meaning for Women?" Origins 21 (Sept. 12, 1991): 225–29. But other Catholic feminists support the traditional practice; see Rousseau, "Real Fems," Catholicism in Crisis 2 (Feb. 1984): 17–22.

11. If it be argued that in order to satisfy its "right" to the Eucharist, a local church can decide what the qualifications for its celebrant are to be, and thus can ordain women or married persons, it must be recalled that priests are ordained to the presbyterium of the whole church, not merely for a local church. Hence their qualifications must be accepted by apostolic authority. The suggestions made by Edward Schillebeeckx, O.P., Ministry: Leadership in the Community of Jesus Christ (New York: Crossroad, 1981), about the power of local churches to ordain their own ministries, have been well answered from an exegetical and historical point of view by Pierre Grelot, Église et Ministères: Pour un dialogue critique avec Edward Schillebeeckx (Paris: Éditions du Cerf, 1983), and by Albert Vanhoye, S.J., and Henri Crouzel, S.J., "The Ministry in the Church: Reflections on a Recent Publication," The Clergy Review 5.68 (May 1983): 156–74; and from a more theological point of view by Walter Kasper, "Ministry in the Church: Taking Issue with Edward Schillebeeckx," Communio, Summer 1983, 185–95. Schillebeeckx tried to answer these criticisms as well as to satisfy the Congregation for the Doctrine of the Faith (unsuccessfully) in The Church with a Human Face: A New and Expanded Theology of Ministry (New York: Crossroad, 1985); cf. Congregation for the Doctrine of the Faith, "Letter to Fr. Schillebeeckx Regarding His Book

by offering themselves as candidates, by generosity in parenthood, by fostering the ideal of priestly vocation in their children, by inviting promising young men to be candidates for priesthood, or, in the early church, by electing married candidates on condition they promise to live after their ordination as celibates.[12] Thus it is argued that the present lack of vocations in certain countries is not inevitable but has resulted from the influence on the Catholic laity of the mode of living common in their secular milieu and the growing pressures to conform to it. Hence this shortage can only be remedied by increased participation by the laity in the church's authentic life. Moreover, the decline of priestly vocations is matched by an even greater decline of vocations

---

Ministry," *Origins* 14 (Jan. 24, 1985): 523, and "Note on Response of Fr. Schillebeeckx," *Origins* 14 (Apr. 4, 1985): 683.

12. See Christian Cochini, S.J., *Origines apostoliques du célibat sacerdotal* (Paris: P. Lethielleux, Le Sycomore, 1980), and the review of this book by Ch. Martin, S.J., *Nouvelle Revue Théologique* 105 (1983): 437–38. Cochini argues that while married men were usually chosen for deacon, priest, and bishop, contrary to what is often assumed, the known cases in the first three centuries are not proved to have children after ordination. In the fourth century councils begin to require abstinence after ordination both in East and West. The retention of wives after ordination (but not for bishops) was *tolerated* in the East only by the Council of Trullo in the seventh century by an act never approved by Rome. Thus the oft repeated claim that clerical celibacy in the West was a medieval innovation is erroneous, based on the efforts of Gregory VII strictly to enforce the ancient practice of the Latin church. Roman Cholij, *Clerical Celibacy in East and West* (Herefordshire, UK: Fowler Wright Books, 1989), a priest of the Ukrainian Catholic church, confirms the canonical part of Cochini's argument. Other scholars, not contesting these canonical facts, attribute them to an exaggerated enthusiasm for virginity and celibacy, which they say arose in the fourth century and think it must have been more an ideal than a reality; see Roger Gryson, *The Ministry of Women in the Early Church,* trans. Jean Laporte and Mary Louis Hall (Collegeville, MN: The Liturgical Press, 1976). See the review of the original French edition by H. Crouzel, *Nouvelle Revue Théologique* 93 (1971): 649–53; and R. Gryson, "Dix ans de recherches sur les origines du célibat ecclésiastique: Reflexion sur les publications des annees 1970–1979, *Revue Théologique de Louvain* 11 (1980): 157–85. See also Pierre Grelot, *Église et Ministères,* 153–61 who criticizes Cochini's reading of 1 Tm 3:2 and Ti 1:6. Clifford Stevens, "The Law of Celibacy: Some Historical Corrections," *The Priest* 50 (1994): 42–44, favors celibacy but attacks Cochini both on theological and historical grounds, but in a rather popular article does not substantiate his case. Vatican II, "On the Ministry and Life of Priests" *(Presbyterorum Ordinis),* no. 16 says, "Celibacy was at first recommended to priests. Then, in the Latin Church, it was imposed by law on all who were to be promoted to sacred orders."

among women religious. What is the proof, it is asked, that opening priesthood to women will really lead to a more than temporary increase in the total number of persons dedicating their lives to the service of the church?[13] May it not further decrease male vocations while adding only a handful of female vocations?

Pragmatic arguments from the shortage of priests for women's ordination resemble the parallel arguments for supplying more priests by abolishing mandatory celibacy. Those who reject this solution say that such proposals ignore the fact that priestly vocations decline where priesthood is not sufficiently honored among the faithful. In most cultures men are encouraged much more than women to pursue sexual gratification, so the willingness of males to sacrifice sexual activity is generally recognized as even more extraordinary than for women to do so. Hence, not only in the Catholic tradition but in many of the world religions, for example Hinduism and Buddhism, the dignity of religious leadership seems to have been greatly enhanced by the witness of men dedicated totally by celibacy to a spiritual mission.

The fourth argument is that if priesthood is a calling from God, then, since some women do in fact experience that calling, to refuse them ordination is to stifle a divine charism.[14] Did not St. Paul command, "Do not quench the spirit" (1 Th 5:19)? Yet it must be admitted that while some male candidates for priesthood report such a subjective interior experience of God's call, others who be-

13. A recent study of over a thousand women members of religious congregations reported that only two percent said they "definitely" would seek ordination if the church allowed for women priests and this response was highest among middle-aged sisters. Elizabeth Durkin and Jule Durkin Montague, "Surveying U.S. Nuns," *America* 172 (1995): 11–17.

14. See Sister Fran Ferder, C.F.S. P.A., Ph.D., *Called to Break Bread?* (Mt. Rainier, MD: Quixote Center, 1978); see also her article, "An Experience of Priesthood," in *New Women, New Church, New Ministry* (Chapter II note 37 above), 101–8, which lists six characteristics of this experience: (1) an "excitement for the sacred"; (2) a call "to reveal" oneself to others; (3) "a clear, unmistakable call from God"; (4) a courageous desire "to rise above structure—to refuse to be bent low under the weight of tradition"; (5) a decision "to choose the better part" like Mary rather than Martha; (6) and a yearning "to be a pontifex, a bridge builder." These are certainly signs of a call to serve God in some special way, but is that way specifically the priesthood?

come excellent priests do not. Nor, even for males, have such subjective experiences been considered in the church to be valid unless
confirmed by the judgment of the ordaining bishop who must act
on more objective criteria.[15]

The fifth argument, therefore, is that there *is* an objective criterion on which ordination should be based, namely the biblical
teaching of Genesis that both men and women are created in the
image of God (Gn 1:27), and St. Paul's declaration in Galatians
that "There is neither Jew nor Greek, there is neither slave nor free
person, there is not male and female, for you are all one in Christ
Jesus" (Gal 3:28).[16] For some, these texts even imply the need to
level all "hierarchy" in the church in the name of "the discipleship
of equals."[17]

15. The New Testament states objective criteria for presbyters and deacons (1
Tm 3:1–12) and *episkopoi* (Ti 1:5–9) and advises "Do not lay hands too readily
on anyone, and do not share another's sins" (1 Tm 5:22).

16. If one needs an example of "proof-texting," the abuse of Gal 3:28 in the
ordination controversy is a splendid example. Note the context: Paul has been
speaking of how faith frees Christians from the obligations of the law (he has
circumcision and dietary regulations principally in mind), and he then writes,
"Consequently, the law was our disciplinarian for Christ, that we might be justified
by faith. But now that faith has come, we are no longer under a disciplinarian. For
through faith you are all children of God in Christ Jesus. For all of you who were
baptized into Christ have clothed yourselves with Christ. *There is neither Jew nor
Greek, there is neither slave nor free person, there is not male and female; for you
are all one in Christ Jesus.* And if you belong to Christ, then you are Abraham's
descendant, heirs according to the promise" (Gal 3:24–29). The parallel passage
in Col 3:11 is in the context of the death to sin and the new way of life: "Stop
lying to one another, since you have taken off the old self with its practices and
have put on the new self, which is being renewed, for knowledge, in the image of
the creator. *Here there is not Greek and Jew, circumcision and uncircumcision,
barbarian, Scythian, slave and free; but Christ is all in all.*" (Italics added to both
passages. See Chapter I note 27 above on the omission of "male and female" from
the parallel text in Colossians.) These texts say only that all the baptized are equally
members of the church, free of the Old Law, and of the old way of life. They cannot
be forced to support a rejection of functional hierarchy within the Christian community.

17. See Chapter I note 2 above. For a somewhat extreme statement from a
radical feminist: "Theologically speaking, then, we might say that the maleness of
Jesus has no ultimate significance. It has social symbolic significance in the frame-
work of societies of patriarchal privilege. In this sense Jesus as the Christ, the representative of liberated humanity and the liberating Word of God, manifests the
kenosis of patriarchy, the announcement of the new humanity through a lifestyle
that discards hierarchical caste privilege and speaks on behalf of the lowly. In a

If, however, to confuse personal equality with functional equality undermines the very foundations of basic human rights, as I argued in my first chapter, then to treat women as in some respects *functionally* unequal to men in no way derogates from their *personal* equality with men. We must, therefore, formulate our problem not in terms of equality, but of qualification for a particular function in the church.[18]

The sixth argument is that women are just as well qualified as men to teach, to preach, to administer, to lead liturgy, to counsel, etc., and indeed today are often better educated and more competent.[19] Yet to base the argument for women's ordination on this fact assumes that such functions as these are the essential ones that qualify for priesthood, an assumption still to be examined.

---

similar way, the femaleness of the social and religiously outcast who respond to him has social symbolic significance as a witness against the same idolatrous system of patriarchal privilege. This system is unmasked and shown to have no connection with favor with God" (Rosemary Radford Ruether, *Sexism and God-Talk: Toward a Feminist Theology* [Boston: Beacon, 1983], 138). For a critique of such views see Susanne Heine, *Women in Early Christianity: A Reappraisal*, (Minneapolis: Augsburg Publishing House, 1987). Heine is professor in the Protestant Faculty of Theology at the University of Vienna.

18. In using the term "function" in this context, I have no intention of adopting the purely "functional" theology of priesthood according to which to be a priest is merely to carry out certain functions, a mode of doing, as opposed to an "ontological" theory of priesthood as first of all a mode of being and living, which I would defend. As baptism constitutes a person in a new ontological state as a member of the church united to Christ, its head by grace; so analogically ordination constitutes the priest, already a baptized member of the church, in a certain ontological state *within* the body of the church, as sacramentally representing primarily Christ, its head and mediator with the Father in the Spirit, and secondarily representing the church, Christ's Body. As the baptized persons by their ontological status of grace are enabled to live as Christians, so the priest is enabled to perform certain functions within the church that its other members cannot perform, but he does so in their service not for himself.

19. Elisabeth Schüssler Fiorenza, in "To Console or Challenge," says with apparent approval of what she reports, "The pre-conference responses abundantly diagnose the destructive impact of sexism on the present ecclesial structures. Characterizations abound that speak of the present priesthood as 'distant, judgmental, opinionated, ritualistic, hierarchical instead of pastoral, exclusive, sterile, stifled, regressive, paternalistic, male-dominated, full of (expletive deleted), patriarchal, impersonal, frustrating.' These characterizations can be summarized in the following statements: 'The institutional church no longer mediates between the people and God.' 'The official church consolidates the existing structures in society thus oppressing women and other groups'" (p. 52).

A seventh and final argument for ordination of women is based on the principle of participation for which I argued in my first two chapters: women have the right equally with men to participate in decisions of the church; therefore, they must have equal access to the most powerful offices in the church. This argument seems to me to have greater force than any of the others, and I will deal with it at some length in my last chapter, but it too depends on the issue of functional qualification since, as I have already shown, there are other ways than holding offices of power to participate fully in decision making in a community.[20]

20. Sister Sara Butler, M.S.B.T., "The Findings of the Research Team of the Catholic Theological Society of America," in *New Women, New Church, New Ministry*, 117–25, summarizes the CTSA's *Research Report: Women in Church and Society* (Mahwah, NJ: Darlington Seminary, 1978), which she edited. The research team first considered the *praxis* of Jesus, the apostles, and the church, and concluded that (1) the New Testament does not decisively support nor exclude women's ordination, but does "in fact invite women to a situation of equality with men in their ministry and mission"; (2) "the constant practice of later centuries" is "an unexamined manner of acting, not a genuine theological tradition," while the Anglican and Protestant ordinations of women are evidence of a legitimate development; (3) the anthropology which supported exclusion, e.g., that women are in a "natural state of subjection . . . can no longer be seriously maintained"; and (4) "Injustice is done when women are excluded, "*unless* it can be established that this matter had been settled by divine will," so that "the pertinence of the 'justice argument' turns on the resolution of these two questions: the nature of pastoral office and the nature of women." The report also challenges "the Thomistic theology of the eucharistic ministry of the ordained" for three reasons: (1) it overemphasizes the "moment of consecration," (2) it treats the Eucharist as a "sacred drama" in which the priest plays the role of Christ and the members of the congregation are simply spectators, and (3) it fails to make clear that "priest acts 'in persona Ecclesiae' as well as 'in persona Christi,'" thus failing to show "that Christ is present to his church through the exercise of the church's *faith*, and not by an 'institution' (in this case, apostolic succession) which operates independently of that faith." To these three points I would reply in order: (1) Liturgists' insistence on the consecratory character of the whole eucharistic Prayer does not contradict St. Thomas's teaching that the Words of Institution (or something equivalent to them) are the *minimum* form required for sacramental validity. But how is this relevant to the issue at hand? (2) Does the fact that the whole congregation offers the Eucharist with and *through* the priest prove that it is not a "sacred drama"? Are the spectators at a drama always "simply spectators," or may there not also be "audience participation"? And where does St. Thomas Aquinas relegate the laity to being "simply spectators" at the Eucharist? (3) the question is, Faith in what? Is it not faith in Christ's promise to remain present in the church he instituted? And again, when did Thomists deny that priests act not only *in persona Christi* but also *in persona ecclesiae*? These "challenges" are addressed only to caricatures

Sacramental Development

Thus all these arguments stand or fall on the fundamental question whether the nature of the priesthood is such that for it male gender is a necessary qualification. If it is not, then the vagueness of the biblical data, the cultural conditioning of the tradition, and the need of the church to inculturate itself into a society where democratic values predominate, make the case for ordination the more probable to many theologians today.[21]

Furthermore, in taking up this question I am very aware that I am dealing with a kind of problem that is always difficult, perhaps impossible, to solve simply by theological reasoning. Since the sacraments were established by Christ and receive their validity from him, it is certain that the church has no power to change the sacraments he instituted in their essentials. Nevertheless, the church does have the power, as history attests, to make quite notable changes in the manner in which these holy rites are celebrated.[22]

The arguments that I propose to give are offered only for discussion, subject, of course, to the judgment of the magisterium,

---

of classical theology. See the reply of (now Bishop) John R. Sheets, S.J., "The CTSA and the Ordination of Women," *Communio* 5 (1978): 382–88.

21. See references in note 3 above.

22. Examples: Holy Communion for the laity was originally given under both kinds, then for a long time refused them, then restored by Vatican II. Alcoholic priests are allowed to use lightly fermented grape juice in substitution for regular wine in the Eucharist. Baptism of adults was originally by immersion, then by pouring, and then after Vatican II immersion was again permitted. Confirmation was originally (and always in the Eastern Rites) given at baptism and only by the bishop, later as an entirely separate rite and often by the pastor. Cases are known where popes permitted abbots who were priests but not bishops to ordain priests. Theologians in the Middle Ages taught that sacred orders are conferred by the *tradition instrumentorum* (Bible, chalice, paten, etc.), but Pius XII declared they were henceforth given by the laying on of hands. Confession and absolution of serious sins in the early church were performed publicly, only much later privately. Vatican II permitted the anointing of the sick to be given to some who formerly would have been refused because not in immediate danger of death. On this topic see Aimé Georges Martimort, *The Signs of the New Covenant*, rev. 2nd ed. (Collegeville, MN: The Liturgical Press, 1968), 32–34 and 39–40, and Paul J. LeBlanc, "Substantive Changes in Sacraments?" in *Women Priests: A Catholic Commentary*, ed. Leonard and Arlene Swidler, 216–20. On post-Vatican II theology of the sacraments see Michael G. Lawler, *Symbol and Sacrament: A Contemporary Sacramental Theology* (New York: Paulist Press, 1987).

which has warned, "As we are dealing with a debate which classical theology scarcely touched upon, the current argumentation runs the risk of neglecting essential elements."[23] Certainly, the magisterium could not permit a change in its sacramental practice until it had assured itself that the validity of the sacraments would be conserved.[24]

Meaning of Priesthood

One Priest Only

The theological starting point for this inquiry must be the fact that in the Scriptures Christ alone is called a priest of the New Covenant.

It was fitting that we should have such a high priest, wholly innocent, undefiled, separated from sinners, higher than the heavens. He has no need, as did the high priests [of the old covenant] . . . to offer sacrifice day after day, first for his own sins, and then for those of the people, he did that once for all when he offered himself. . . . Now he has obtained so much more excellent a ministry as he is mediator of a better covenant, enacted on better promises. (Heb 7:26–27; 8:6)

Probably the title of "priest" (hiereus) was not given to the apostles, bishops, and presbyters in the New Testament lest they be confused with the priests of the Old Law or those of the pagan religions.[25] An expectation was current among some Jews, how-

23. Inter Insigniores, proem.
24. Manfred Hauke, Women in the Priesthood?, 472–80, discusses "The Degree of Theological Certainty" of his case against ordination and concludes that "at the least . . . the qualification fidei proxima would seem to be appropriate: only a baptized male can validly receive ordination to priesthood" (p. 479). See John Paul II's conclusion in Ordinatio Sacerdotalis, quoted at the beginning of this Chapter.
25. Instead the term presbyteros or elder, common for synagogue leaders, was used. The evidence is discussed and analyzed in depth in Jean Colson, Ministère de Jésus Christ ou le sacerdoce de l'Évangile (Paris: Beauchesne, 1966), and Albert Vanhoye, S.J., Old Testament Priests and the New Priest According to the New Testament, trans. Bernard Orchard (Leominister, England: Fowler Wright, 1986). On the later development see Jean Galot, Theology of the Priesthood (San Francisco: Ignatius Press, 1984), 31–37, and Nathan Mitchell, Mission and Ministry: History and Theology in the Sacrament of Order (Wilmington, DE: Michael Glazier, 1982).

ever, that the "Messiah of Aaron," when he came, would receive the priestly anointing.[26] The Epistle to the Hebrews, therefore, argues that Christ excels all former priests by a unique kind of priesthood. Christ is a priest because he is the sole mediator between God and humanity, sent by God to us, and in return representing us to God.

Christ can represent God to us because he is the Son of God, anointed by God the Holy Spirit. He can represent us to God because he is the New Adam, the spiritual father of the redeemed human race (Rom 5:15–19; 1 Cor 15:21–22), the Head of the church which is his Body and his Bride (Eph 1:22–23; 5:29–31), typified in Mary, the virgin mother of the church (Rv 12:1–5; 21:9). As mediator, Jesus Christ offers sacrifice to God with us and on our behalf, the perfect sacrifice of himself on the Cross which is made present to us in the eucharistic sacrifice. Thus as Father of humanity, Head of the church, mediator with God, and offerer of the only sacrifice worthy to worship God, Jesus is the sole priest in the church.[27]

Yet it is also certain that this priesthood of Christ is in some very real way shared by the church as a whole, and hence by its baptized members. Thus, 1 Peter, which some exegetes believe was addressed to the newly baptized,[28] says, "Like living stones, let yourself be built into a spiritual house to be a holy priesthood to offer spiritual sacrifices acceptable to God through Jesus Christ. . . . You are a chosen race, a royal priesthood, a holy nation, a people of his [God's] own" (1 Pt 2: 5, 9, quoting Ex 19:6), and Vatican II says,[29] "Christ also gives them [the laity] a share in his priestly function of offering spiritual worship for the glory of God and the salvation of all." Yet Vatican II also says,

---

26. Raymond E. Brown, S.S., "Dead Sea Scrolls," in *New Jerome Biblical Commentary,* 1076–77, and John J. Collins, *The Apocalyptic Imagination: An Introduction to the Jewish Matrix of Christianity* (New York: Crossroad, 1984), 122–26.

27. See Vatican II, *Lumen Gentium,* no. 7.

28. William J. Dalton, S.J., *New Jerome Biblical Commentary,* 904, who says, however, that it is "a real letter."

29. *Lumen Gentium,* no. 34.

Though they differ from one another in essence and not only in degree, the common priesthood of the faithful and the ministerial or hierarchical priesthood are nonetheless interrelated. . . . For the distinction which the Lord made between sacred ministers and the rest of the People of God entails a unifying purpose, since pastors and the other faithful are bound to each other by a mutual need.[30]

Jesus empowered the Twelve among his disciples to *represent* him in a special way, both during his earthly ministry and after his departure.[31] Their reward for carrying out this perilous task was to be that in Christ's Kingdom they would "sit on twelve thrones judging the twelve tribes of Israel" (Mt 19:28; Lk 22:29–30) and were to be, according to Ephesians 2:19–20 (cf. Mt 16:18; Rv 21:14), the "foundation" of the church.[32] St. Paul also

30. Ibid., nos. 10 and 32.

31. For a defense of this statement see Appendix 1, where the argument over whether Christ is a "representative" of the church or "represents" Christ is discussed.

32. Raymond E. Brown, "The Twelve and the Apostolate" in *New Jerome Biblical Commentary,* 1377–81, is cautious about whether we can definitively prove that Jesus separated "exactly twelve very close friends or was the specification of *the Twelve* a later idea?" (p. 1380), but he points out that already Paul speaks of "the Twelve" (1 Cor 15:5) as witnesses of the Risen Christ. In "*Episkopē* and *Episkopos,*" he says, "There is little reason to doubt that Jesus chose the Twelve. Why did he do this? We have only one saying attributed to Jesus himself about the purpose of the Twelve: he had chosen them to sit on (twelve) thrones judging the twelve tribes of Israel (Mt 19:28; Lk 22:28–30). The idea seems to have been that in the renewed Israel which Jesus was proclaiming there were to be twelve men, just as there were twelve sons of Jacob/Israel at the beginning of the original Israel. The Dead Sea Scrolls community of the New Covenant adopted the same symbolism, for they had a special group of twelve in their Community Council (1QS 8:1)" (pp. 323–24). But does not the idea that the Twelve are to be "judges" in the "new world" (Mt) or "kingdom" (Lk) like the progenitors of the twelve tribes of Israel mean that they were to share in Jesus' own authority over the new Israel, his church? The fact that they, except for Peter, James and John, soon disappear from the biblical record does not alter this significance. For *Inter Insigniores* the theological task is not to establish Jesus' intentions simply by historical evidence (which is hardly possible with such scanty data) but by the canonical witness of the inspired Scriptures as to the meaning of these events for the faith of the church. The churches he addresses seem to recognize the tradition, but they need to be encouraged to live up to it. On the problems about the terms "Twelve" and "Apostles" see the lengthy discussions in Miguens, *Church Ministries,* 3–31, and Galot, *Theology of Priesthood,* 155–59. For the current questioning on whether the bishops of the Catholic church are the successors of the Twelve—as asserted by *Inter Insigniores,* following Vatican II, *Lumen Gentium,* nos. 19 and 24—see Appendix 1, notes 26 and 27.

dared to say to the Corinthians, "Be imitators of me, as I am of Christ" (1 Cor 11:1), in the context not of his personal sanctity, of which he dared not boast, but as he was an authorized witness of apostolic tradition (11:2).[33]

Jesus did not choose the Twelve among his disciples to set them outside and above his community, since Jesus himself is "head of the body, the church" (Eph 5:23), and the head and the members of a body live by one and the same life and in mutual service. Yet Jesus is indeed Head of the Body, and he chose and empowered the Twelve to represent him in the church, not to divide it but to unify it, as a shepherd gathers together his flock.

Priest as Symbol

The essential meaning of this ordained priesthood derived from the special role to which Christ called the Twelve and shared both by bishops and by presbyters, is still subject to much theological controversy.[34] To be on firm grounds, we need to follow the four

33. Hans Conzelmann, *1 Corinthians*, 179–80, says that this verse is "a summons to the imitation of Paul, grounded in his imitation of Christ. Paul does not make his own person the content of his preaching. His exemplariness consists in the fact that—in himself, objectively, on the basis of his calling—he is nothing. In all the passages on the *imitatio Pauli* the paradox of this exemplariness appears. And v. 2 then emphasizes that what is essential and exemplary is the *teaching* which he has transmitted to the Corinthians. The imitation *of Christ* takes its bearings not on the person of the historical Jesus, not on his way of life, but—in the sense of Phil 2:6 ff.—on his saving work." And Conzelmann adds in a note, "The primary factor is Christ as *sacramentum*, not as *exemplum*."

34. St. Thomas Aquinas defined priesthood in relation to the Eucharist. The Council of Trent followed the same course, but did not deal with the priest's prophetic and governing functions. Vatican II, *Lumen Gentium*, no. 28, describes the priest's various functions without explicitly saying which is supreme, but it places the offering of the Eucharist first in order. Vatican II, *Presbyterium Ordinis*, no. 2 (which I will quote later in the text) is explicit. Moreover, since the Council's *Sacrosanctum Concilium*, no. 10, says "Nevertheless, the liturgy is the summit toward which the activity of the church is directed: at the same time it is the fountain from which all her power flows," it is difficult to see how some other activity of the priest could be more important or define him more specifically. Nevertheless, theologians dispute the Thomistic view. Jean Galot, *Theology of the Priesthood*, 129–37, briefly surveys current opinions: Congar, Bouëssé, and Lécuyer make the cultic or sacramental aspect primary. Dillenschneider, Bouyer, Rahner, Olivier, and Dianich give priority to preaching. Kasper, and Dodd opt for "leadership" (governance). Patrick J. Dunn, *Priesthood: A Re-Examination*, 151–64, surveys American authors. He discusses the influential works of Edward Schillebeeckx and Hans

principal documents of Vatican II that dealt with this question from different perspectives.[35] The Synod of 1971 in its final document on *The Ministerial Priesthood* synthesized the teaching of the Council as follows:

> The essential structure of the church—consisting of a flock and of pastors appointed for this purpose (Cf. 1 Pt 3:1–4)—according to the tradition of the church herself, was always and remains the norm. Precisely as a result of this structure the church can never remain closed on herself and is always subject to Christ as her origin and Head.
>
> Among the various charisms and service, the priestly ministry of the New Testament, which continues Christ's function as mediator, and which in essence and not merely in degree is distinct from the common priesthood of all the faithful (*Lumen Gentium*, no. 10), alone perpetuates the essential work of the Apostles: By effectively proclaiming the gospel, by gathering together and leading the community, by remitting sins, and especially by celebrating the Eucharist, *it makes Christ, the head of the community, present in the exercise of his work of redeeming humanity and glorifying God perfectly.*[36]

The phrase I have italicized seems to me an excellent definition of the essential purpose of priestly ordination. The Christian priest *makes Christ present* as *head of the community,* a Christ who mediates between God and humanity, bringing the graces of God in Word and sacrament to the people and "especially" (i.e., above all) leading them in turn to worship God both in the sacrifice of praise and the sacrifice of their lives. This does not imply, of course, that *all* graces or *all* sacrifice require the priest's mediation, but only that his mediation serves the corporate life of the church as such.

Küng whose pneumatological conception of the church leads to a "low" conception of the presbyterate (pp. 26–27, 31–44, 166–71), and also provides an up-to-date bibliography on the question (pp. 225–32). For a recent but not entirely satisfactory history of the topic see Kenan B. Osborne, O.F.M., *Priesthood: A History of the Ordained Ministry in the Roman Catholic Church* (New York: Paulist, 1988). A still more recent survey is Daniel Donovan, *What Are They Saying about the Ministerial Priesthood?* (New York: Paulist, 1992).

35. Vatican II, *Lumen Gentium*, nos. 10, 18–20, 34, 41.

36. "The Ministerial Priesthood" *(Ultimis temporibus),* Synod of Bishops, November, 30, 1971, I.4, p. 679, included in Flannery, ed., *Vatican II Postconciliar Documents,* no. 118, pp. 672–94. This summarizes very neatly what is said in Vatican II, *Lumen Gentium,* no. 28.

There has been much discussion as to whether in this three-fold ministry of "sanctifying, teaching, and governing"[37] (priest, prophet, king or shepherd), granting that all are essential, any one predominates. Certainly we should avoid any "reductionist" understanding that would minimize the specificity of each of these three offices.[38] Nevertheless, the documents do support the classical view that the sanctifying (cultic) function, especially the offering of the eucharistic sacrifice, is the supreme act of the priesthood, both universal and ministerial, which sublates the others.[39] Preaching calls the community into existence, governance builds it up in love, but the community's supreme act is by the power of the Holy Spirit to join in Christ's praise of the Father. Vatican II declared:

Through the ministry of priests the spiritual sacrifice of the faithful is made perfect in union with the sacrifice of Christ, the sole Mediator. Through the hands of priests and in the name of the whole Church, the Lord's sacrifice is offered in the Eucharist as an unbloody and sacramental manner until He Himself returns. The ministry of priests is directed toward this work and is perfected in it. For their ministry, which takes its start from the gospel message, derives it power and force from the sacrifice of Christ.[40]

37. "The Ministerial Priesthood," in Flannery, ed., *Vatican II Postcounciliar Documents,* 679.

38. Galot, *Theology of the Priesthood,* 40–49, argues that the title "Shepherd" is better than that of any of the three ministries, because it includes all of them in their specificity without subordinating one to another. I find this unsatisfactory since it does not designate the principle of unity which holds them together. Others use "shepherding" for the "governing" ministry.

39. The tendency, formerly common in Old Testament exegesis, to oppose "cultic" to "prophetic" acts as religiously inferior is now passé, but it still influences some thinking about ministry. On this see Bruce Vawter, "Introduction to Prophetic Literature," *New Jerome Biblical Commentary,* who concludes, "The prophetic attitude to the cult was like the prophetic attitude to everything—one in which forms were always secondary to the realities they signified. It was only when forms no longer signified anything that they demanded condemnation" (p. 192–93).

40. Vatican II, *Presbyterium Ordinis,* no. 2. Vatican II also emphasized that the hierarchical priesthood is not in competition with the universal priesthood of all the baptized but mediates and completes it; cf. *Lumen Gentium,* nos. 10 and 35. Raymond E. Brown, S.S., *Priest and Bishop: Biblical Reflections* (Paramus, NJ/ New York, 1970), 13–20, argues that the New Testament church did not yet think of itself as having any other priesthood than that of the Old Law nor of itself as a

In Persona Christi Capitis

What qualifications, then, are essential for a candidate for priesthood to be suitable to preside at the Eucharist, as well as to preach and govern? The explicit New Testament passages about the qualifications of presbyters and deacons speak primarily of the pastoral office, i.e., the capacity to govern the flock (e.g., 1 Tm 3:1–13). From many other passages it is clear that a leader in the church must be an orthodox minister of the Word (e.g., 1 Tim 1:3–11). Nothing is said explicitly about the qualifications to perform the sacraments, the Eucharist in particular.

Consequently some today want to say that only those who have the gifts of leading a community should be ordained, and only because they are the ordained leaders of a community should they preside at the Eucharist.[41] For centuries the church was reluctant to permit other than "absolute" ordinations, i.e., the ordination of a bishop who was not first chosen to head a local church.

Nevertheless, it must be recalled that early in church history and not a few times later the question has arisen whether the incompetency or bad character of a candidate for priesthood invalidates ordination, and that in spite of hesitancies, the answer has always been negative.[42] Thus the argument of those who point out that today many women are as competent or more competent than many male priests as preachers, teachers, administrators, and liturgical performers and the claims of women to experience a call to priesthood are not decisive for our question. Certainly, the church has a grave responsibility to seek out competent and virtuous persons, gifted in the Holy Spirit, for the office of priest-

---

"royal priesthood" (1 Pt 2:9; Rv 1:6; these texts refer simply to the *holiness* of the church). The notion of Christian priesthood, he believes is a valid but post-biblical development. I would add that an ancient people could be called "priestly," not because each of its members is a priest but simply because it had priests to lead it in worship, just as it could be called a "royal people" if it had a king (cf. I Sm 8:5).

41. For a detailed historical discussion of this issue see Hervé Legrand, "The Presidency of the Eucharist According to the Ancient Tradition," *Worship* 53:5 (Sept. 1979): 413–38.

42. Thus Canon Law states no other qualification for valid ordination except that "Only a baptized man can validly receive sacred ordination" (Canon 1024).

hood. Undoubtedly in the early church such qualities were required for liceity as they are still by Canon Law.[43] Yet pastoral
competence and personal holiness do not define the essential purpose of ordination, because the ordained priest does not act in his
own name but *in persona Christi et persona ecclesiae,* continuing
"Christ's function as a mediator," the Son of God made like us in
all things but sin, who alone is truly The Priest.[44]

As Yves Congar has written:

> For some the priest is the man of the Eucharist, acting *in persona Christi
> (Capitis)* and, therefore, president of the community. For others, the priest
> is the president of the community, and, therefore, the minister of the Eu-
> charist, that is to say, of the supreme sacrament of the community. This
> formulation is obviously too simple to show the working of the dialectic
> of headship vs. conciliarity; rather the truth is symphonic. The *in persona
> Christi* and the *in persona ecclesiae* are both true: sacramental ordination
> makes the presidency of the community something other than if a simple
> initiative by a member based on his gifts and the trust of the assembly
> had placed him there. But if the ordination, which joins the ordinand with
> the apostolicity of the minister happens to consecrate one chosen by all
> to lead the whole community, one has what Christian antiquity considered
> and practiced as its ideal.[45]

43. Canons 1025–52.

44. "Though they differ from one another in essence and not only in degree,
the common priesthood of the faithful and the ministerial or hierarchical priesthood are nonetheless interrelated. Each of them in its own special way is a participation in the one priesthood of Christ. The ministerial priest by the sacred power
he enjoys molds and rules the priestly people. Acting in the person of Christ, he
brings about the eucharistic sacrifice, and offers it to God in the name of all the
people. For their part, the faithful join in the offering of the Eucharist by virtue of
their royal priesthood. They likewise exercise that priesthood by receiving the sacraments, by prayer and thanksgiving, by the witness of a holy life, and by self-
denial and active charity" (Vatican II, *Lumen Gentium,* no. 10).

45. "Collège, primauté . . . conférences épiscopales: quelques notes," *Ésprit et
vie,* 96 (10 serie), 27 (July 3, 1986): 390 (my translation). The dialectic of which
Congar speaks, is illustrated by the different sacramental formulas of the Eastern
and Western churches. The East emphasizes the *in persona ecclesiae* when it says
this formula is the *epiclesis* of the Eucharist prayer, i.e., the petition of the congregation led by the priest for the Holy Spirit to consecrates the elements; likewise,
that absolution from sins should be given by the priest in petitionary form. On the
contrary, in the West, eucharistic consecration is attributed to the priest saying *in
persona Christi,* "This is my Body. This is my Blood." Likewise the Latin priest
says, "I absolve you." Theologically both kinds of formulas are correct. The Latin
form, however, appears more developed, making explicit that the *ex opere operato*

These two aspects of the priestly ministry are complementary and inseparable, as they must be in a mediator. Yet the principal reality symbolized by the priest as mediator is not the church he leads in prayer to God, but Christ the Mediator without whose grace no prayer and no sacrament is efficacious. The bishop in ordaining acts not simply as an agent of the church, but as an instrument of Christ who alone can incorporate the candidate through the sacramental character into the priestly college. Thus it is not *primarily* because he represents the people that an ordained priest represents Christ when he leads the people in prayer, but because through ordination he represents Christ that he is empowered to lead them.

Some accuse recent documents of the magisterium, including *Inter Insigniores*, of *Christomonism*, i.e., excessive insistence on the apostolic succession through a chain of ministers from the earthly Jesus, rather than on apostolic succession through the church as a whole animated by the Holy Spirit sent by the Risen Christ. It is argued that the Holy Spirit empowers a local church to ordain its own ministers when necessary, perhaps even when the insistence of central authority on unessential qualifications such as celibacy or male gender deprive it of its "right to the Eucharist."

Certainly, the Holy Spirit is the very life of the church and its ministry, but the Holy Spirit is sent by the Incarnate Son, whose Body is the church in whom he remains visible to us in the sacramental symbols—the first of which is the visible church itself.

How then can there be an apostolic succession that is not visible

---

efficacy of the sacrament is not due to the faith *(ex opere operantis)* of the *individual* members of the church but to Christ in whose name the priest is ordained to speak. Nevertheless, the *whole* church as Body of Christ prays in the Holy Spirit with infallible result for the efficacy of the sacraments when led by the priest *in persona ecclesiae*. These different approaches can be reconciled if we recall that both the church and the priest, as a member and minister of the church, perform the sacraments not by their own power but only as instruments of the same Christ—the church as Christ's Body animated by his Spirit, the priest as Christ the Head of that same Body, *in persona Christi Capitis* through the same Spirit (see *The Catechism of the Catholic Church*, nos. 1548–53).

in the hierarchical structure of the church? A local group of Christians is a local *church* only potentially, until it receives authorization by ministers of the universal Catholic church vested with apostolic authority. No doubt the Holy Spirit is at work in this group of Christians moving them to ask for apostolic recognition, but they cannot presume to claim this recognition simply by the inspiration of the Holy Spirit. Hence the priestly ministry in the church provides it with the visible symbol of the invisible presence of the Holy Spirit, as the human body is symbolic of its spiritual soul.

Thus the essence of ordination and its validity depend only on the fittingness of the candidate to represent Christ in the community and the unity of the community in Christ. The essential function of priesthood, therefore, is representational, iconic, symbolic, sacramental. Yet precisely because the priest acts *in persona Christi* he also has the responsibility to seek holiness and to perform his duties in humility, making full use of whatever gifts God has bestowed upon him in the service of his flock. He must always remember that the essential meaning of his vocation is to be "transparent" to Christ who alone acts through him.

When St. Paul says, "Thus should one regard us: as servants of Christ and stewards of the mysteries of God. Now it is of course required of stewards that they be found trustworthy" (1 Cor 4:1–2), clearly he is emphasizing that simple fidelity in witnessing to apostolic tradition in his pastoral charge of a community is the principal and minimally essential duty of the priest.[46] This fidelity requires of the priest a *kenosis*, an emptying of all merely personal hopes and projects, all vanity and ambition, as the classic writings on the spirituality of priesthood have constantly insisted.[47] The

46. It is not necessary to go so far as Luther, who translated 4:2 as "Now no more is required of stewards than that they prove trustworthy. . . ." (cf. Conzelmann's commentary, 83 n. 12) but simply to understand this as indicating that trustworthiness is fundamental and indispensable in a steward.

47. The French school of spirituality, especially of the Sulpicians, so vital to the development of the seminary system for training priests, has been much criticized for its notion of the "selflessness" of priests and the dubious Christological arguments used to support it. Certainly priests need full psychological "individ-

priest's personal defects, incompetence, and sinfulness are of course scandalous, but to the eyes of true faith they only serve to make evident that the priest in his human weakness represents the all-holy Christ and not himself.

It is obvious, therefore, why the candidate must be a human being, created in God's image, and a baptized member of the Body of Christ. But it is far from obvious today that to act *in persona Christi* requires some gender qualification. In our culture it seems absurd to many that gender should have anything to do with qualification for ministry, any more than for being a teacher, a mayor, or the head of a business corporation. To put it crudely, as some objectors have done, "How can the possession of male genitals possibly be a requirement for ordination to a spiritual office?"[48]

Incarnation and Gender

Political and Symbolic Power

In contrast to the centrality of preaching in the churches of the Reformation, for the older churches of East and West the proclamation of the Word stirs up a faith that centers in Christ present in the sacraments, above all in the Eucharist. God reveals himself

---

uation," initiative and creativity, friendship, appropriate recreation, and closeness to the people they serve. Yet this school contributed importantly to the theology of priesthood by identifying priesthood with Christ's *servanthood*. See E. A. Walsh, *Priesthood in the Writings of the French school: Bérulle, de Condren, Olier* (Washington, DC: Catholic University of America Press, 1949), and Michael J. Buckley, S.J., "Seventeenth Century French Spirituality," in *Post Reformation and Modern Spirituality*, ed. Louis Dupré and Don E. Saliers, 28–68. In Appendix 1, an article of Dennis Michael Ferrara is discussed which argues from this "kenotic," "self-effacing," instrumental or "apophatic" character of priesthood that the priest cannot "represent" Christ, but only be his "representative." In my opinion the priest does re-present Christ precisely as Christ is Servant.

48. This often raised objection betrays a Platonistic spirituality that I have studied in my *Theologies of the Body: Humanist and Christian*. According to Francine Cardman, "The Medieval Question of Women and Orders," *Thomist* 42 (Oct. 1978): 582–99, the speculative question why women could not be ordained was first raised by Bonaventure, then by Thomas Aquinas, both strongly influenced by Gratian and liturgical practice. She also notes that in citing Scotus against women's ordination *Inter Insigniores* fails to note that he qualifies his own opinion not as certain but simply as "more probable" (*probabilior*).

most fully in the sacramental *symbols* because the Divine Mystery can be communicated to earthly humanity only in terms of earthly, human experience—symbolically, analogically.[49] Even the biblical and preached Word, therefore, is largely a texture of symbols.[50]

Of course, the Bible also contains many literal statements which enable us to avoid arbitrary and erroneous interpretations of its symbols. It is the task of the magisterium, assisted by theologians, to carry this exegetical work of literal interpretation still further. Nevertheless, the plenitude of what is signified in biblical and sacramental symbols can never be exhausted in literal propositions.

As we have already seen, many today object to arguments from symbolism, because such arguments seem to them a mere cover-up to conceal the real issue of "patriarchy" in the church.[51] Influenced by liberation theology, and often by the notion that sexism is the primordial form of political oppression, some theologians want to formulate the problem of women's ordination purely in terms such as "rights," "equality," "oppression," and "empowerment."[52]

49. See *ST* I, q. 1, a. 9. John Henry Newman, "the heir to Keble's sacramental sense of the visible world, also turned increasingly towards analogy, metaphor and symbol as the appropriate vehicles for the living ideas of a community ... for Newman, the Church lived not through its theology, but in its symbols and sacraments" (Stephen Prickett, *Words and the Word: Language, Poetics and Biblical Interpretation* [Cambridge: Cambridge University Press, 1986]), 217).

50. Thus Vatican II, *Dei Verbum*, after reaffirming the doctrine of biblical inspiration and inerrancy (no. 11), goes on to say: "For the words of God, expressed in human language, have been made like human discourse, just as of old the Word of the eternal Father, when he took to Himself the weak flesh of humanity, became like other men" (no. 13). Popular, nontechnical discourse, especially in traditional cultures, such as produced the Bible, is by no means flatly literal, but rich in metaphor. Moreover, as Prickett, *Words and the Word,* speaking of Bible translations, asks, "how far is it possible, in the words of the *Good News Bible,* 'to use language that is natural, clear, simple, and unambiguous,' when the Bible is *not about* things that are natural, clear, simple, and unambiguous?" (p. 10).

51. See Chapter II note 36 above.

52. David Hein, "Women's Ordination Redivivus," *Liturgy* 23 (March 1978): 34, quotes Anne Carr, B.V.M., as saying at the 1975 Detroit Women's Ordination Conference that "the ordination of women will not mean admission to the clerical caste, as some fear.... Rather it would further the transformation of the priesthood: by admission of those who have traditionally only served, the sign will be clear. It will help to transform the ministry *from a predominantly cultic role to a ministerial one,* from a symbol of prestige to a symbol of service, releasing the

The real reason, therefore, that the controversy on ordination is so bitter is because the priesthood seems to be a *symbol* of what feminism rightly opposes, i.e., male oppression, not the reality of clerical life itself, since the clergy are by no means the most powerful or oppressive males in our society. Indeed the church today, bereft as it is of political, legal, economic, and cultural influence, has no considerable power except that of manipulating certain symbols of a unique "numinosity," much envied by politicians and the public media.[53] Hence the church cannot simply change its symbols to accommodate cultural changes without asking whether, like Samson shorn, it will be left impotent.

Archetypical and Revelatory Symbols

Perhaps the chief reason the arguments of *Inter Insigniores* and *Ordinatio Sacerdotalis* lack credibility to many theologians today is that they tend to view any claim of transcultural permanence with a "hermeneutic of suspicion." For them human historicity implies that all symbols inevitably change their meaning and are relative to the particular culture in which they are used.[54] Hence

---

imagination of half the church's population into fuller operation as the church moves into the future" (my italics). Would a priesthood that was not "predominantly cultic" be truly priesthood? As to "hierarchy," Sandra Schneiders, in her influential book *New Wineskins: Re-Imagining Religious Life Today* (New York: Paulist Press, 1986), says, "the principle of hierarchy, which is the nerve of both secular and religious obedience as they have been traditionally understood, is being radically questioned and the principle of participation is supplanting it in more and more sectors of life," and supports this "rejection of hierarchy" (p. 106). In fact "hierarchy" and "participation" are not opposed but mutually supportive, as I showed in Chapter II. Of course the "hierarchical structure" of the church was strongly confirmed by Vatican II, *Lumen Gentium*, no. 18.

53. The term "numinosity," meaning the supernatural power of a symbol, person, or thing, was used by Rudolf Otto in his *The Idea of the Holy*, 2nd ed. (London: Oxford, 1950), and popularized by the Jungians. For the continuing role of symbols in today's secularized culture and politics see Gregor T. Goethals, "TV's Iconic Imagery in a Secular Society," *New Theology Review* 6 (Feb. 1993): 40–53, which was excerpted from his *The Electronic Golden Calf: Images, Religion, and the Making of Meaning* (Cambridge, MA: Cowley Publications, 1990). See John Saward, "The Priest as Icon of Christ: A Thomist Concept," *The Priest* 50 (1994): 37–47, for a discussion of the priest as a "symbol-person."

54. See Sallie McFague, *Metaphorical Theology: Models of God in Religious Language* (Philadelphia: Fortress Press, 1982), and *Models of God: Theology for an Ecological, Nuclear Age* (Philadelphia: Fortress Press, 1987). McFague dis-

to survive and remain effective, they believe, the church must be able to change its sacraments as radically as may be necessary to fit the needs of the times. For such theologians the argument that Jesus never chose women among the Twelve and that the church has an unbroken tradition of never ordaining women merely provokes them to exclaim, "Well, it is about time the church caught up with the 'signs of the times!' "

We must, however, distinguish among symbols those that are permanent from those that the church has the power to change for the sake of pastoral accommodation and of doctrinal development. *Inter Insigniores* recalls the words of the Council of Trent: "In the Church there has always existed this power, that in the administration of the sacraments, *provided that their substance [substantia] remains unaltered,* she can lay down or modify what she considers more fitting either for the benefit of those who receive them or for respect towards those same sacraments, according to various circumstances, times or places."[55]

The sacraments of the church can have a permanent "substance" for two reasons. The first reason is that there are in fact archetypical, transcultural, transhistorical symbols grounded in *universal human experiences,* especially of the body and fundamental biological and environmental relationships, notably human gender and the family.[56] While feminist scholars struggle valiantly

---

cusses many symbols from which the church might choose so as to better express currently popular theological attitudes.

55. Session 21, chap. 2, DS 1728; cf. DS 1061 which speaks of the power of the Pope to change rites "saving the necessity and integrity of the sacraments."

56. Without accepting Jung's theory of a "collective unconscious," I do accept the evidence he and other students of comparative religion cite to show the existence of transcultural symbols; see Carl Gustave Jung, et al., *Man and His Symbols* (Garden City, New York: Doubleday, 1964). See also Naomi Goldenberg, "A Feminist Critique of Jung," and Demaris Wehr, "A Feminist Perspective on Jung's Concept of the Archetype," both in *Women's Spirituality: Resources for Christian Development,* ed. Joann Wolski Conn (New York: Paulist Press, 1986), 150–58, 158–73. These theories are applied exegetically by Robert Annechino, "Song of the Groom: Spiritual Marriage and Masculinity," *Review for Religious* 50 (1991): 822–38, and Nancy M. Cross, "The Bible's Use of Sexual Language," ibid., 839–48. See also Donald J. Keefe, S.J., "Gender, History and Liturgy in the Catholic Church," *Review for Religious* 46 (1987): 866–81.

to overcome restricting stereotypes that have developed in various cultures from a too-literal interpretation of these *natural* symbols, they have ended by themselves using such symbols in their glorification of the power of women. Why call God "Mother"[57] or "Fatherly-Motherly Spirit"[58] except because of the numinosity of these archetypes?

57. See Elizabeth Moltmann-Wendel's, *A Land Flowing with Milk and Honey,* especially chap. 6, "God our Mother," 91–102. In chap. 3, "The Forgotten Goddess," 42–59, she accepts the dubious arguments for primitive matriarchy. See also Starhawk, *The Spiral Dance: A Rebirth of the Ancient Religion of the Great Goddess* (San Francisco: Harper and Row, 1979), favorably reviewed by Rosemary Radford Ruether, "The Way of Wicca," *The Christian Century* 97, 6 (Feb. 20, 1980): 208–209; Christine Downing, *The Goddess: Mythological Images of the Feminine* (New York: Crossroads, 1981); Virginia Ramey Mollenkott, *The Divine Feminine: The Biblical Imagery of God as Female* (New York: Crossroad, 1983); Carol Olson, *The Book of the Goddess Past and Present* (New York: Crossroads, 1983). Rosemary Radford Ruether, ed., *Woman Church: Theology and Practice of Feminist Liturgical Communities* (San Francisco: Harper & Row, 1985), applies these ideas to prayer. Probably for these writers, as Denise Lardner Carmody says in her *Femininity and Christianity: A Two Way Reflection* (Nashville, Abingdon Press, 1982), what is "more important than the question of the Goddess's objective reality, then, is her symbolic function" (p. 27). See also Carmody's *Women and World Religions* (Englewood Cliffs, NJ: Prentice-Hall, 1989). For criticism of this trend see Susanne Heine, *Matriarchs, Goddesses and Images of God*

58. "Fatherly-Motherly Spirit" is the name for God proposed by Jürgen Moltmann, *The Trinity and the Kingdom* (San Francisco: Harper and Row, 1981), 57 and 164–65. But Elizabeth Johnson, C.S.J., "The Incomprehensiblity of God and the Image of God Male and Female," *Theological Studies* 45 (1984): 441–65, argues that "image-breaking is a part of religious traditions, because focusing on a fixed image not only compromises the transcendence of God, but petrifies and stultifies human beings into the likeness of the image worshipped, inhibiting growth by preventing further searching for knowledge of God. Calling into question the exclusively male idea of God does not spell the end of male imagery used for God; what has been destroyed as an idol can return as an icon evoking the presence of God. Using female imagery for God does not introduce a distraction from belief in the one God of the Judaeo-Christian tradition; the use of startling metaphors opens up the possibility of new religious experience of the one Holy Mystery" (pp. 464–65). But has not the Incomprehensible God achieved self-revelation in the Incarnation, by which, in the famous phrase of St. John of the Cross, "God has said it all"? Johnson, with whom McFague, *Models of God,* 204, agrees, seems to have derived her approach from Rosemary Radford Ruether, *Sexism and God-Talk.* Ruether speaks of a "God/ess" who is both male and female, and argues that prior to the rise of nomadic herding societies with their patriarchal monotheism the gods were both male and female and there was no "dualizing of gender metaphors" (pp. 53–61). She asserts that a feminist God should be free of all dualisms: matter vs. spirit, male vs. female, upper and lower class status, etc. (pp. 68–71). For Ruether, Jesus' gender is of no significance, because his kingdom is one of earthly liberation. Ruether is agnostic about a future life (pp. 235–58).

The second reason for the permanence of the church's symbols is their origin in unique *historical* personages and events—their narrative aspect. If we take human historicity seriously, then we must concede that the historical origin of the sacraments has determined these universal symbols in a unique way. "Do this in memory of me" (1 Cor 11:25–26), Jesus said in instituting the Eucharist. Indeed, it can be argued that every sacrament is rooted in revelatory events that are unique and unrepeatable.[59] Therefore, biblical and sacramental symbolism cannot be essentially altered without losing its character as *anamnēsis* (commemoration), its reference to the male Jesus of history and his male Twelve. Thus I believe this argument can withstand any criticism that it is arbitrary or limited to one age or culture. It is rooted in a universal symbolism confirmed by particular historical commemoration.

It is this historicity that gave rise to "the scandal of particularity" during the Enlightenment and Modernity, which led to the effort to "demythologize" or "remythologize" Christian symbols into abstract "values" having no unique, historical referent. For not a few theologians, Jesus has become the "Christ figure" or the "Christ event," or the "Christ story," more than a unique historic individual. Some argue, therefore, that it is not the historic male Jesus that is important for us, but the values embodied in the central character of the biblical narrative, the historical basis of which escapes our scholarly quest.[60]

59. Although we cannot historically verify that Jesus by a specific act intended the institution of several of the sacraments, nevertheless, biblically based tradition associates them with events in his life. For example the anointing of the sick is associated with Jesus' own healing miracles and the tradition that the disciples also healed by anointing with oil (Mk 6:13, cf. Jas 5:13–15); marriage is associated with the miracle at the wedding at Cana (Jn 2:1–2; cf. Eph 21:33), etc. Thus the practice of the church was shaped by symbols rooted in biblical narratives believed to be historically grounded. The sacrament of ordination, however, is grounded very firmly in the historical event of the institution of the Eucharist at the Last Supper mentioned both by Paul (1 Cor 11:20, 23–27) and the synoptic Gospels (Mk 14:22–25; Mt 26:26–30; Lk 22:14–20), although only Paul (v. 24) and Luke (v. 19) mention the command "Do this in memory of me." The fourth Gospel is silent on the Eucharist, but seems to substitute for it the event of the Risen Christ bestowing the power to forgive sins (Jn 20:21–23).

60. See Patricia Wilson-Kastner, "Who is the Christ?" chap. 5 in *Faith, Fem-*

Underlying these two reasons is a third which grounds the other two. As the Greek Orthodox theologian Kallistos Ware insists, the symbols that faith applies to God, "are not chosen by us but revealed and *given*."[61] God has chosen those that are fitting to be *revelatory* in view, on the one hand, of God's order of creation, and on the other, of God's providence over history. Yet God chose them not necessarily but freely. Hence they are not subject to human choice or substitution, any more than we can dictate to another human person the words she or he selects to communicate with us. We have only to listen respectfully and in our own turn respond freely and fittingly.

It can also be objected that it is dangerous to rest a theological argument on a single symbol, since every analogy limps and must be corrected by other analogies.[62] True, but as I will show in what follows, what the phrase *in persona Christi capitis* involves is not a single symbol, but as structuralist theory has enabled us to per-

---

inism, and the Christ (Philadelphia: Fortress, 1983), 89–119, who deprecates the "quest for the Jesus of history" and urges emphasis on the "values" embodied in the Christ figure that transcend all "dualism." Other feminists speak of the "Whole Christ," the risen, purely spiritual Christ living in the Christian community in which gender has been transcended, or the "Cosmic Christ" who has existed from the beginning and is Sophia, Wisdom become incarnate in the universe and for a time in the earthly Jesus. How odd that today when Christologies "from below" are popular, such *docetic* Christologies are also proposed!

61. "Almost always the symbolism used of God by the Bible and in the Church's worship has been male symbolism. We cannot prove by arguments why this should be so, yet it remains a fact of our Christian experience that God has set his seal upon certain symbols and not upon others. The symbols are not chosen by us but revealed and *given*. A symbol can be verified, lived, prayed—but not 'proved' logically. These 'given' symbols, however, while not capable of proof, are yet far from being arbitrary. Like the symbols in myth, literature and art, our religious symbols reach deep into the hidden roots of our being, and cannot be altered without momentous consequences. If, for example, we were to start saying, 'Our Mother who art in heaven,' instead of 'Our Father,' we should not merely be adjusting an incidental piece of imagery, but replacing Christianity with a new kind of religion. A Mother Goddess is not the Lord of the Christian Church" (Kallistos Ware, *The Orthodox Way* [Crestwood, N.Y.: St. Vladimir's Seminary, 1979], 42–43).

62. This point is made by Dorothy Irvin, "*Omnis Analogia Claudet*," in *Women Priests: A Catholic Commentary*, ed. Leonard and Arlene Swidler, 271–77.

ceive, a *system* or complex of mutually interpretative and rein-
forcing symbols.

A final objection to my argument is that it rests on symbols and
metaphors that are very shifting in meaning and easy to manipu-
late in arbitrary ways, as the medievals did with their "spiritual
senses" of the Scriptures.[63] Such arguments depend, it is alleged,
more on the imaginative ingenuity of the interpreter than on the
Word of God. Yet, biblical exegesis and theology, especially sacramental theology, cannot avoid the use of analogy and symbolism. The only question is how well grounded are the analogies and
symbolisms that are used.

Here again some theologians object because their methodology
of "correlation" does not admit of any literal "revelation" by God,
but only of a "religious experience" which is a human construct
projected on a silent God.[64] Nevertheless, it is only by the submission of faith that the church recognizes in the symbols of the
Bible and tradition what is essential and what is not. For pastors
of the church, vested with apostolic authority, to make this discernment definitive they must determine first the primary reality
which this symbol signifies, and then the natural and historical
appropriateness of the sign that points to this primary reality. Because in our culture we are used to the free manipulation of images
to sell products and create reputations, we suppose that the church

63. *ST* I, q. 1, a. 10, ad 1, insists that only the "literal" sense of scripture can
be directly the basis of theological argumentation. This "literal" sense is "that
intended by the [human] author." To arrive at this literal sense, therefore, one has
to reduce the three "spiritual senses" (allegorical, moral, and anagogical) to the
literal sense on which they are based, and furthermore reduce any metaphors in
the text to terms which involve *proper* analogy. Aquinas, however, also shows in
his *Librum Beati Dionysii De divinis nominibus Expositio* that in theology this
reduction cannot usually be to univocal terms, but only to analogical ones, which
cannot make entirely explicit (univocal) the entire content of the biblical symbols.
On the permanent importance of "spiritual exegesis" and its hermeneutic canons
see Henri de Lubac, *Exégèse mediéval: Les quatre sens de l'Écriture* (Paris: Aubier,
1960), 2 vols. (4 parts), especially "Symbolisme," chap. 8 of vol. 2, pt. 2, as well
as vol. 2, pt. 2, pp. 125–262, and the comparison of Bonaventure and Aquinas,
pp. 263–301.

64. I am grateful for insights on feminist hermeneutics to Father Francis Martin, *The Feminist Question: Feminist Theology in the Light of Christian Tradition*
(Grand Rapids, MI: Eerdmans, 1994).

must be free to change its symbols to meet the mood of our times. But the pastors of the church know they cannot validate a sacrament simply by an act of human power. The performance of a sacrament in an abusive manner contrary to its divinely given purpose would only result in an invalid and indeed sacrilegious travesty. To ordain a woman to priesthood, *if* this is contrary to the divinely designated and essential symbolism of ordination, would not make her a priest, even if she were "ordained" by the pope. Such an occasional and local abuse is not impossible and may actually have occurred, although rarely,[65] but the doctrine of the infallibility of the church is not compatible with error in *definitive* magisterial judgments on the validity of the sacraments.[66] How then is the magisterium to establish the permanent requirements of ordination?

The Father Symbol

The foregoing discussion has led to the conclusion that to answer the question of the validity of female ordination theologically we must first ask *whether Jesus' maleness was and is significant for his mission.* No doubt one of the reasons that the magisterial documents have appeared to some unpersuasive is that they have not addressed this crucial question directly. Only if the answer to

65. In claiming a constant tradition against woman's ordination, *Inter Insigniores* did not deny occasional local deviations: "A few heretical sects in the first centuries, especially Gnostic ones, entrusted the exercise of the priestly ministry to women: this innovation was immediately noted and condemned by the fathers, who considered it unacceptable in the Church" (no. 1). See note 7 above for references to historical studies.

66. The definitive judgment of the Holy See or an ecumenical council on the valid performance of the sacraments *in the abstract* pertains to a matter of faith (dogma) and therefore according to Vatican I and II is infallible. *In the concrete* it may be a question of "dogmatic fact" which theologians generally hold to pertain to the secondary object of infallibility (though this thesis has not yet been explicitly defined by the church). All this does not imply, however, that the sacraments may not be invalidly performed in particular cases or for a time in a local church. See Francis Sullivan, S.J., *Magisterium: Teaching Authority in the Catholic Church* (Ramsey, NJ: Paulist, 1984), 131–36 on dogmatic facts; but he does not treat the question of the validity of the sacraments. On "reordinations" in patristic times see Joseph Lécuyer, *Le sacrement de l'ordination: Recherche historique et théologique* (Paris: Beauchesne, 1983), 237–39. See also Appendix 3.

this question is yes does it becomes evident why to symbolize Christ the priest must be a man and not a woman.

The mission of Christ was to reveal God to us fully as a God "who so loved the world that he gave his only Son, so that everyone who believes in him might not perish but might have eternal life" (Jn 3:16). This self-revelation of God in his most intimate Trinitarian life is communicated to us in the crucified and risen Christ, re-presented in and to the Christian community in the symbol of the priest anointed in the power of the Holy Spirit.

Today it is generally agreed by theologians that the reality of the Trinity (the "ontological" Trinity) is revealed to us by the manifestation of the Divine Persons in the plan of salvation (the "economic Trinity").[67] Thus the First Person is especially revealed through the creation, the Second through the incarnation, the Third through the life of the church. Moreover, in the incarnation, Christ in his visible, earthly life revealed his relations to the other two persons of the Trinity and thus revealed them to us, and in so doing revealed his "centrality" in the Trinity.[68]

The Bible, in outlining the order of creation, teaches the equality of man and woman as images of God, but also differentiates their roles in the human community by the narrative of the creation of Eve from Adam (Gn 2:18–25), thus picturing Adam as the origin and representative, the "head" of all humanity (Rm 5:12–21; 15:21–23).[69] Moreover, in many places in the moral instruc-

67. See William J. Hill, O.P., *Three-Personed God* (Washington, DC: The Catholic University of America Press, 1982), and Walter Kasper, *The God of Jesus Christ*, trans. Matthew J. O'Connell (New York: Crossroad, 1986), 243–49. To the contrary, however, Catherine Mowry LaCugna, *God For Us: The Trinity and Christian Life* (San Francisco: Harper, 1992), argues that "there is neither an economic or an immanent Trinity, there is only the *oikonomia* that is the concrete realization of the mystery of *theologia* in time, space, and personality" (p. 223), and states that "an immanent' trinitarian theology of God is nothing more than a theology of the economy of salvation" (p. 224). See the review by Joseph A. Bracken, S.J., *Theological Studies* 53 (1992): 558–60. This same apophatic theology is found in Elizabeth Johnson, *She Who Is*, analyzed in Appendix 2.

68. This "centrality" of Christ the Divine Son is a major theme in the symbolic theology of St. Bonaventure. See Zachary Hayes, O.F.M., *The Hidden Center*, (New York: Paulist Press, 1981).

69. On the "head/body" imagery in the New Testament see Stephen F. Miletic,

tions in the New Testament (as well as in the Old), it is declared that the headship of the man over the family pertains to the order of creation, distorted by sin and restored in Christ (1 Cor 11:3–16; Eph 5:21–32; Col 4:18–21; 1 Tm 2:8–15; Ti 2:3–5).[70]

Relying on what he considers this natural symbolism, St. Paul then explains that the universality of both the Fall and the Redemption imply that Jesus is the New Adam (Rm 5:12–21; 1 Cor 15:21–28, 45–49), the origin and head of the human race, who represents the whole of humanity, male and female.[71] Hence, when

---

"One Flesh" (Eph 5:22–24; 5:31): Marriage and the New Creation, Analecta Biblica (Rome: Biblical Institute Press, 1988), chap. 4, and see also Stephen B. Clark, Man and Woman in Christ: An Examination of Man and Woman in the Light of the Scriptures and the Social Sciences (Ann Arbor: Servant Books, 1980); Dietrich Von Hildebrand, Man and Woman (Chicago: Francisco Herald Press, 1966); and Jean Vanier, Man and Woman He Made Them, (Mahwah, NJ: Paulist Press, 1985). Two exhaustive studies, Kari Elisabeth Børresen, Subordination and Equivalence: The Nature and Role of Woman in Augustine and Thomas Aquinas (Washington, DC: University Press of America, 1981), and Prudence Allen, The Concept of Woman: The Aristotelian Revolution 750 BC–1250 AD (Montréal: Eden Press, 1985), analyze the influence of Aristotle on the theological concept of the relation of the sexes. Allen promotes man-women "complementarity" and attributes it first to Hildegard of Bingen (1098–1179) who "corrected" Aristotelian "polarity." See also her "Hildegard of Bingen's Philosophy of Sex Identity," Thought 64 (1989): 231–41. Aristotle, however, did not speak of "polarity," since as Allen herself shows, Aristotle held this relation to be analogous to that of form to matter, a purely complementary relation, since it produces an unum per se.

70. A thorough study of these texts is contained in Miletic, "One Flesh," and the as yet unpublished dissertation of Salvatore M. Ballacchino, The Household Order Texts: Colossians 3:18–4:1; 1 Peter 2:17–3:9; 1 Timothy 2:8–15 (5:1–2) and Titus 2:1–10: Present State of the Question and Assessment (Washington, DC: John Paul II Institute for Studies in Marriage and Family, 1992). See also Philip H. Towner, The Goal of Our Instruction: The Structure of Theology and Ethics in the Pastoral Epistles (Sheffield, ISOT Press, 1989). John Meier, "On the Veiling of Hermeneutics (1 Cor 11:2–16)," Catholic Biblical Quarterly 40 (Apr. 26, 1978): 212, criticizes Inter Insigniores for neglecting the historical-critical method in its use of biblical texts, and shows that Inter Insigniores arbitrarily dismisses Paul's arguments for the veiling of women (or, as other exegetes think, a simple coiffeur) and their silence in church. Joseph Komonchak, "Theological Questions on the Ordination of Women," argues to the same effect. If the hermeneutic of Inter Insigniores can be faulted, it is rather for failing to make explicit that, although Paul's pastoral precepts in these cases no longer bind, they were his temporary application of a permanently valid principle, namely, the husband's headship of the family. What is historically conditioned is how "headship" is appropriately expressed.

71. The objection often raised is that the principle of the Church Fathers that "what has not been assumed in the Incarnation, is not redeemed" implies that in

the Church Fathers in their christological arguments used the principle "What is not assumed, is not redeemed," they found no difficulty in the fact that Christ assumed a male humanity in order also to redeem female humanity, because they understood that the male has the natural office of representing his children of both sexes since he is their primal source. Thus, in the symbol system of the Pauline churches, Jesus' maleness was an important element in revealing that he as the New Adam was the beginning of the new creation.

Of course it is precisely this "patriarchal" or "headship" symbolism that many feminists indignantly reject. Correctly advocating the equal dignity of woman and man in marriage, they believe they must deny the differentiation of roles in the family as inimical to this equality and mutuality. Nevertheless, they also emphatically declare that male oppression has been and still is a major feature of human history. Some even identify it with the original sin.[72] In this they have biblical support in the original curses on Adam and Eve, which prophesy that sin will produce a world in which men toil in poverty and women bear the burden of childbirth and of dependency on their husbands (Gn 3:16–19).

Feminists attribute this universal subjugation of one sex by another to woman's unfair disadvantage in "the war of the sexes" because of her smaller size, lesser physical strength, liability to rape, and disablement by pregnancy and nursing, as compared to the male's greater strength, freedom of movement, and aggressiveness, and his ability to impregnate the woman and then desert her. But do not these sinful abuses of women by arrogant and brutal men reflect a natural differentiation that has to be recognized

---

the Incarnation what was assumed was a *humanity* whose gender was irrelevant. But for the Bible, Adam is the source of all humanity, including Eve, and thus the New Adam is the spiritual *father* of both sexes, whom the priest represents equally in the one mother, the church. Thus Jesus, precisely because he was male, has assumed all humanity, female and male, as its spiritual father. According to modern biology, the male produces two kinds of sperm *determinative* of both daughters and sons although both sexes have one mother.

72. See Rosemary Radford Ruether, "Original Sin and Sexism," in *Sexism and God-Talk*, 173–83.

in nonabusive ways in successful marriage? It is this natural differentiation of sexual roles in the family that Scripture, while acknowledging human liability to sinful abuse, expresses by the etiological narrative of the creation of Eve from Adam and by the concept of the father's "headship" in the family.

As I will show later, the Bible strives to show how this "headship" can be freed of abuse and reconciled with the still more fundamental equality of husband and wife, which it must support not contradict. Moreover, the way in which this "headship" is rightly expressed differs in different times, cultures, and economic conditions. To say, therefore, that even today the man is "head" of his family in no way justifies his exercising this headship in the manner of a Victorian father, nor indeed in any way that derogates from the equal personal dignity of his wife. The concept of male "headship" realistically recognizes that, because of the natural physical and psychological differentiation of the sexes and their relations to their offspring, some differentiation in their roles in the service of family unity must be acknowledged.

Thus maleness is essential to Jesus as New Adam, head and father of redeemed humanity, and therefore to the priest who symbolizes him.[73] The Christian priest has not in all places and cultures been given the title "Father," as is now customary in the United States, but it has commonly been applied to him, as St. Paul applies it to himself (1 Cor 4:15; 2 Cor 6:13; 1 Thes 2:11), and it is most fitting. While feminists frequently use the term "patriarchy" as if the word "father" connotes tyranny, in fact it implies that the violent and sexually exploitative male can be tamed by his tender love and care for his children and their mother.

It was in this sense of intimate trust that Jesus prayed to God

73. Joseph Komonchak, "Theological Questions on the Ordination of Women," 21, argues that "theological emphasis on the maleness of Christ's humanity is foreign to the New Testament," because there are only three texts (Lk 24:19; Jn 1:30; Acts 2:22) that use the term *anēr* (male) of Jesus and "none of them exploits Christ's maleness." Even the reference to Christ as New Adam (Rm 5) calls him *anthrōpos* (human). This argument ignores the symbolic significance of the terms "Son," "Adam," "Bridegroom" to which masculinity is intrinsic. Komonchak's important critique fails to distinguish the major symbols of the New Testament from its *occasional* use of gender metaphors (see pp. 79–82).

as "Abba" (Dear Father), invited us to pray the "Our Father," and in the great parable of the Prodigal Son (Lk 15:11–32) portrayed what a real father ought to be. The beautiful text of Isaiah, often cited by feminists to justify naming God "Mother," "Can a mother forget her infant, be without tenderness for the child of her womb? Even should she forget, I will never forget you (Is 49:15)," loses all its paradoxical, rhetorical force unless one notes that it is the patriarchal God, Yahweh, the Almighty Lord of Hosts, who is pleading with us so gently.[74]

The Son Symbol

It can be conceded that Jesus called God "Father" because in the patriarchal society of the Old Testament the prophets preferred to speak of Yahweh as male not female. But they did so also because they believed that this Name was the one that God himself had commanded them to use, "This is my name forever, this is my title for all generations" (Ex 3:15). "I am Yahweh, this is my name; my glory I give to no other, nor my praise to idols" (Is 42:8).[75]

Jesus seems to have felt no need to correct this understanding, as he did other Old Testament views (Mt 5:21–48). It was his own way of speaking of his relation to God: "No one knows the Son except the Father, and no one knows the Father but the Son and

74. On this topic see George T. Montague, *Our Father, Our Mother: Mary and the Faces of God*, (Steubenville, OH: Franciscan University Press, 1990).

75. See John W. Miller, "Depatriarchalizing God in Biblical Interpretation: A Critique," *Catholic Biblical Quarterly* 48 (1986): 609–16, who notes that according to Felix Donahue, "The Spiritual Father in the Scriptures," in *Abba: Guides to Wholeness and Holiness East and West*, ed. John R. Sommerfeld (Kalamazoo, MI: Cistercian Publications, 1982), pp. 3 and 6, God is referred to as father 21 times in the Old Testament, but 255 times in the New Testament. Miller concludes "Yahweh, then is not simply male, but father to his worshipers, as the name Yahweh itself may imply ('he causes to be'). True, Yahweh as father is pictured occasionally as acting with tenderness and care that is mother-like. But nowhere is it ever said or suggested that he *is* mother. According to Jesus his very 'name' is father and the hallowing of that name the focal point of religious devotion," and quotes Raphael Patai, *The Hebrew Goddess* (see note 94 below), p. 9, as saying that Yahweh's fatherhood is "possibly the greatest such symbol and image conceived by man. . . . Nor can there be any doubt as to the psychological need answered by the image. This together with the great moral imperatives, was the unique contribution of prophetic Judaism to mankind."

anyone to whom the Son wishes to reveal him" (Mt 11:27; Lk 10:21–22).[76] Jesus not only reveals the Father as Creator, but also manifests himself as Son sent by the Father on our behalf. But Jesus as Son of God and New Adam is the image of the Father, the First Person, "from whom every family *[patria]* in heaven and on earth is named" (Eph 3:15).[77]

Why then does the Bible prefer to symbolize God as Father, rather than Mother?[78] The reason is not hard to find if we remember that human language cannot be applied literally to God, but only analogically. Furthermore, for the Old Testament the analogy to be employed, as we have already seen, had to be based on a natural and therefore universal symbolism, namely, the best known relations in universal human experience, the relations within the family closely connected with the life of the body—a "theology of the body."[79]

76. Generally attributed to the hypothetical Q document which the majority of scholars believe represented very early tradition. "If the crucial v. 27 is authentic, as it may well be, it would give a most important clue to Jesus' self-understanding as absolute Son of the absolute Father. There is a Marcan-overlap of idiom here; cf. Mk 13:32" (B. T. Viviano, *New Jerome Biblical Commentary*, 653).

77. The traditional translation of this text is "from whom all *paternity* [or 'fatherhood'] in heaven and earth is named." This translation reflects the root *pater*, "father," implying that the father is source and representative of the family. But according to U. Hutter, *Exegetical Dictionary of the New Testament*, ed. Horst Balz and Gerhard Schneider (Grand Rapids, MI: W. B. Eerdmans, 1993), *patria* more precisely means "family, people, nation," as in Lk 2:4. Paul J. Kobleski, *New Jerome Biblical Commentary*, remarks, "God, the creator of all the families of beings, established his power and control over all creatures in the act of naming them (Ps 147:4; Is 40:26; cf Gn 2:19–20)" (p. 888).

78. Many feminists realize that to call God "Mother" and ascribe to deity "feminine" traits opens them to the charge of stereotyping. McFague, *Models of God*, 97–123, objects to what she calls the "dualism" between Creator and creation and hence to *creatio ex nihilo*, and accepts the notion that creation is the "Body" of God who, however, can also be thought of as its "Parent." It is true that the Holy Spirit has sometimes been regarded by Christian writers influenced by Platonism or Stoicism as the *Anima mundi*, but this expression tends to pantheism. Trenchant criticisms of such language can be found in Donald G. Bloesch, *Is The Bible Sexist: Beyond Feminism and Patriarchalism* (Westchester, IL: Crossway Books/Good News Publishers, 1982), and *The Battle for the Trinity: The Debate Over Inclusive God-Language* (Ann Arbor: Servant Publications/Vine Books, 1985).

79. I have developed this theme at length in my *Theologies of the Body: Humanist and Christian*.

We live in the time of the so-called Generation X and the widespread breakup of the family. Often we are weary of the prattle of reactionary politicians and pundits extolling "family values" while promoting a for-profit, consumerist culture which has undermined these same "values." Moreover, a large section of our population has never personally experienced a family with two parents permanently committed to each other in marriage. To such deprived persons the universality and archetypal power of symbols drawn from natural family relations may not at all seem obvious. In our times we are also experiencing in our culture, alienated as it is from nature, a very strong ecological movement, which for all its occasional extravagances, is proof that our human need for a natural physical environment cannot be destroyed. How much more real, then, is our need for a natural family environment? One of the tasks of any vital religion is to heal these natural relationships. Catholic Christianity, which has retained both the Bible and the sacraments, and especially sacramental marriage, has always been profoundly aware of this responsibility.

The principal Old Testament revelation, which is the foundation of the New Testament and the first article of its Creed, is that there is only one God, the Creator Almighty, who brought into being the People of the Covenant but also the heavens and the earth. Therefore, the First Person had to be symbolized as Father and not Mother in order to express the absolute transcendence of the Creator, utterly *other* than the cosmos of which he is the origin. This relation of *otherness* is not well expressed by the child's relation to its mother because she is more *same* than other, since her children develop within her body and are nourished at her breast. On the contrary, the relation of the child to its father is more a relation to the Other, but an Other who is still caring.[80] As

80. This is expressed somewhat differently by Mary and Leon J. Podles, "The Emasculation of God," *America* 161 (Nov. 25, 1989): "Why is God the Father a Father and not a mother? Maleness is a symbol of transcendence because the fundamental male experience, that of fatherhood, of reproduction through ejaculation, is one of separation, while the fundamental female experience is one of prolonged and intimate union with the offspring through the long months of gestation and nursing. The male experience of the world is one of 'either/or,' 'this, and not that,'

Aristotle said, "Male is what we call an animal that generates into another, female that which generates into itself. That is why in the universe as a whole the earth's nature is thought of as female and matter, while the sky and sun or such others are called begetters and fathers."[81]

A more technical explanation of why "Father" is to be preferred to "Mother" as names of God, can be developed from the distinction (frequently neglected in current discussions) between *metaphorical* analogy, based on a merely *accidental,* extrinsic resemblance, and *proper* analogy based on an *essential,* intrinsic resemblance.[82] Thus when the Bible calls God "my Rock" (Ps 18:3), "Rock" is taken metaphorically, because the point of comparison is "solidity," but "solidity" is not the very nature of a rock, nor of God, so that the comparison is very superficial. But when we call God "Light" (1 Jn 1:5) the analogy is proper and essential, since it is based on the comparison of what is essential and intrinsic to both "light" and "God," i.e., as it is the very nature of light to reveal the visible, material world to us, so it is the very nature of God to know and to reveal the truth of all things,

---

one of separation" (p. 373). Should not, however, the child's experience of its parents, which imprints the child with the archetypal symbol of God, be the analogue, rather than the parents' experiences? Elisabeth Schüssler Fiorenza, "You are not to be called Father," *Cross-Currents,* fall 1979: 356–58, argues that women's sense of being treated as *not* godlike has preserved in women, much more than in men, the sense of God's utter "otherness" and uncontrollability. May not the converse be the case: that women, because they correctly think of God as "other," think of him as a father rather than a mother like themselves?

81. *Generation of Animals,* trans. A. L. Peck, Loeb Classical Library, (Cambridge, MA: Harvard University Press, 1953), 1.2.716a14.

82. When a term is used to mean one thing only it is *univocal.* When used in several senses it is *equivocal.* When these diverse senses are nevertheless related, it is *analogical.* When the relation between them is based on a similarity that is extrinsic to their essences it is *improper analogy* (metaphorical); when it based on an intrinsic, essential likeness it is *proper* or *proportional analogy;* and when proper analogy results from giving the name of an effect to its cause or vice versa it is *attributive analogy.* In proportional analogy there are four terms and the relation between terms 1 and 2 is similar to the relation between terms 3 and 4, e.g., "As a *father* is to his *child,* so an *author* is to his *book.*" Thus the relationship of "fatherhood" and "authorship" are compared and seen to be both similar and different, i.e. analogous, and by a similarity that is intrinsic and essential, since it is essential to fatherhood that one produce a child, and to authorship that one produce a book.

visible and invisible, to us. As we see the material world only by light, so we know the spiritual world only by God's word. Hence the Psalmist can say, "In your light we see light" (Ps 36:10).[83] Thus the fundamental terms of the Bible, of worship, and of theology are not mere metaphors but proper analogies by which we know the Creator through his works of creation and redemption. St. Paul says, "Ever since the creation of the world, his [God's] invisible attributes of eternal power and divinity have been able to be understood and perceived in what he has made" (Rm 1:20; cf. Wis 13:1–9).

The fundamental fact on which our use of sexual terms is based is that, while both male and female are equally "parents" of their children, the term "father" is defined as the one who makes the mother pregnant, not the mother the father. Whatever the complexities of the reproductive process as revealed by science, the defining biological difference between male and female will always be that in reproduction the male role relative to the female is that of agent to patient. The male is the parent who impregnates the female, not the female the male; nor does the female impregnate herself.[84]

83. See *ST* I, q. 13, for a very detailed analysis of how analogical names of God can be applied in Scripture and in theology, a topic that goes back to the Pseudo-Dionysian, *De Divinis Nominibus*, on which St. Thomas Aquinas and his teacher St. Albert the Great wrote profound commentaries. Neither Pseudo-Dionysius nor Thomas, however, give much attention to the name "Father" as applied to the One God, but see *ST* I, q. 33, on the name as applied to the First Person of the Trinity.

84. Aristotle's biology is often blamed for degrading women because of his statements in *Generation of Animals* that in all sexually reproducing animals, "A female is as it were a deformed *(peperomenon)* male" (737a26), and that "We should look on the female state as being as it were a deformity *(anaperian),* though one which occurs in the ordinary course of nature" (775a15–16). In context these words actually mean "unformed," "incomplete," "undeveloped," rather than Peck's translation "deformed." Aristotle argues that since male semen actively generates life and "like produces like," if semen produces not a male but a female its effect is "incomplete." This he attributes to a lack of proportion *(symmetria)* of the semen's activity to the resistance to formation of the matter supplied by the female parent. Modern biology also holds that the sperm actively initiates reproduction, though its effect is to trigger the already highly organized ovum rather than, as Aristotle thought, to form it *ab initio;* see Keith L. Moore, *Before We Are Born: Basic Embryology and Birth Defects* (Philadelphia: W. B. Saunders, 1989), 1–28. Modern biology, like Aristotle, attributes sex determination to the sperm,

Hence, if the term "Father" is applied to God so that the comparison is between the human male's impregnation of the female and God's creative act, the analogy is merely metaphorical, since impregnation is intrinsic to the human male, but not to God who creates *ex nihilo*, and therefore the resemblance is merely extrinsic and accidental. But if we abstract from the dependence in reproduction of the human male on the female he impregnates and use the term "Father" as an analogy to God who creates out of nothing, we are using an analogy that is proper, since the point of comparison (active agency) is essential and intrinsic both to the human father and the Divine Father, although of very different types. The Bible and art sometimes use male, anthropomorphic images of God, as when Daniel beholds God as "the Ancient One" whose "clothing was snow bright, and the hair on his head as white as wool" (Dn 7:9). But the Bible also makes clear that such language is metaphorical, and must be interpreted theologically. The term "Father" used of God in no way implies that he is male, but only that as our father gave us life and loves and cares for us, so does God.

On the contrary, the term "Mother" cannot be applied to God by a proper analogy, but only as a metaphor. We can speak of women having traits (accidental attributes) such as nurturing, caring, tenderness which make them splendid metaphors for God, but precisely as mothers their defining role (relative to their male mate) is not to be the active cause of the child, but to supply and conserve the matter out of which the child is generated. This material causality cannot be the basis of a proper, essential, and intrinsic analogy with God because God creates out of nothing, i.e., without a correlative material cause—without a female partner. It makes sense to say "God the Father made the world." It is not true to

---

but explains this not by the proportion of the sperm's activity to the ovum's resistance, but to the male's production of both X and Y chromosome sperms. Ova supply only X chromosomes, and so require a Y chromosome sperm to produce a male. Thus Aristotle could easily accept the modern explanation without changing his basic principles. His intention was not to evaluate the role of gender in determining personal value, but to understand embryological processes in physiological terms.

say, "The world was made out of God the Mother." This latter expression implies the error of pantheism, the metaphysical oxymoron of a *causa sui*, something making itself out of nothing. Furthermore, the name "Father" can be used as a name especially appropriate to the First Person of the Trinity. In this case the analogy is not "As a human father is efficient cause of his child, so God is the efficient cause of the universe," but rather "As the human father is *principle* of his child, so the First Person, God the Father, is the *principle* of the Second Person, God the Son."[85] For this to be a proper analogy, the human father must not be seen as "cause." There is no *causal* subordination (since this would imply that the Divine Persons are not equal in the one Godhead), but there is subordination of *origin* by which the Second Person proceeds from the First Person as his principle of being.[86]

Feminists who want to call God "Mother" have themselves made the point that the world religions other than Judaism and its offshoots Christianity and Islam, all tend to be monistic and appropriately picture the Supreme Being as the Great Goddess who is identical with the cosmos, Mother Nature or Mother Earth.

The primary symbol for "That-Which-Cannot-be-Told" is the Goddess. The Goddess has infinite aspects and thousands of names—She is the reality behind many metaphors. She *is* reality, the manifest deity, omnipresent in all of life, in each of us. The Goddess is not separate from the world—She is the world, and all things in it: moon, sun, earth, star, stone,

---

85. In patristic Trinitarian theology the terms "principle" and "cause" were often used interchangeably because both mean a "source" or "origin." Later, however, they were distinguished so that "principle" is taken to mean "origin," abstracting from causality, e.g., a point can be the "principle" of a line in the sense of its beginning, but does not cause the line to be. In the Trinity, the Father is source and origin of Son and Holy Spirit, but does not create them, since they are equally the One God.

86. It is not usual to speak of a "hierarchy" among the Three Divine Persons, and some have claimed that to do so would be the heresy of "subordinationism." But while it is true that their hierarchy involves inequality among creatures, this need not be the case in every hierarchy. In the Trinity there is a sacred order (hierarchy) of origin that in no way contradicts the perfect equality of the Son and the Holy Spirit with the Father (Monarch or sole principle or fount of Divinity) from whom they proceed. The theology of the Eastern church especially insists on the divine monarchy of the First Person as the source of the divine unity.

seed, flowing river, wind, wave, leaf and branch, bud and blossom, fang an claw, woman and man. In Witchcraft, flesh and spirit are one.[87]

Hence quite logically some feminists propose to revive this ancient pantheistic (or "panentheistic") conception and therefore reject theism.[88] Any religion that worships a transcendent Creator, they maintain, is irredeemably patriarchal. Christianity, however, cannot tear out its roots in Judaism whose great contribution to the world is precisely its witness to a God who creates *ex nihilo* in opposition to the gods and goddesses of the Canaanites and other pagan peoples who surrounded Israel.[89] Since, then, to free the Jews and all humanity from the error of pantheism, the Divine First Person chose to reveal himself as related to us as Father rather than Mother (though he is of course also the origin of motherhood), the Second Person, in order to be revealed as God's image and absolute equal had to be the Son not the Daughter of God.

87. Starhawk, *The Spiral Dance,* 8.

88. The term "panentheism" seems to have been coined by Carl C. F. Krause (1781–1832) who loved neologisms. "Krause claimed to be developing the true Kantian position. . . . The system was intended to mediate between pantheism and theism, hence Krause called his position 'Panentheism' to suggest the idea that God or Absolute Being is one with the world, though not exhausted by it" (Arnulf Sweig, "Krause," in *Encyclopedia of Philosophy.*) Given theological currency by disciples of the process philosophy of Alfred North Whitehead, panentheism has been adopted by some feminist theologians. They hope by this term to avoid *pantheism,* on the one hand, by affirming with the Judaic, Islamic and Christian faiths that God creates freely and hence is really distinct from the world, and on the other hand, to avoid *theism,* because they think it implies that "the world is really related to God, but not God to the world" (cf. *ST* I, q. 3, a. 7). But this misunderstands the highly nuanced scholastic uses of the term *relatio;* see Anthony Kelly, "God: How Near a Relation," *The Thomist* 34 (1970): 191–229; and William Hill, "Does the World Make a Difference to God," *The Thomist* 38 (1974): 146–64. Aquinas only meant that God does not depend for his existence on the world, since then the world would be uncreated. But he clearly held that God is "really related" (in the modern sense of that term) to the world by causality, knowledge, love, intimate presence, providence, and compassion. Thus a "panentheistic Creator" is an oxymoron that contributes only confusion to theological discourse.

89. "The three principal goddesses [of Canaanite religion] were Asherah (*qnyt ilm* . . . perhaps 'creatress of the gods') and of a strongly sexual stamp, Astarte (Ashtoreth) and Anath ('the virgin' and of warlike nature) whose exploits are well known from the Ugaritic texts. Canaanite religion was marked by fertility rites, which involved sacred prostitution" (Roland E. Murphy, *New Jerome Biblical Commentary,* 1227). On these three goddesses see David Noel Freedman, ed., *Anchor Bible Dictionary,* (New York: Doubleday, 1990), s.v. "Anath," by Walter A. Maier III, and "Ashtoreth (Astarte)" and "Asherah," by John Day.

To argue that this divine act of self-revelation had significance only in the particular culture of the Jews because of their patriarchy is to belie the universality of God's self-revelation through the Incarnation to all peoples and all times. As the revelation of God's Name to Moses was fundamental to the religion of the Jews, so Jesus is said in the New Testament to be the very Name of God for all humanity. "Because of this [his sacrificial death] God highly exalted him and bestowed on him the name that is above every other name" (Phil 2:9). Hence Jesus, as God's Name, must include in his identity the male gender of Yahweh by which the transcendent Creatorship of the Father is symbolized.

Some have been outraged that *Inter Insigniores* denies to women the capacity to act *in persona Christi*. Do not women as Christians image Christ to the world? Of course women image him as he is human, but they are not well qualified to represent him precisely as he is the New Adam and the image of God as Father.[90] Thus we can conclude that because *women cannot be fathers, they cannot be priests.*

Men alone are qualified for this particular function in the church not because they are superior as persons, but because they are qualified to be spiritual fathers, and women to be not spiritual fathers, but spiritual mothers. The exclusion of women from

90. St. Paul's statement, "A man, on the other hand, should not cover his head, because he is the image and glory of God, but woman is the glory of man. For man did not come from woman, but woman from man, nor was man created for woman, but woman for man" (1 Cor 11:7–9), has led some to say that woman is *not* the image of God, but instead the image of man. Yet there are other texts (Rm 8:29; 3 Cor 3:18; Eph 4:24; Col 3:10) addressed to all Christians, both men and women, that imply that women also are images of Christ. I think that Paul in the quoted text is saying that, like Adam, the Christian man has a certain dignity (glory) as head of the family (image of the Father, head of all families) and the family's representative before God. The wife shares in this dignity and contributes to it (she is the husband's "glory"), but she is not head of the family nor symbol of the Father as such. On the many meanings of *kephalē* (head) in Pauline usage see Balz and Schneider, *Exegetical Dictionary of the New Testament.* Its core meaning seems to be "a principle of life" which is exactly what the head of a family ought to be. See J. A. Fitzmyer, "Another Look at *kephalē* in 1 Cor, 11:3," *New Testament Studies* 35 (1989): 503–11, against the suggestion that Paul uses the word to mean "source" rather than "authority"; but, since "authority" is a "source" (it is from Latin *auctor*, "originator"), and the father of the family, as I have argued, is both, it comes to the same.

priesthood, therefore, is not an injustice, but a simple recognition of the woman's special gifts and special contribution to the church. In fact the church would be unjust to women if it were to call them to a function inappropriate to their special gifts, just it would be if it called men to an inappropriate role and ignored their special gifts as men. To deny the complementarity of these gifts is to deny human sexuality, or to see in it no other significance than a mere physical fact like differences in height, weight, or skin color.

The Male Slave Symbol

One of the sources of this controversy about women's ordination has undoubtedly been the arrogant clericalism of some priests, a sinful manifestation of male pride and aggressiveness that has obscured the symbolism of priesthood. While representing Christ as the revelation of the Father, a priest even more visibly represents him in his *kenosis* (emptying) as he became a lowly human being, a servant of the Father and of his fellow human beings, sent on a mission that involved humiliation, suffering, and death. The power of God is manifested in the priest not so much in victory as in powerlessness, or rather, "power perfected in weakness" (2 Cor 12:9; cf. Heb 4:15).

Women who think that ordination will "empower" them do not realize what the experience of being a priest usually amounts to. Few priests, even bishops, feel "powerful," since they live every day with tasks that seem to produce no results at all! Indeed, clerical abuse of the power of office, arrogance, ambition, or pomp are as often as not the reflection of the frustration that male aggressiveness feels in a position which by its very nature is so countercultural and lacking in prestige. If we may use the gender differences cited by many feminists, it seems that it would be far more humiliating for a proud, aggressive male to acknowledge himself an obedient slave than it would be in most cultures for a woman to acknowledge herself a "lowly servant" or "handmaid" as Mary did (Lk 1:48).

When St. Paul says, "Thus should one regard us: as servants of Christ and stewards of the mysteries of God" (1 Cor 4:1), he is speaking of the only power a priest can claim. Presiding at the Eucharist or reconciling the sinner is not an exercise of power by the priest in his own right but by Christ and by the church through him. A priest acting in the name of Christ and the church is gravely obliged to act simply as their servant. On Holy Thursday when the church celebrates the institution of the Eucharist and of the Christian priesthood and instructs the faithful liturgically as to what a priest is, the Gospel and the ritual reenact how Jesus washed the apostles' feet as their slave (Jn 13:1–20).

Christ had to be male because of the very fact feminists proclaim, namely, the universal oppression of woman by man, foretold but not condoned by God after the Fall (Gn 3:16). To overcome this oppression it was necessary that a man, not a woman, should demonstrate that true manhood is not characterized by *machismo*, that is, violence and sexual prowess. Jesus, by being the New Adam yet a male who was nonviolent and virgin, gave this proof in his heroic life and death. If the Second Person had been incarnate as a woman, the *kenosis* of the Master choosing to be the servant would have been missing, and incarnation of God as Suffering Servant would have seemed just another example of woman's victimization. A feminist theologian, Elizabeth A. Johnson puts it well,

On the cross Jesus symbolizes the exact opposite of male dominating power. Rather on the cross power is poured out in self-sacrificing love. The cross is the *kenosis* of patriarchy. Looking at the cross, some feminists have reflected sociologically it was probably better that the incarnation happened in a male human being; for if a woman had preached and enacted compassion and given the gift of self even unto death—is not this the way women are supposed to do anyway?—but for a man to live and die this way in a world of male privilege is to challenge the patriarchal idea of the dominating male at the root.[91]

91. *Consider Jesus: Waves of Renewal in Christology* (New York: Crossroad, 1990), 111. David Hein, "Women's Ordination Redivivus," surely misses the point when he argues in the opposite sense, "Can a male person represent the suffering servant better than a female person? That is not at all obvious. . . . Who could more faithfully represent service than those who have always served? By virtue of never having had worldly power, women possess the power to convey images

Thus Christ and the priest who images him symbolically reveal the Trinity in that the Son stands in relation to the Father as having nothing of his own, but receiving all from the Father, who is the very principle of the Son, who, as the Athanasian Creed says, is "one in Being with the Father." Sent to us in total obedience to the Father, he prayed in Gethsamane, "Abba, Father, all things are possible to you. Take this cup away from me, but not what I will but what you will" (Mk 14:36).

Feminists complain of the use of the term "submission" in the New Testament texts relating to the role of the wife in the family (e.g., Col 3:18; Ti 1:5), overlooking that Christ totally submitted to the Father, and that the husband as representing Christ in the family is by that very fact also called on to submit himself to his wife by sacrificing for her as Christ sacrificed himself for the church.[92] Thus in the Christian scheme of things "submission" is in no way degrading, but is "self-giving." Moreover, it is *mutual*, since to give oneself in love calls the other to the reciprocal act of self-giving.

Feminists do not like the notion of the "complementarity" of

---

of faithful and humble love" (p. 34). If male priests are so oppressive, will women continue to represent "humble service" once they become hierarchical priests?

92. The verb *hupotassō*, "to place under, subject, subordinate, submit," is used in several of these texts of slaves (Ti 2:9; 1 Pt 2:18) and of wives (1 Cor 14:34; Eph 5:22, 24; Col 3:18; Ti 2:5; 1 Pt 3:1), and similarly *hupotagē* ("subjection") (1 Tm 2:11) is used of wives. But in Eph 5:21 just before speaking of the submission of wives, all Christians, both husbands and wives, are exhorted: "Be subordinate to one another *(hupotassomenoi allēlois)* out of reverence for Christ," and in 1 Cor 11:3, Paul writes, "But I want you to know that Christ is the head of every man and a husband the head of his wife, and God the head of Christ." Thus the early church did not see *subordination* as taking away anything of the equal dignity and mutual respect of persons, but rather as contributing to it, because its model was Jesus who with regard to his humanity subordinated himself in obedience to the Father and in service to all and by that was exalted to the right hand of the Father (Phil 2:6–11). The temptation to refuse a due subordination ("You shall be as gods," Gn 3:5) was the original sin. This Christian subordination is the proper analogue of the ordering (but not *causal* subordination) of the Divine Son to the Father, and of the Holy Spirit to the Father through the Son, which implies order but not inequality because the order is precisely one of *total* self-giving, by which recipient becomes absolutely equal to giver.

the sexes, because, they say, it is often used to imply the incompleteness and therefore inferiority of the woman, and hence feminists prefer "mutuality."[93] But mutuality is generic to all truly Christian and humane relationships and in the case of the sexual relationship requires to be made more specific by the additional term "complementarity" or "complementary equality," which implies not only that woman is in one sense incomplete without man, but that man is incomplete without woman. Yet both woman and man are complete persons and only when mature as persons they are ready to enter into the self-giving covenant of marriage. To be a complete person is to be social, but to be social is to find completion in other persons. This is precisely what Genesis 1–2 teaches, what Jesus affirms in quoting Genesis 1–2 (Mk 10:6–9), and what St. Paul sums up when he says, "Woman is not independent of man or man of woman in the Lord. For just as woman came from man, so man is born of woman; but all things are from God" (1 Cor 11:11–12).

The Messiah (Spirit-Anointed) Symbol

In the third phase of the economy of salvation, Christ reveals the Holy Spirit by sending the Spirit from the Father to his disciples to form them into a church. In the Old Testament the prophets foretold that the restoration of God's Reign would be through a Messiah, an anointed king of the line of David. Christian tradition also saw him as an anointed priest "of the line of Melchizedek," i.e., no longer of the Aaronic priesthood. This anointing of Jesus by the Holy Spirit and his acknowledgement by the Father as his Beloved Son was manifested in his baptism (Mt 3:16–17).

When the heart of Jesus was pierced after his death on the Cross, blood and water flowed out (Jn 19:34), symbols of the sacraments of the Eucharist and baptism through which the life-giving

---

93. See Eugene C. Bianchi, *From Machismo to Mutuality: Essays on Sexism and Woman-Man Liberation* (New York: Paulist, 1976) and Beverly Wildung Harrison, "Human Sexuality and Mutuality," in *Christian Feminism: Visions of a New Humanity,* ed. Judith L. Weidman (San Francisco: Harper and Row, 1984), 158–80.

Spirit is to be offered to all humanity. This action of the Holy Spirit, sent by the Son ascended to the Father, became manifest at Pentecost in the Spirit's animation of the apostles and the holy women, constituting them as the church.

The priest, who in ordination receives the Holy Spirit and is permanently consecrated (i.e., receives the sacramental "character") for his role in the community of the church, is thus a symbol of the presence of the Messiah (in Hebrew, "the Anointed One"; in Greek, "the Christ"), on whom the Holy Spirit rests as did the *Shekinah* or "glory of the Lord" on the Holy of Holies in the Tabernacle and the Temple.

When we recall that Jesus the Messiah was a poor carpenter, and in the eyes of the world nothing more, it becomes understandable why the priest who stands for Christ can be a very ordinary human being dedicated to the service of his people and yet be consecrated in the Spirit. It is only because the members of the church have the faith to perceive this invisible yet real presence of Christ through the Spirit in their priests that they can listen to their preaching with trust, confess their sins, and receive the Eucharist in faith.

The Bridegroom Symbol

The Fathers of the Church thought the church was born from the side of the Jesus dead on the Cross in fulfillment of the symbol of the creation of Eve from the side of the sleeping Adam. Certainly *Genesis* wished to show that although the man heads and represents the family as the basic community, the woman is equal to the man in nature, yet complementary to him as his covenant partner. Between man and woman there is a certain natural ordering relationship, as between the different members of a living organism. Yet precisely because men and women have different gifts to contribute they can form a perfect unity in which they equally share one being and life. Moreover, this is a unity of *love*, of self-giving, by which each submits (is subordinated) to the other, so that all that belongs to one belongs to the other. They thus image the Trinity in which, although it could be misleading to speak of *sub*-ordination, there is nevertheless a divine *order* of First, Second, Third, yet only one Divinity, One Being, One Life.

Thus the sacrament of marriage symbolizes the church, which is itself constituted through the sacrament of holy orders, because in ordination the priest becomes the consecrated symbol of the presence of Christ, the Head, and the people become the Body of Christ. If it be objected that the people are already members of Christ by the sacrament of baptism, which can be performed even by a non-priest, this of course is true, but there would be no Christian community into which one could be baptized if it had not been constituted by priestly authority continuous with that which the apostles received from the Risen Christ.

In the Old Testament, Yahweh as sole author of creation, had no goddess-wife.[94] Therefore, metaphorically, the Creation itself was his wife. Hence, in the Old Testament the order of creation and the order of the law were personified as a woman, "Wisdom" (cf. Job 28; Prv 1:8–9; Sir 24; Wis 7–9; Bar 3:9–4:4). In the New Testament, Jesus is called "the power and wisdom of God" (1 Cor 1:24) by St. Paul, since in Jesus, the New Adam, creation is restored (Rm 5:12–21), and the New Law of Love ("the law of Christ," Gal 6:2; "the law of faith," Rm 3:27) is manifested to all nations.

Yet more properly it is to the Third Person of the Trinity, who proceeds from the Father and the Son, who is Love, wise Love, that the Old Testament descriptions of a feminine Wisdom are applied. In the New Testament the Holy Spirit, although named by a grammatically neuter term (*pneuma*, spirit), nevertheless as a Divine Person is designated by masculine terms (Jn 16:7, 12, 14, etc.).[95] Yet as the creation and the Law are the wife of Yahweh

94. See Raphael Patai, *The Hebrew Goddess* (New York: KTAV Publishing House, 1967), on the rabbinic concept of *Shekina* or glorious presence of God, conceived as the bride of God (pp. 137–56) and the Kabbalistic figure of "Matronit" or Maternal Presence (pp. 157–206); see also Mark S. Smith, "God Male and Female in the Old Testament: Yahweh and his 'Asherah'," *Theological Studies* 48 (1987): 333–40.

95. An Orthodox theologian and ecumenist, Paul Evdokimov, has suggested that the Holy Spirit is feminine and with the Father begets the Son. He urges that

because they are the works of his wisdom, so the church is the Bride of Christ because she is the creation of his wisdom through the Holy Spirit. Thus, although the Holy Spirit, as all the Divine Persons, is named as masculine, the church to which as its very soul the Spirit gives life is feminine and complements Christ as his Bride.[96]

Therefore, it is in the covenant relation of the church to Christ, in their union of love, that the Holy Spirit is especially revealed. This Spirit descending on Christ in his baptism, making him the Messiah or Anointed One, the Beloved Son of the Father (Mt 3:16–17), overflows from the Head to the members, and gives life to the church, which is then united to him as the Bride of the Lamb (Rv 21:9). The Old Testament theme by which Yahweh is the Bridegroom of Israel, who forgives her unfaithfulness and reunites her to himself in mutual love, marvelously making her his *equal* in the covenant relationship (Hos 1–3), is manifested in its fullness in Christ and the church, with the difference that by the guidance

---

the Western church accept a *Spirituque* so that the Eastern church can accept the *Filioque;* see Evdokimov, *La Femme et la salut du monde* (Paris/Tournai: Ed. Caterman, 1958), and also Peter C. Phan, "Gender Roles in the History of Salvation: Man and Woman in the Thought of Paul Evdokimov," *Heythrop Journal* 31 (1990): 53–66. For other theories on this subject see Donald Gelpi, S.J., *The Divine Mother: A Trinitarian Theology of the Holy Spirit* (New York: University Press of America, 1984), and *God Breathes the Spirit in the World* (Wilmington, DE: Michael Glazier, 1988); and Leonardo Boff, O.F.M., *Trinity and Society,* trans. Paul Burns (Maryknoll, NY: Orbis Books, 1988), and *The Maternal Face of God,* trans. R. R. Blair and W. Dieckmeier (San Francisco: Harper and Row, 1987).

96. Some feminists theologians seek to develop a "Spirit Christology" (see Appendix 2). They propose that Christ be named "Wisdom" or "Sophia," which is incarnated as the "Word made flesh" (Jn 1:14) in Jesus of Nazareth. Hence, they say, the maleness of Christ's flesh is less significant than the femininity of Christ as Divine Spirit. But when Paul says in 1 Cor: 1:24 (a phrase without parallel in the New Testament) that Christ is "the power and wisdom of God" *(theou dunamis kai theou sophia)* there is no reason to think "power" and "wisdom" are understood as proper names of God rather than as attributes of God communicated to Jesus. Jerome Murphy-O'Connor, *New Jerome Biblical Commentary,* paraphrases the expression as meaning "The authentic humanity of Jesus makes visible God's intention for the human race and radiates an attractive force that enables response" (p. 801). Only twice in the New Testament, at Lk 7:35 (with parallel Mt 11:19) and Lk 11:49, is "Wisdom" used in the personified manner of the Old Testament and then without reference to Jesus. Thus although the attributes of Old Testament "Wisdom" are assigned to Jesus in the New Testament, he is not named "Sophia"; cf. H. Hegermann, *Exegetical Dictionary of the New Testament,* 258–61.

of the Holy Spirit the church is always kept faithful to Christ in its infallibility and indefectibility (Eph 5:25–27).

Within the Christian community, therefore, the invisible presence of Christ, Husband of the church, is made visible by the selection and ordination of one of its members to be the symbol or icon of Christ, as the people as a whole is the icon of the church, Bride of Christ. Some may object that the laity, of course, consists of men as well as women. It is not, however, the sometimes unfaithful faithful as individuals who *symbolize* Christ in this relationship but the ever faithful church as a *corporate whole*. The presiding priest is the only individual in the eucharistic assembly who stands for Christ in relation to the corporate congregation as church.[97] Other individual Christians do symbolize Christ and also the church but in different individual ways according to their various vocations and charisms.

Priesthood in the Family

Married Priests

Sometimes it is claimed that the exclusion of women from priesthood is an affront to their personal equality with men. It is forgotten that most men are also excluded from priesthood because in one way or another, other than maleness, they are not qualified for it. This is not usually regarded as an affront to their personal dignity. In particular many males are disqualified for ordination by the law of mandatory celibacy for priests. Consequently, we often find arguments for optional celibacy for priests linked with the arguments for ordination of women. In our American culture, both laws seem arbitrary and contrary to justice. Moreover, these opinions are frequently linked with "liberal" views on sexual orientation. In all these questions the influence of secular humanism, with its denial that gender as a biological fact

97. The traditional term for the priest as *alter Christus,* "another Christ," can be benignly explained, but it is not really proper, since a priest is not *another* Christ, but symbolically Christ himself, just as, in another way, the poor man who needs our compassion is Christ himself (Mt 25:40).

need play any determinate role in the evaluation of human behavior, is very evident. For Christians, however, the relations within the family, which are grounded in human nature both in its bodily and spiritual character, shape all of human life according to a God-given dynamic.[98]

The arguments for optional celibacy for the clergy are based on the frequent failures in this regard, sensationally publicized by the media,[99] and the popular supposition that the practice of sexual abstinence is even more difficult for men than for women. Thus feminists charge that the sexual aggressiveness of men is the paramount source of female oppression and exploitation.[100] We often hear it argued that it is utterly unrealistic to expect male sexual drives to remain unexpressed.

What does historical experience have to say on this question?

98. See Chapter II nn. 22 and 24 above. For a Protestant view of the man-woman relation, which comes to somewhat different conclusions, see the favorably reviewed work of Paul King Jewett, *Man as Male and Female: A Study in Sexual Relationships from a Theological Point of View* (Grand Rapids, MI: Eerdmans, 1975), and *The Ordination of Women: an Essay on the Office of Christian Ministry* (Grand Rapids, MI: Eerdmans, 1980).

99. An attempt at a clinical approach has been made by A. W. Richard Sipe, *A Secret World: Sexuality and the Search for Celibacy*(New York: Brunner/Mazel, 1990). James J. Gill, S.J., reviewing it in *Commonweal* 118 (Feb. 8, 1991): 108–10 writes, "Sipe makes clear at the beginning he has not conducted his study according to the canons of scientific research. He says, in other words, that he is not looking at the behavior of a sample of priests that adequately represents the Catholic clergy of the United States or any specific region within the country." H. Vernon Sattler, "An Agenda to Reject Celibacy," *Homiletic and Pastoral Review* 91 (June 1991): 72–77, is even more critical. Certainly the historical section of the book is inaccurate.

100. Yet some feminists also argue that women should have the free choice of contraception and abortion so that they can have the same sexual freedom as men. A noted feminist writer, Marilyn French, *Beyond Power*, says, "Sex is the core of pleasure, which is the realm in which freedom lives. Freedom is the state in which the greatest possible harmony and sense of rightness obtains among body, emotions, and mind. Freedom and pleasure are among the values that feminism upholds. Many people deplore the unhappy consequences of an age they see as sexually 'free': but sexual freedom does not exist now and has never existed as a cultural standard in history. (It may have existed in prehistory). To achieve it, we must get beyond the worship of power, a sense that hierarchy is the only possible structure, and our sense of sex as tainted. To get to freedom of any sort, we must get beyond gender roles and the definition of man as the controller, woman as the controlled" (p. 528).

Recent research has brought out a fact, often ignored,[101] that in the early church priests were ordinarily chosen from married men who, in accordance with the advice in the Pastoral Epistles (1 Tm 3:1–13; Ti 1:5–11), had proved their prudence as fathers of families. Yet, once ordained, these heads of families were often required either to separate from their wives, or at least to abstain henceforth from marital relations.

This mandatory clerical celibacy was certainly in force at least in some regions from the beginning of the fourth century, when it appears in the canons of both the Eastern and Western churches. While a lack of data makes it difficult to trace the origins of this requirement back earlier, there is a good case for it having apostolic origins and no decisive evidence to the contrary.[102]

In the Latin church this requirement for priests has been constantly maintained in principle, and its admittedly sometimes wide-spread violation has always provoked reform movements to restore the tradition. In the Eastern church, on the other hand, the marriage of the lower clergy was tolerated after the Council of Trullo in the seventh century, a council never accepted by Rome. Evidence that before this time the Eastern clergy was also required to be celibate is to be found in the fact that even now in the Eastern churches a bishop must be unmarried and a priest may not marry after ordination even if his wife dies. Moreover, priests are urged to abstain from marital relations for a time before celebrating the Eucharist.[103]

The reason for this requirement of celibacy is sometimes said to be merely "cultic," and now obsolete.[104] It is true that the reason

101. Sipe, in his chapter, "The Origins of Celibacy," in *A Secret World,* lists popes in the ancient church who were married or were sons of clergy as evidence that clerical celibacy was not then in force, without mention of the discipline noted in the text.

102. See the works of Cholij and Cochini, and the different view of Gryson in note 12 above.

103. Details on these regulations and actual practice in the Eastern churches are discussed in Cholij, *Clerical Celibacy in East and West,* 106–94.

104. See Jean Paul Audet, *Structures of Christian Priesthood* (New York: Macmillan, 1968), 77–92. Audet, a priest who has now married, believes clerical celibacy had its origins in a tendency to "sacralization" of religious things and persons,

often given by the Church Fathers was that since priests under the
Old Law, although married, were required as a matter of ritual
purity to abstain from sex for a period before offering the sacrifices, the New Testament priest who offered the Eucharist frequently, even daily, should abstain perpetually. Since the Gospel
abolished the laws of ritual purity, it is argued, why should Christian priests be bound to this obsolete rule? This objection overlooks the fact that when these canons were written the bishops
were perfectly well aware that the ritual prescriptions of the Old
Law were no longer in force and they generally opposed Judaizing
tendencies.[105]

Therefore, it was not the Old Law itself that led the church to
require celibacy of the clergy, but an understanding of the perpetually valid purpose behind the Old Law. The reason for temporary
abstinence by the Old Law priests and the permanent abstinence
of the New Law priests was the perception that the offering of
sacrifice requires a priest to transcend earthly concerns so as to
give total attention to heavenly ones. In the New Testament this
transcendent attention of the offering priest is eschatological and
absolute in a way that was only hinted at in the Old Testament. It
demands of the priest who represents Christ, now present at the
right hand of the Father, a permanent state of consecration.[106]

---

which he believes is incompatible with the "secularizing" tendencies (of which he
approves) of modern culture and, he claims, of the Gospel. See also Bernard Verkamp, "Cultic Purity and the Law of Celibacy," *Review for Religious* 30 (1971):
199–217. On the Biblical roots of priestly celibacy see Barbara Thiering, "The
Biblical Source of Qumran Asceticism," *Journal of Biblical Literature* 93 (Sept. 3,
1974): 429–44.

105. See Daniel Callam, C.S.B., "Clerical Continence in the Fourth Century,"
Theological Studies 41 (March 1980): 3–50. Priests did not celebrate the Eucharist
every day. Hence the notion of cultic purity does not satisfactorily explain why
clerical abstinence was perpetual. Callam details the other motives.

106. As both Cochini and Cholij argue (see note 12 above), while the notion
of "cultic purity" undoubtedly was a strong influence in the development of clerical
celibacy, it was not fundamental. What *was* fundamental was the conviction that
the leaders of a Christian community ought to be *totally* dedicated to the service
of God and the community. Some church historians say that the fourth century
canons on clerical abstinence originated in an "excessive" praise of virginity by
certain Church Fathers. But why "excessive"? I would suggest that this renewed
emphasis on the value of virginity and celibacy was part of the monastic reaction

This clerical celibacy is a matter of appropriateness not of validity, as is the requirement that priests be men. Since the ordination of noncelibates is not invalid, the Catholic church has accepted the age-old discipline of the Eastern churches, and also the ordination of some married converts for ecumenical reasons. Nevertheless, the appropriateness of mandatory celibacy rests on solid theological foundations. If it were to be further weakened by circumstances, this would still more obscure the nature of the priesthood. Nor is there any proof that in the long run the permission to seek domestic happiness would inspire more men to enter a Christian priesthood,[107] which seeks only to imitate the celibate Christ and looks for no other happiness except what Jesus promised the apostles when he said, "Amen, I say to you, there is no one who has given up house or wife or brothers or parents or children for the sake of the kingdom of God who will not receive an overabundant return in this present age and eternal life in the age to come" (Lk 18:29–30).

Priests of the Domestic Church

Who denies that chastity is difficult for men? Or who can ignore such facts as that most adolescent males masturbate, that polygyny, prostitution, pornography, and active male homosexuality have existed in most cultures and still exist in ours? It is generally conceded that men more than women tend to promiscuity and to seek selfish satisfaction rather than binding relationships. Hence societies have found it necessary to institute and sanction marriage as a way of committing males to responsibility for the female and his offspring. Attacks on the institution of marriage are often a

---

to the worldliness of the Constantinian Establishment. If David G. Hunter, "Resistance to the Virginal Ideal in Late-Fourth-Century Rome: The Case of Jovinian," *Theological Studies* 48 (1987): 45–64, is correct, St. Jerome, a fourth-century leader in the exaltation of virginity, may have been defending a traditional Christian value imperiled by Jovinian's too one-sided defense of marriage, another traditional Christian value, against the Manichees.

107. On a recent trip to Greece, I was told that the Greek church, probably the most vital of the Eastern churches, was suffering from a clergy shortage in spite of its married lower clergy. Some Protestant churches have the same experience, others have an excess of clergy, due to the decline in membership.

covert male device for escaping its responsibilities, as is evident
from the present American experience of single-parent households,
predominantly female-headed, with the husbands gone and their
child support or alimony payments in arrears.[108]

This does not mean, however, that men are simply sexual
brutes. A man's love for his wife and children, once aroused—
which it cannot be by casual sexual encounters—is one of the
deepest responses of the human heart, one for which life is often
sacrificed. It is this husbandhood and fatherhood that is sanctified
by the sacramental covenant of Christian marriage, and by it the
man is constituted head of the family, as Christ is of the church.
As such he becomes the mediator between the family and God,
the priest of the *ecclesia domestica*.[109]

This can be achieved only when the wife sees in the husband's
commitment to the marriage covenant the commitment of God to
her in protection of her life and child-bearing. The sad experience
of women who have not found in their own fathers, or in their
lovers and husbands this security based on faith in God and commitment to the permanency of marriage is, I would suggest, the
prime source of feminist outrage.[110]

108. On the crisis of fatherhood in the United States see Nancy R. Gibbs,
"Bringing Up Father," *Time*, June 28, 1990, 52–61. On the personal and social
consequences see Clayton Barbeau, *The Head of the Family* (Chicago: Regnery,
1961); Henry B. Biller, *Paternal Deprivation* (Lexington, MA: Lexington Books,
1974); Michael Lamb, ed., *The Role of the Father in Child Development* (New
York: John Wiley & Sons, 1976); L. McKee and M. O'Brien, eds. *The Father
Figure* (London/New York: Tavistock Publications, 1983); John W. Miller, *Biblical
Faith and Fathering: Why We Call God "Father"* (New York: Paulist, 1989).

109. The term *ecclesia domestica* is used by John Paul II in his encyclical, "The
Role of the Christian Family in the Modern World" *(Familaris Consortio)*, November 22, 1981, no. 51. He also emphasizes the "priestly" character of the family,
i.e., its special participation in the universal priesthood of the faithful (no. 55). He
does not distinguish the role of the man and the woman in the family in this respect,
but if we accept the biblical view of the husband as in some sense "head of the
family," it follows that he is in a special sense "priest of the family" as Christ, Head
of the church, is priest. See also William E. May, "Marriage and the Complementarity of Male and Female," *Anthropotes* 8 (June 1, 1992): 41–60.

110. This sense of outrage was eloquently expressed by Simone de Beauvoir:
"Woman recognizes that the world is masculine on the whole; those who fashioned
it, ruled it, and still dominate it today are men, as for her, she does not consider
herself responsible for it; it is understood that she is inferior and dependent; she

The husband, because he is constituted head of the family, has the responsibility for its worship of God, not only by encouraging family prayer or Mass attendance, but for instruction in the Christian faith and in disciplined moral life. If he carries out these tasks with love and true concern for the good of each member of the family, and not for his own aggrandizement, he will be a true father and a true priest of the home.[111] This is not the picture of fatherhood that we find often on television, but we can be grateful that even there occasional glimpses of it are seen and usually find an affectionate popular response. On the other hand the tyrannical father, the abusive father, the incestuous father, the neglectful or

---

has not learned the lessons of violence, she has never stood forth as a subject before the other members of the group. Shut up in her flesh, her home, she sees herself as passive before these gods with human faces who set goals and establish values. In this sense there is truth in the saying that makes her the 'eternal child'. . . . The lot of woman is a respectful obedience. She has no grasp, even in thought to the reality about her. It is opaque to her eyes" (*The Second Sex,* trans. H. M. Parshley [New York: Bantam Books, 1953], 563).

111. "In revealing and in reliving on the earth the very fatherhood of God, a man is called upon to ensure the harmonious and united development of all members of the family; he will perform this task by exercising generous responsibility for the life conceived under the heart of the mother, by a more solicitous commitment to education, a task he shares with his wife, by work which is never a cause of division in the family but promotes its unity and stability, and by means of the witness he gives of an adult Christian life which effectively introduces the children into the living experience of Christ and the Church" (John Paul II, *Familaris Consortio,* no. 25). The literature on the role of the human male is much thinner today than the abundant feminist literature, but some significant works are: Willi Moll, *Father and Fatherhood,* trans. E. Reinecke and P. C. Bailey (Notre Dame, IN: Fides, 1966); Leonard G. Benson, *Fatherhood: A Sociological Perspective* (New York: Random House, 1968); David B. Lynn, *The Father: His Role in Child Development* (Monterey, CA: Brooks Publishing Co., 1974); Joseph H. Pleck and Jack Sawyer, eds., *Men and Masculinity* (Englewood Cliffs, NJ: Prentice-Hall, 1974); Lionel Tiger and Robin Fox, *The Imperial Animal* (London: Secker and Warburg, 1977); James A. Doyle, *The Male Experience* (Dubuque, IA: W. C. Brown Co., 1983); George Gilder, *Men and Marriage* (Gretna: Pelican Publishing Co., 1986); Michael E. Lamb, ed., *The Father's Role: Cross-Cultural Perspectives* (Hillsdale, NJ: L. Erlbaum Associates, 1987); Phyllis Bronstein and Carolyn Pape Cowan, eds., *Fatherhood Today: Men's Changing Role in the Family* (New York: John Wiley, 1988); Stanley M. Cath, Alan Gurwitt, and Linda Gunsberg, eds., *Fathers and Their Families* (Hillsdale, NJ: Analytic Press, 1989); Robert L. Moore and Douglas Gillette, *King, Warrior, Magician, Lover: Rediscovering the Archetypes of the Mature Masculine* (San Francisco: Harper, 1990); Sam Keen, *Fire in the Belly: On Being a Man* (New York: Bantam Books, 1991).

indulgent father, the foolish father, and the absent father are images that too often appear both in fiction and reality.

Men Ready for Marriage

What is the preparation of a man to be a good husband and father? Fundamental to that preparation is the practice of chastity while he is still living a single life.[112] The idea that a man must "sow his wild oats" is a delusion, because its effect can only be to addict him to selfish sexual pleasure, to brutalize him, and to make him unfit for the sensitive, unselfish relationships of the family. Does not the woman who gives herself to a man who is romantically exciting because he has learned the arts of "good sex" and who thinks she can satisfy him, deserve his subsequent infidelity? Does not the man who binds himself to a woman because of her sexual attractions without regard to her character and practical good sense also deserve to lie in the uneasy bed he has made?

Single Men

Sexual Orientation

Most single men are preparing for marriage, and as I have argued, this realistically requires the practice of chaste celibacy. But there are many men, whether they have been married or not, who are not suited for marriage or who freely do not choose to marry. Of these the most discussed today are the perhaps two or three percent of males who ought not to marry because their sexual orientation is not sufficiently heterosexual to make marriage a workable option.

I do not say they are "homosexual" and especially I do not say

---

112. "Such a situation [the increasing prevalence of cohabitation without marriage] cannot usually be overcome unless the human person, from childhood, with the help of Christ's grace and without fear, has been trained to dominate concupiscence from the beginning and to establish relationships of genuine love with other people. This cannot be secured without a true education in genuine love and in the right use of sexuality, such as to introduce the human person in every aspect, and therefore the bodily aspect too, into the fullness of the mystery of Christ" (*Familaris Consortio*, no. 80).

they are "gay" because I believe these labels create a destructive stereotype.[113] Sexual orientation is not an all-or-none matter as if persons were created either "gay" and "lesbian" or "straight." While gender is naturally determined, probably sexual orientation is learned in the interaction of nature and culture. Even if it be established—and it has not yet been proven—that there is a significant genetic factor in homosexual orientation, it is still not probable that this is absolutely determinant. Certainly the "gay-life style" is a cultural artifact.

The Congregation for the Doctrine of the Faith has been angrily denounced for its "insensitivity" in calling homosexuality an "objective disorder," but it is not cruel to speak the truth, no matter how much it is denied or resented.[114] The real cruelty was the action of the American Psychiatric Association in removing homosexuality from its manual of psychopathologies, thus excluding homosexuals from the list of those wounded in life's battle who await healing care based on continuing research.[115]

113. See Alan P. Bell and Martin S. Weinberg, *Homosexualities: A Study of Diversity Among Men and Women* (New York: Simon and Schuster, 1978), one of the most extensive statistical studies on the subject. "Psychoanalytic research is most decidedly opposed to any attempt at separating off homosexuals from the rest of mankind as a group of special character. By studying sexual excitations other than those that are manifestly displayed, it has found that all human beings are capable of making a homosexual object-choice and have in fact made one in their unconscious" (Sigmund Freud, *Three Essays on the Theory of Sexuality*, trans. James Strachey [New York: Basic Books, 1962], 11).

114. Gareth Moore, O.P., "Are Homosexuals Sick?" *New Blackfriars* 70 (1989): 15–19, answers his own question negatively and makes the following claims: (1) to say homosexuals are "sick" is only "an effective way of excluding them from integration in the normal situation"; (2) "sick" is a term of abuse and doesn't apply because sickness is suffered involuntarily, while active homosexuality is voluntary; and (3) sickness is a "condition," but homosexuality is not a condition but a "difference" or "way of life." But see my article "Compassion and Sexual Orientation," in Jeannine Grammick and Pat Furey, eds., *The Vatican and Homosexuality: Reactions to the "Letter to the Bishops of the Catholic Church on the Pastoral Care of Homosexual Persons"* (New York: Crossroads, 1988), 105–111 (the Letter itself is translated on pp. 1–12). See also Bruce Williams, O.P., "Homosexuality: The New Vatican Statement," *Theological Studies* 48 (1987): 259–77. On the contrary, Derrick S. Bailey, *Homosexuality and the Western Christian Tradition* (Hamden, CT: Shoe String Press, 1975), and J. McNeill, *The Church and the Homosexual* (Kansas City: Sheed, Andres and McMeel, 1976), argue that the biblical texts against homosexuality do not apply today.

115. While the debate on this issue was going on among psychiatrists, the

In truth homosexuals are victims of a condition that is "objectively" (abstracting from all questions of moral responsibility) "disordered," i.e., not ordered to the purpose for which God created sexuality and to which it intrinsically tends, namely, the family community. An element in this disorder, as in many other human disorders, is the felt need to deny that it is a disorder. Yet the recognition of the truth is the first step to dealing with any disorder realistically.

The denial that homosexuality is a disorder has been reinforced by the way in which sex has been separated in our culture from family life. Yet, from the Christian point of view it is clear that without the human need for the family we would not have been created sexual at all. Isolated from the family, sex becomes a disintegrating force contributing to the decadence of the American community. This trend has been reinforced by some feminists' denial that the appropriate relation between the sexes is one of gender complementarity, which is lacking in same-sex relationships.[116]

In this debate there is once again the confusion between per-

---

International Journal of Psychiatry 10 (March 1972), 77–128, published a debate, "Homosexuality as a Mental Illness," which stated the opposing opinions very clearly. The critique from a scientific point of view of the arguments for regarding homosexuality as a "normal variation" by Arno Karlen (pp. 108–113) is in my opinion sound. On the great range of views among theologians see Edward Bachelor, Jr., ed. *Homosexuality and Ethics* (New York: Pilgrim Press, 1980). On the etiology and psychotherapy of this condition see Ruth Tiffany Barnhouse, *Homosexuality: A Symbolic Confusion* (New York: Seabury, 1977); Elizabeth R. Moberly, *Psychogenesis: The Early Development of Gender Identity* (London: Routledge and Kegan Paul, 1983), and "Counseling the Homosexual," *The Expository Times* June 1985, 261–66; see also Joseph Nicolosi, *Reparative Therapy of Male Homosexuality: A New Clinical Approach* (Northvale, NJ: Jason Aronson, 1991); and on pastoral care of homosexuals see National Conference of Catholic Bishops, "Principles to Guide Confessors in Questions of Homosexuality," (Washington, D.C.: National Conference of Catholic Bishops, 1973).

116. Thus Elisabeth Schüssler Fiorenza in "To Console or Challenge," argues that a feminism that bases itself on "woman's nature" rather than on women's "experience of oppression" by tending to emphasize "the unique gifts that feminine persons can offer to leadership and ministry in the church" only reinforces the notion of the "complementarity of the sexes" rather than their equality (pp. 47–48). A radical feminist, Sylvia Walby, *Theorizing Patriarchy* (Oxford: Basil Blackwell, 1990), even claims that "heterosexuality is an important patriarchal structure" (p. 127)! For a good presentation of the case for complementarity see Germain Grisez, et al., *Living a Christian Life*, 387–90.

sonal equality and functional inequality. Homosexual orientation does not diminish personal dignity, but pertains instead to the ability to function in a family. The functional disability to enter successfully into a complementary, heterosexual marriage is a disorder. Homosexual behavior reinforces this disorder. Hard as it may seem, the only moral option for homosexuals, just as for many heterosexuals who are physically or psychologically unable to marry, is chaste celibacy.[117]

Those lonely persons yearning for a sexual relationship but frustrated by a disordered sexual orientation for which they were not responsible certainly deserve deep sympathy. Their problem, however, is no greater than the problems of many other persons who are disabled in other ways, for example by a manic-depressive temperament, and yet courageously learn not only to live with their handicap but to make it the occasion of the development of character and of special service to others. Such persons do not indulge in self-pity, and neither should the homosexual. Heterosexuals need to be compassionate and supportive toward those suffering from this disablement, and should greatly honor those who struggle to live with their disability chastely and courageously.

Permanent Celibates

The single male who for whatever reason is not preparing for marriage can conform himself to the celibate Christ by that very fact. In the case of the man who chooses celibacy by a religious vow, this constitutes a way of life that witnesses to the eschatological character of all Christian living. Christians know that they must be in the world but not of it (cf. Jn 17:14–18; Rm 7:31–34), because this world is passing away and human destiny ultimately is in the world to come. Jesus in many parables kept exhorting his followers to keep vigil, to be prepared for death and

117. See John F. Harvey, O.S.F.S., *The Homosexual Person: New Thinking in Pastoral Care* (San Francisco: Ignatius Press, 1987); Elizabeth Moberly, *Homosexuality: A New Christian Ethic* (Greenwood, S.C.: Attic Press, 1987); and Benedict J. Groeschel, O.F.M. Cap., *The Courage to be Chaste* (Mahwah, NJ: Paulist Press, 1985).

judgment, and to look forward beyond suffering to the real life of the kingdom (e.g., Mk 13:32–37; Mt 24:45–51; 25:1–13; Lk 12:35–40, 42–48). That kingdom was already present in this world in Jesus himself, and is now beginning in his church. We pray, "Thy kingdom come . . . on earth as it is in heaven" (Mt 6:10). Yet it is a kingdom that will be consummated only with the passing of this order of things.

It is not easy to keep our goal in mind in the midst of the interests and events of this life. Consequently, in the church there is need of the witness of some who devote themselves singlemindedly to preparation for the kingdom and to remind others of their transcendent goal. Already there were such male ascetics in St. Paul's time. In the third century this vocation became institutionalized in the monastic movement, and it has continued to generate communities of men in vows, who as such are not priests but penitents keeping watch for the Lord's coming. Originally only a few of the monks became priests.[118] Today there are congregations of religious brothers, and in every religious order there are also members who do not seek ordination as priests. Religious celibacy and priestly celibacy, even when they concur in one person, have different motives: the former is undertaken primarily for the sake of witness, the latter for ministry.[119]

Spiritual Fatherhood

What of the single man who does not choose to marry or to become a religious? It may very well be that many men ought not to marry because they are not prepared to accept the responsibilities of fatherhood. It is an injustice that single men should be pressured to marry lest their sexual orientation be suspected or their morals questioned. Marriage, like religious consecration, ought to

118. See the article by Jean Gribomont, "Monachisme," *Dictionnaire de spiritualité*, tom. 10, cols. 1524–1617. From the beginning, however, clerics were admitted to monastic life, and many bishops were chosen from among the monks.

119. On the special character of clerical celibacy see Paul VI's encyclical, "On Priestly Celibacy" *(Sacerdotalis Coelibatus)*, June 24, 1967, no. 95 (in Flannery, ed., *Vatican II Postcounciliar Documents*, pp. 285–317).

be a free choice, and the individual's privacy in making it should be sensitively respected.

Yet the single man does have a responsibility to society to use his freedom from domestic cares to be of service to society just as married people make a contribution by forming a family. Such a bachelor life should not be the occasion of violations of chastity, nor of the pursuit of purely private and selfish pleasures and ambitions. We must all give an account to God if we have wasted the gifts given us for service to society (Mt 25:14–30; Lk 19:12–27). The single man thus realizes the gifts of his masculinity (this applies whatever the man's sexual orientation) by the services to others that such gifts make possible.[120]

For all men, the model of what it is to be a man is Jesus, not the violent and sexually rapacious heroes of fiction. While Jesus did not marry, he gave to married men as a model his own spiritual father St. Joseph, husband of Mary, the virgin mother of Jesus, for in Joseph we see the beauty of true fatherhood transcending every taint of selfishness.

120. See John Paul II, "On The Dignity and Vocation of Woman" *(Mulieris Dignitatem)*, August 15, 1988 *(Origins* 18 [Oct. 6, 1988]: 261–83), no. 21, on spiritual parenthood.

CHAPTER IV

Women and Worship

contemplative vs. active life

Mary and Priesthood

Contemplation and Ministry

In the last chapter I defended the position of recent popes who have supported the tradition excluding women from ordination to priesthood. The obvious question this stance raises, however, is: If only men are qualified for the office of such dignity as the priesthood, is there any office of equal dignity for which only women are qualified? It would seem there is not, since what office is higher in the church than priest, bishop or highest of all, the Bishop of Rome?

In order to approach this problem I first turn to a debate, classical in the Catholic tradition, the controversy over whether the contemplative or the active life is superior. Plato attempted to show that both might coincide in the same person, since his "philosopher-king" was a king (i.e., a practical man of prudence) precisely because he was a philosopher (i.e., a man of theory, a contemplative).[1] Alas, Plato demonstrated in his own life the dif-

---

1. "The next question is this. If philosophers have the ability to grasp eternal and immutable truth, and those who are not philosophers are lost in multiplicity and change, which of the two should be in charge of the state?" (*Republic* 6.484b2). Then after a description of the qualities necessary for a philosopher, Socrates says, "Can you, then possibly find fault with an occupation for the proper pursuit of which a man must combine in nature good memory, readiness to learn, breadth of vision and versatility of mind, and be a friend of truth, justice, courage, and discipline? . . . Grant, then, education and maturity to round them off, and aren't they the only people to whom you would entrust your state?" (487a2). The translation is that of H. D. P. Lee in the Penguin Classics edition.

ficulty of this combination, since his own attempts to be the counselor of rulers failed.[2]

Aristotle, who also failed to influence politically his pupil Alexander the Great, more realistically argued that although the contemplative and the active cannot be conveniently joined, the active life in which the moral virtues are acquired by exercise is the necessary preparation for the contemplative.[3] Augustine and other Church Fathers found the answer to this question in Jesus' words to Martha, type of the active life, concerning Mary, type of the contemplative life. Jesus said to Martha, who complained that Mary sat listening at his feet, while she, Martha, prepared the meal for him, "You, Martha, are busy about many things, but only one thing is necessary. Do not trouble Mary, she has chosen the better part" (Lk 10:38–42).[4] Thus for the Christian it seemed obvious that the contemplative life directed toward eschatological heavenly matters is superior to the active life directed toward this world. This tradition continues in the church, and certain recent magisterial documents at least implicitly affirm the superiority of the contemplative life over the active.[5]

St. Thomas Aquinas, a friar and a member of the Order of Preachers, had to defend the friars both against the monks who exalted their contemplative life and against the diocesan clergy who exalted their active ministry. Hence, he expressed the relation

2. See Ronald B. Levinson, *In Defense of Plato* (Cambridge, MA: Harvard University Press, 1953), which treats at length of Plato's political experiences and theories.

3. *Nicomachean Ethics* 6.12–13; 10.6–8.

4. Modern exegesis of this text notes that Jewish women were not permitted to study the Torah as men were required to do, but in this pericope women receive Jesus into their home (the house-church) and are free to listen to the Gospel. See Ben Witherington, *Women in the Ministry of Jesus*, 100–3.

5. See Vatican II, "Decree on the Appropriate Renewal of the Religious Life" *(Perfectae Caritatis)*, no. 7, which speaks of contemplatives as "the glory of the Church and an overflowing fountain of heavenly graces," and the Congregation for Religious and Secular Institutes, "*Instructio de vita contemplativa et de monialium clausura,*" Nov. 10, 1969, *Acta Apostolicae Sedis* 61 (1969): 674–90, and "The Contemplative Dimension of Religious Life," Feb. 12, 1981, *Origins* 10: 550–60; and the Post-Synodal Apostolic Exhortation following the Synod of Bishops, Rome 1995, "The Consecrated Life" *(Vita Consecrata)*, Washington, DC: United States Catholic Conference, nos. 7–8, 32, 34, 59.

between contemplation and action in a nuanced way.[6] Contemplation, he argued, is certainly superior to action, but the mixed life of contemplation and action is best of all, since "light that illumines is better than light which merely shines." This answer, which seemed to be that of Plato, he then reconciled with the objections of Aristotle by showing that while contemplation is difficult to reconcile with many kinds of action, this is not the case when the action is that of teaching or preaching, since the task of this kind of active ministry is "to contemplate and then to communicate what one has contemplated to others *(contemplare et contemplata aliis tradere)*."[7] Nevertheless, Plato, Aristotle, Augustine, and Aquinas all agree that contemplation *per se* is superior to action; or, to put it another way, it is the consummate form of activity and hence a completion and rest.[8]

In view of this teaching if one asks whether priesthood, and particularly the papacy, is the highest office in the church, it becomes apparent that the answer is not so obvious. Pope Gregory the Great complained in a famous passage that as pope he no longer had the leisure for contemplation he had enjoyed as a monk.[9] Ecclesial ministry as such pertains to the active not the

6. *ST* II–II, q. 182; q. 187, a. 1; q. 188.
7. *ST* II–II, q. 188, a. 6 c.
8. See Josef Pieper, *Happiness and Contemplation,* trans. Richard and Clara Winston (New York: Pantheon, 1958), and *Leisure, the Basis of Culture,* trans. Alexander Dru (New York: New American Library, 1963), for excellent discussions of this point in the thought of Aquinas.
9. "When I was in the monastery I could curb my idle talk and usually be absorbed in my prayers. Since I assumed the burden of pastoral care, my mind can no longer be collected; it is concerned with so many matters. . . . With my mind divided and torn to pieces by so many problems, how can I meditate or preach wholeheartedly without neglecting the ministry of proclaiming the gospel? . . . And because I too am weak, I find myself drawn little by little into idle conversation, and I begin to talk freely about matters which once I would have avoided. What once I found tedious I now enjoy" (St. Gregory the Great, *Homilies on Ezekiel* [Lib. 1, 11: CCL 142, 170–72] from *The Liturgy of the Hours According to the Roman Rite* [New York: Catholic Book Publishing Co., 1975], 4:1366). St. Thérèse of Lisieux wrote that she at one time desired to be a priest so as to be a missionary and a martyr, but at last she understood: "When I looked upon the mystical body of the Church, I recognized myself in none of the members which Saint Paul described [1 Cor 12], and what is more, I desired to distinguish myself more favorably within the whole body. . . . Indeed, I knew that the Church had a

contemplative life.[10] On the other hand, it could be argued that the priest lives a mixed life, since this ministry must be based on prayer, and its chief acts are preaching and leading the people in offering the sacrifice of the Mass. Worship is a contemplative act. Nevertheless, priesthood, episcopacy, and papacy also necessarily include the office of shepherding, which clearly pertains to the active life and it was of this that Gregory was complaining.

Does this mean, therefore, that those who lead the contemplative life rank higher in the church than pope, bishop, and priest? Since the ministry of the hierarchy has as its end the sanctification of the people and their eternal salvation, and since the Christian contemplative life is an eschatological or proleptic anticipation of heaven, I believe that we can answer in the affirmative,[11] granting of course that contemplatives as obedient members of the church remain subject to the pope and bishops as regards doctrine and discipline.

The goal of the church is holiness, and in heaven persons will rank according to their love of God, not according to earthly office, even ecclesial office.[12] Ecclesial office does not automatically confer

---

body composed of various members, but in this body the necessary and more noble member was not lacking; I knew that the Church had a heart and that such a heart appeared to be aflame with love. . . . Then nearly ecstatic with the supreme joy in my soul, I proclaimed: O Jesus, my love, at last I have found my proper calling: my call is love. . . . In the heart of the Church, my mother, I will be love" (*Manuscripts autobiographique* [Lisieux: 1957], 227–29; translated in *Liturgy of the Hours*, 4:1451).

10. *ST* q. 188, a.4.

11. Vatican II declared that religious life "not only witnesses to the fact of a new and eternal life acquired by the redemption of Christ. It foretells the resurrected state and the glory of the heavenly kingdom" (*Lumen Gentium*, no. 44) and this is eminently true of contemplatives. What is also said in *Lumen Gentium*, nos. 61–65 concerning the supreme position of the Blessed Virgin Mary in the church also applies in a remarkable way to contemplatives who by prayer share in the mediation of Christ and the spiritual motherhood of Mary. On the ancient Christian view that the life of virginity was a "realized eschatology" see Ton H.C. Van Eijk, "Marriage and Virginity: Death and Immortality," in *Epektasis: Mélanges offerts au Cardinal Jean Danielou*, ed. Jacques Fontaine and Charles Kannengiesser, (Paris: Beauchesne, 1972), pp. 209–35.

12. Aquinas, *ST* Suppl. q. 96, a.1 argues that rank in heaven is essentially according to the degree of charity, but that to it can be added an additional reward (*aureola*) for the performance of particular tasks. The second kind of reward, however, is not comparable to the first.

sanctity, although, according to Aquinas,[13] the episcopal state is one of perfection, i.e., it demands the bishop's total commitment to his flock. Yet one who is bishop is bishop even when he is not holy; his priestly acts sanctify others but they do not always sanctify himself. The life vowed to contemplation, however, is also a state of perfection, and although those vowed to it also may fail to be holy, they cannot truly contemplate without being themselves sanctified by contemplation which consists essentially in acts of the theological virtues of faith, hope, and love.[14]

Mary as Contemplative

My thesis is confirmed when we consider the religious significance of the Mother of Jesus who is above all the type of the contemplative life in the church.[15] It is true that Mary exercised an active ministry in bearing the Son of God and raising him to manhood. As she did so, however, she "pondered all these things in her heart" (Lk 2:19; cf. 2:51), that is, she constantly meditated on the mysteries which were the events of Jesus' life, events which were indeed mysteries to her since neither she nor Joseph fully understood them (Lk 2:50).[16]

13. *ST* II–II, q. 184, aa. 6–8 says that as religious are committed totally to God by their three vows to observe the counsels, so bishops are committed by their office totally to the service of the church and hence are also *in statu perfectionis,* but the lower clergy are only committed by their ordination to specific obligations. But Vatican II, *Presbyterorum Ordinis,* no. 12 teaches that while all the baptized are bound to seek perfection, the ordained have a very special obligation to do so.

14. See Antonio Royo, O.P., and Jordan Aumann, O.P., *The Theology of Christian Perfection* (Dubuque, IA: Priory Press, 1962), 531.

15. "Mary was involved in the mysteries of Christ. As the most holy Mother of God she was, after her Son, exalted by divine grace above all angels and men" (*Lumen Gentium,* no. 66). "The Council emphasizes that the Mother of God is already the eschatological fulfillment of the Church" (John Paul II, Encyclical Letter, "The Mother of the Redeemer" *[Redemptoris Mater],* March 25, 1987 [Washington, DC: U.S. Catholic Conference, 1987], no. 6, p. 12).

16. John Paul II, *Redemptoris Mater,* no. 17, pp. 35–36, remarks on this text, "Jesus was aware that 'no one knows the Son except the Father' (cf. Mt. 11:27); thus even his Mother, to whom had been revealed most completely the mystery of his divine sonship, lived in intimacy with the mystery only through faith! Living side by side with her Son under the same roof, and faithfully persevering in her union with her Son, she *advanced in her pilgrimage of faith,* as the Council emphasizes [*Lumen Gentium,* no. 58]. And so it was during Christ's public life too

After Jesus began his active ministry, we no longer find his mother playing an active role in that ministry. Nothing is left to her but to contemplate his words and deeds, to stand at the foot of the Cross, and pray with the Twelve for the coming of the Holy Spirit.[17] As a widow, deprived of her only son, Mary's life became one of contemplation and prayer. It was like the life of that other woman whom Mary met in the temple when she offered her infant son to God—the widow Anna of whom Luke says, "She never left the temple, but worshiped night and day with fasting and prayer" (Lk 3:37).

Some devotees in the past wanted to give Mary the title of priestess and had her portrayed in priestly robes, but the magisterium rejected this pious error.[18] Mary is not a priest, nor a bishop, or a pope, nor even an apostle, but something greater than these. She is Mother of God, the New Eve, Mother of priests and of the whole

---

(Cf. Mk 3:21–35) that day by day there was fulfilled in her the blessing uttered by Elizabeth at the Visitation: Blessed is she who believed."

17. "But since it pleased God not to manifest solemnly the mystery of the salvation of the human race until He poured forth the Spirit promised by Christ, we see the apostles before the day of Pentecost 'continuing with one mind in prayer with the women and Mary, the Mother of Jesus, and with his brethren' (Acts 1:14). We see Mary prayerfully imploring the gift of the Spirit, who had already overshadowed her in the Annunciation" (*Lumen Gentium*, no. 59). On this see *Redemptoris Mater*, no. 26, pp. 55–59.

18. Decree of the Holy Office, March 29 (Apr. 8), 1916, DS 3632. See also *Redemptoris Mater*, no. 26, p. 57: "The mission of the Apostles began the moment they left the Upper Room in Jerusalem. The Church is born and then grows through the testimony that Peter and Apostles bear to the Crucified and Risen Christ. . . . Mary did not directly receive this apostolic mission. She was not among those whom Jesus sent 'to the whole world to teach all nations' (cf. Mt 28:19). But she was in the Upper Room, where the Apostles were preparing to take up this mission with the coming of the Spirit of Truth: she was present with them. In their midst Mary was 'devoted to prayer' as the 'mother of Jesus' (cf. Acts 1:13–14), of the Crucified and Risen Christ." Leonard Swidler, "Goddess Worship and Women Priests," in *Women Priests: A Catholic Commentary*, 167–82, refutes *Inter Insigniores*'s claim that Jesus, although aware of pagan priestesses, did not choose women as priests, by saying that Jesus was bound by the Jewish opposition to women priests because they served the mother goddesses, although this exclusion did not express his own attitude to women, which now should be our norm. Swidler seems unimpressed by the claim of the magisterial documents that Jesus was able to free himself from Jewish attitudes of which he disapproved.

church.[19] Her Assumption not only placed her in heaven, but joined her with her Son in anticipation of the final resurrection of all humanity, so that in her the work of salvation is already complete.[20] This is symbolized in her rosary by the mystery of her coronation as Queen, or as the church, Bride of the Lamb (Rv 21:2, 9) with the King, her Son.[21]

Thus, Mary, virgin, mother, and contemplative in the plan of God is not a passive, submissive cipher, as sentimental piety has often portrayed her, but a figure of cosmic power to whom the liturgy applies the words of the psalmist, "Who is this that comes forth like the dawn, as beautiful as the moon, as resplendent of the sun, as awe-inspiring as bannered troops" (Sg 6:10)[22] and of Revelation (12:1), "A great sign appeared in the sky, a woman clothed with the sun, with the moon under her feet, and on her head a crown of twelve stars."[23]

Virgin and Prophet

Consecrated Virgins

From the beginning of the church other women have followed Mary by vowing themselves to virginity and to a contemplative life of prayer in the church, as we read in 1 Corinthians and as is

19. These titles and others are explained in *Redemptoris Mater*, with reference to the teaching of Vatican II, *Lumen Gentium*.

20. "In the bodily and spiritual glory which she possesses in heaven, the Mother of Jesus continues in this present world as the image and first flowering of the Church as she is to be perfected in the world to come. Likewise, Mary shines forth on earth, until the day of the Lord shall come (cf. 1 Pt 3:10), as a sign of sure hope and solace for the pilgrim people of God" (*Lumen Gentium*, no. 68; cf. *Redemptoris Mater*, no. 41, pp. 87–91).

21. See *Redemptoris Mater*, no. 43, pp. 93–95.

22. Luis Stadelmann, *Love and Politics: A New Commentary on the Song of Songs* (New York: Paulist, 1992), 164, translates "bannered troops" as "constellations" of the stars (thus parallel to Rv 12:1), and in accordance with his interpretation of the Song as a political allegory, thinks that the bride is a symbol of "the triumphant Jewish nation."

23. For a contemporary appreciation by feminist writers see Carol Frances Jegen, B.V.M., ed., *Mary according to Women* (Kansas City, MO., Leaven Press, 1985).

amply illustrated in the writings of the Church Fathers.[24] Theological students today when they read these early writings are often puzzled to see the magnificent praise of the early church, still enshrined in the liturgy, for virgins and especially for the virgin martyrs. "Why all this fuss about virginity?" one student asked me recently. To our culture virginity seems like something merely negative, a lack of a maturing human experience, to be promptly shed not cherished.[25]

Feminists are quick to explain the ancient church's cult of virginity as a product of male possessiveness, which led husbands to demand virginity in the women they were to wed, although they contemned it for themselves.[26] But this falls short of explaining even pagan Greek and Roman admiration for female virginity in their goddesses Athena and Artemis or in their vestal priestesses. For Christians, virginity, both female and male, was first of all an imitation of Jesus and of Mary who were virgins, which had been foreshadowed in the biblical symbolism of the Old Testament in

24. On the history of the "ecclesial orders for women" see Sister Mary Lawrence McKenna, S.C.M.M., *Women of the Church: Role and Renewal* (New York: P. J. Kenedy & Sons, 1967), especially chap. 5, "The Order of Virgins," pp. 95–110; Janine Hourcade, La Femme dans L'Église, 247–322; and Karl Suso Frank, "Le consécration des vierges," section in "Vie consacrée," in *Dictionnaire de spiritualité*, fasc. 104, cols. 655–61. On the patristic notion of virginity and marriage see T. H. C. Van Eijk, "Marriage and Virginity, Death and Immortality" (cited in note 11, above). On the meaning of the cloister, see Emmanuele Boazo, O. Carm., "La Clasura: Origine e sviluppo storico-giuridico-spirituale," *Vita Consecrata* 29 (July–Aug. 1993): 492–512.

25. This is why William E. Phipps, *Was Jesus Married?* (New York: Harper and Row, 1970) could use as his principal argument for the affirmative that since Jesus was the Perfect Man he must have married. Two of the best contemporary defenses of virginity and celibacy are Ida Frederike Görres, *Is Celibacy Outdated?* trans. Barbara Waldstein-Wartenberg in collaboration with the author (Westminister, MD: Newman Press, 1965); and Paul M. Quay, S.J., *The Christian Meaning of Human Sexuality* (Evanston, IL: A Credo House Book, 1985), 85–109.

26. Marilyn French, *Beyond Power,* however, sees something positive in Christian celibacy, although she thinks it was rooted in St. Paul's "hatred of sex" (p. 153): "A celibate life freed women not only from the burden of domesticity and childbearing but from subjection to men. To many of us renunciation of sex seems a sacrifice, but it is questionable whether it seemed so to women of the time, married not by their own choice, while they were still children, to much older men who were strangers and expected to be fertile, hard-working and obedient. Under such circumstances marital sex is a form of rape" (p. 154).

the ritual purity required of the priest and the virginity required of his bride (Lv 21:14–15). The bride of the Song of Songs (4:12) is praised, "You are an enclosed garden, my sister, my bride, an enclosed garden, a fountain sealed," as a pledge of fidelity in marriage.²⁷ Vowed virgins in the church, therefore, were Christians who had consecrated their entire life, including all the energy and intimacy of love of which they were capable, to Christ with whom they hoped to live for all eternity on the Great Wedding Day. What was celebrated, therefore, was not a negative lack of earthly sexual experience, but the positive love of exclusive engagement to Christ.²⁸

To be virgin was not merely never to have engaged in intercourse (as the word is often used today), but not to have deliberately consented to any genital satisfaction of any sort even in a purely mental manner. The consecrated Christian virgin had thus entirely re-

27. This meaning is not to be confused with that of such expressions when they are used to personify a city or country as a young woman, as the Greeks personified the city of Athens as the virgin war goddess, Athena: "She laughs you to scorn, the Virgin Daughter Zion" (2 Kgs 19:21; Is 37:22); "Horrible things has Virgin Israel done" (Jer 18:13); "You shall be rebuilt, O Virgin Israel" (Jr 31:4); "Turn back, O Virgin Israel" (Jr 31:21). As John L. McKenzie, S.J., *Dictionary of the Bible* (Milwaukee, WI: Bruce, 1966) notes, very often "the figure represents her helplessness. It is usually employed in contexts of threat, which liken the city or country to a girl who was defenseless against the lust of conquering soldiers" (p. 914): "Virgin Daughter Zion" (Lam 2:13); "Virgin Daughter Judah" (Lam 1:15); "Virgin Daughter Sidon" (Is 23:12); "Virgin Daughter Babylon" (Is 47:1); "Virgin Daughter Egypt" (Jr 46:11); "Daughter of my people" (Jr 14:17). But these personifications are consonant with the symbol of Israel as the betrothed bride of Yahweh (e.g. Hos 2; Is 54:4–5, 62:4; Jer 2:2, 3:20; Ez 16 and 23). Is it possible that the much-controverted *almah* of Is 7:14 (Mt 1:23) was originally not thought of as a particular individual but as a personification of Israel as "mother" of the future Messiah (cf. also Jer 31:22), and hence not identified by name?

28. See Pierre Adnès, "Mariage spirituel," *Dictionnaire de spiritualité*, tom. 10, cols. 387–408, for the history of this concept. One often reads today that celibacy and marriage are regarded as equal vocations by the church, but this is not the case. "This doctrine of the excellence of virginity and of celibacy and of their superiority over the married state was, as We have already said, revealed by our Divine Redeemer and by the Apostle of the Gentiles; so too, it was solemnly defined as a dogma of divine faith by the holy council of Trent, and explained in the same way by all the holy Fathers and Doctors of the Church. Finally, We and our Predecessors have often expounded it and earnestly advocated it whenever occasion offered" (Pius XII, Encyclical Letter, *Sacra virginitas*, March 15, 1954, no. 32, in *The Papal Encyclicals, 1939–1958,* ed. Claudia Carlen [New York: McGrath Publishing Co., 1981], 244).

nounced sexual satisfaction in view of her union with Christ. In the case of women who were no longer physically virgin, widows for example, but lived the contemplative life in a community of virgins, the sign of which I am speaking was still given by the community as a whole, since the *virtue* of virginity can be recovered by repentance of sin or by a new commitment.[29] In the patristic church both men and women might vow their virginity to God. Nevertheless, in that culture, and in fact (considering the prevalence of masturbation among males) the male virgin was considered rare indeed. Females, however, seem somewhat less given to self-abuse, and their physical virginity can be certified by an intact hymen.[30] Yet there was a much more important reason why the vowed female virgin is celebrated in the church. The male ascetic, although he is vowed to perfect chastity and may even, like St. Dominic, remain truly a virgin all his life,[31] cannot supply the symbolic role in the church that the vowed female virgin fulfills. Just as a woman cannot appropriately symbolize Christ, the New Adam, Father of all the redeemed, Bridegroom of the church, as priest, the male virgin cannot appropriately symbolize Mary, the New Eve, Mother of God and of the church, or the church as Bride.

Virginity and Priesthood

Thus while women are excluded from the sacrament of priesthood, men are excluded from consecrated virginity in its full symbolic, i.e., "sacramental" meaning. Why then is the consecration of virgins not, in the proper sense of the term, a sacrament as is

---

29. See *ST* II–II, q. 152; q. 186, aa. 4, 7, 8; Suppl., q. 96, aa. 5, 11–13.

30. See Quay, *The Christian Meaning of Human Sexuality,* 86–91.

31. "Meanwhile at Bologna, Master Dominic began to be seriously ill. . . . He summoned twelve of the more sensible brethren to his sickbed and exhorted them to be fervent and to foster the religious life of the Order and to persevere in the way of holiness, and he advised them to avoid keeping dubious company with women, particularly young women. . . . 'Look at me,' he said, 'God's mercy has preserved me to this day in bodily virginity, but I confess that I have not escaped from the imperfection of being more excited by the conversation of young women than by being talked at by old women'" (Bl. Jordan of Saxony, *Libellus* or *The Origins of the Order of Friars Preachers,* in *Early Dominicans: Selected Writings,* trans. Simon Tugwell, Classics of Western Spirituality [New York: Paulist Press, 1982], 92).

the ordination of men, or the marriage of men and women? The sacraments confer graces to sustain Christians in the struggles of earthly life and to point to the peace of life eternal: the sacrament of matrimony assists the family in its many earthly troubles; the sacrament of holy orders assists deacons, priests, and bishops in their earthly ministry to others. But the consecration to celibacy and especially to virginity, and the contemplative life, in spite of the trials undergone, pertains not so much to earthly life as to the *anticipation* of eternal life. Such a life is not a sacrament but the reality signified by the sacraments.

Therefore, if we ask which of these two roles, priesthood or consecrated virginity, is of greater dignity, we will need to answer with a distinction. If we consider that the priest represents Christ, Head of the church, while the consecrated virgin represents Mary, the church itself, priesthood is superior to consecrated virginity. But if we consider that Mary in her eschatological, contemplative role is superior to the priest in his earthly active ministerial role, and that the consecrated virgin is an eschatological sign of heaven who already stands with the angels at Mary's side, then the consecrated virgin is superior to the priest. At this highest level of comparison, indeed, it is best to say that while Christ as God is infinitely superior to his human Mother, the whole mystery of which we are speaking is precisely that God through Christ has raised Mary and all of us to a genuine *equality* with Him, just as in marriage the headship of the man in no way overrides the mutuality conferred by love but is in its service. One has only to read the Song of Songs to see how true lovers both submit to each another and rule over each other, so that two become one flesh, as Christ and his church become one in the Spirit.[32]

32. Critical opinion is now more and more open to the value of the rabbinical and patristic interpretation of the Song of Songs as an allegory of the covenant of love between God and his people. (See Roland E. Murphy, O. Carm, in *New Jerome Biblical Commentary,* 462–63.) R. J. Tournay, O.P., *Quand Dieu parle aux hommes le langage de l'amour,* Cahiers de la *Révue Biblique* 21 (Paris: Gabalda, 1982), has argued that "Solomon" is the Messianic King for whom Israel longs. Luis Stadelmann, *Love and Politics* tries to show that "the content of the message is the restoration of the Davidic monarchy after the exile" (p. 2), which, of course, had messianic significance.

Thus in the history of the church the dignity of the priest and the dignity of the consecrated virgin are not compared as if one ranked above the other, but as if they complemented one another. The priest stands for the work of Christ sanctifying this world; the nun stands for the already sanctified, glorified church which is Christ's eternal Bride.

Women and Prophecy

The obvious objection to this thesis is that it seems to be just another example of "patriarchy" isolating women in the cloister in a powerless position so that they cannot participate in the decisions of the church. Is it not also inconsistent with the thesis of my second chapter, which declared that it should always be a prime objective of church government and reform to activate all its members to participate as fully as possible in the life of the church, including its decision making? Who is more marginalized in the life of the church than the cloistered nun?

To answer this objection, I first recall that in Chapter II, I also argued that participation in the life of society and of the church is not always nor only achieved by so-called democratic, indiscriminately egalitarian forms of government and social relationship. What is necessary for full participation in social decisions is not that everyone should vote or be endowed with the power of final judgment, but that all be *consulted*, i.e., that according to the principle of subsidiarity the experience and gifts of all be really taken into account in the decisional process. For this reason I fully endorse the proposals of moderate feminists that women play at least a consultative role in ecclesial decisions, especially in matters that directly affect them. Thus even in ecumenical councils where ultimately only the bishops have the apostolic authority to "bind and to loose" by definitive judgment, the voices of women should be heard.[33]

33. Under present canon law only bishops who are members of the College of Bishops (i.e., in union with the Pope) have "the right and duty to take part in an ecumenical council with a deliberative vote" (Canon 339, no. 1), but "the supreme authority of the Church can call others (*alii, aliqui*) who are not bishops to an

Obviously this likewise applies at lower levels, as well as in the papal curia, in the pastoral councils of bishops, and the parish councils of pastors. If it is still argued that when the right to vote is denied such consultation will be ineffectual, I can only reply that the special constitution of the church proper to its origin and mission requires this limitation, just as for example the peculiar Constitution of the United States has vested the Supreme Court with definitive powers, which are not subject to democratic control except in an indirect way. It must be remembered that the truly important decisions of the church are not really "decisions" expressing personal will, but are declarations of the revelation entrusted to the church which none of its officials has any power to change.

But there is another point to be taken into consideration in reply to this difficulty about the empowerment of women. The Scriptures make clear that the gift of *prophecy* is not confined to the priesthood, but is sometimes given to women.[34] This charism is

---

ecumenical council and determine the degree of their participation" (Canon 339, no. 2). Note that "some others" may include women and the degree of their participation, short of a definitive vote, can be maximized. Quotations are from the Latin-English edition of *The Code of Canon Law* (Washington, DC: Canon Law Society of America, 1983).

34. Miriam (Ex 15:20), Deborah (Jgs 4:4), Huldah (2 Kgs 14–20; 2 Chr 34:22), Anna (Lk 2:36), and Philip's "four virgin daughters" (Acts 21:8) are called "prophetesses." Noadiah (Neh 6:14) and Jezabel (Rv 2:20) are false prophetesses. Joel 3:1 (quoted in Acts 2:17) promises "Your sons and *daughters* will prophesy." The apparent contradiction between St. Paul's prohibition of speaking in the Christian assembly by women (1 Cor 14:34–35 [in the Western Text these verses follow v. 40]; cf. 1 Tm 2:11–15) and his apparent presumption that they are permitted to pray and prophesy if they are veiled (1 Cor 11:5) is discussed at length in Hauke, *Women in the Priesthood?* 363–403, who concludes that what is forbidden to women is not prophesying even in the public assembly, but authoritative instruction proper to priests. He also contends that in 1 Cor 14:33–40 St. Paul grounds this rule on: (1) church practice: "As in all the churches of the holy ones, women should keep silent"; (2) the general moral code: "for they are not allowed to speak. . . . But if they want to learn anything they should ask their husbands at home. For it is improper for a woman to speak in church"; (3) what the law "says" about the subordination of women; and (4) a "command of the Lord": "Did the word of God go forth from you? Or has it come to you alone? If anyone thinks that he is a prophet or a spiritual person, he should recognize that what I am writing to you is a commandment of the Lord," which binds under the penalty of excommunication, for "If anyone does not acknowledge this, he is not acknowledged." Hauke attributes the Western Text variation in these verses to Marcion. For a survey of the various views on the text concerning the prophetesses' "veil" see Antoinette

not identical with the function of prophesy with which bishops and priests are endowed by ordination and right of office, which has the binding authority of the apostolic tradition.[35] Rather it is a special gift, usually, but not necessarily, given to persons advanced in holiness, the purpose of which is to build up the church not by some new public or even private revelation, but by arousing the Spirit of conversion, reform, or zeal in the church.

Closely related to the prophetic gift, is that of teaching, *(didache)* especially of religious truth, considered not as authoritative pastoral judgment ("binding and loosing") of doctrine, but as nurturing faith.[36] Mothers have always played this role, and with proper study it becomes the work of the theologian and the spiritual teacher and writer, the preacher of conferences and retreats, and the spiritual director.[37] Women have often excelled in such

---

Clark Wire, "Women's Head Covering," appendix 8 in *The Corinthian Women Prophets: A Reconstruction through Paul's Rhetoric* (Philadelphia, Fortress Press, 1990), 220–223, and her extensive bibliography.

35. "Among the principal duties of bishops, preaching the gospel occupies an eminent place. For bishops are preachers of the faith who lead new disciples to Christ. They are authentic teachers, that is, teachers endowed with the authority of Christ, who preach to the people committed to them the faith they must believe and put into practice. By the light of the Holy Spirit, they make that faith clear, bringing forth from the treasure of revelation new things and old (Cf. Mt. 13:52), making faith bear fruit and vigilantly warding off any errors which threaten their flock (cf. 2 Tm 4:1–4). Bishops, teaching in communion with the Roman Pontiff, are to be respected by all as witnesses to divine and Catholic truth. In matters of faith and morals, the bishops speak in the name Christ and the faithful are to accept their teaching and adhere to it with a religious assent of soul" *(Lumen Gentium,* no. 25).

36. Perhaps this should be connected especially with the charism of "exhortation" *(paraklēsis)* mentioned by St. Paul in Rom 12:8 as distinct from that of "teaching" since the emphasis is on motivation, encouragement. "The 'woman' as mother and first teacher of the human being (education being the spiritual dimension of parenthood), has a special precedence over the man. . . . Motherhood in its personal-ethical sense expresses a very important creativity on the part of the woman, upon whom the very humanity of the new human being mainly depends. In this sense too the woman's motherhood presents a special call and a special challenge to the man and to his fatherhood" (John Paul II, *Mulieris Dignitatem,* no. 19.

37. The liturgical homily is properly the task of the priestly president of the Eucharist or of another priest or deacon as his substitute because of the intimate connection between the symbolism of his preaching and offering *in persona Christi;* cf. Vatican II, *Sacrosanctum Concilium,* nos. 52 and 57 and Canons 766–67.

roles in the church and the opportunities for them to rise to the highest levels in such work are now open.

Two outstanding examples of women endowed with this gift of prophecy for nurturing faith are St. Catherine of Siena and St. Teresa of Avila who exhorted their religious orders to reform and the whole church to a more profound practice of prayer. These two prophetesses were declared Doctors of the Church by Paul VI.[38] St. Thérèse of Lisieux is now being proposed for the same honor. In every century of church history, however, there have been many women who played this role, some locally, some universally in the church. They often counseled, as Hildegard of Bingen, Catherine of Siena, and Bridget of Sweden did so wisely, the highest authorities in the church. Nor did they hesitate to admonish popes for their negligence, cowardice, or imprudence and excoriate priests for their corrupt lives.[39]

There are of course many examples of men also endowed with prophetic gifts, such as the reformer Savonarola or the defender of human rights Bartolomé de las Casas. Yet church history shows that this has been a mode of ministry especially favored by women, not merely because other modes were off-bounds for them, but because it is a ministry so closely associated with the contemplative life for which they have special aptitude.[40] Today the education of women makes it possible for them to engage in this contemplation in a more systematic manner by becoming theologians. Hence they need no longer depend, as did prophetesses in the past, on priest theologians to assist them in giving scholarly formulation to their insights, rather than confine their writing to poetry, autobiography, or correspondence.

Spiritual theologians have frequently pointed out that the con-

38. St. Teresa of Jesus Church, Sept. 27, 1970 (AAS 62 [1970]: 590–96), and St. Catherine of Siena, Oct. 4, 1970 (AAS 62 [1970]: 673–78), were declared Doctors of the Universal Church.

39. St. Catherine of Siena, *The Dialogue,* trans. Suzanne Noffke, O.P., Classics of Western Spirituality (New York: Paulist Press, 1980), chaps. 113–33.

40. In fifteenth-century Italy many towns were protected and guided by prophetesses. For Dominican examples of women following St. Catherine of Siena see my *The Dominicans* (Collegeville, MN: The Liturgical Press, 1990), 102–3.

templative life is in some ways more accessible to women than to men, because men are hampered in it by their tendencies to aggressive drive for power, their excessively "logical" (rationalistic) thinking, and their insensitivity in intimate relationships. Women, on the other hand, gifted with the nurturing, relational skills necessary for motherhood,[41] often do not find it so difficult to do as Mary did, pondering the divine mysteries in their hearts, opening themselves up to the Holy Spirit. Consequently, women who enter on the path of contemplation also open themselves to prophecy. Feminists themselves often attribute these gifts to women, unfortunately too often in the perverse mode of witchcraft ("wicca").

Those who prophesy in the church are not restricted by the requirements of office as are clerics, but can speak with a freedom that priests do not have. It is strange therefore that today some women seem determined to restrict their own freedom by assuming clerical positions in the church where their inspiration will no longer have so free a play.

Of course it is true that every prophet in the church must submit to the judgment of the magisterium on his or her activities, and there are cases such as that of St. Joan of Arc, an authentic prophetess who was suppressed and burned by male ecclesiastical authority. But as St. Stephen said (Acts 7:52), "What prophet did your ancestors not persecute?" Such is likely to be the fate of prophets, whether female like Joan or male like Savonarola.

Thus the objection that to assign to women the role of virgin contemplatives or simply of vowed contemplative is to exclude them from participation in church decision can be answered not only by admitting that reforms giving women more right of consultation are necessary, but also by teaching that what is open to women in a special way is to participate in such decisions by prophecy, which has often corrected the behavior of the male

41. For example, Carol Gilligan, *In a Different Voice: Psychological Theory and Women's Development* (Cambridge: Harvard University, 1982); Mary Field Belensky, et al., *Women's Ways of Knowing: The Development of Self, Voice, and Mind* (New York: Basic Books, 1986). For criticism of such views see Cynthia Fuchs Epstein, *Deceptive Distinctions,* 215–31.

clergy in a most powerful and effective manner. Justice requires that all should participate in the decisions of the church but not that all should do so in the same way.

Active Religious

Another obvious objection to my thesis about the unique role of women as consecrated virgins will be raised by the active sisterhoods in the church whose members also take vows of celibacy. Up to the nineteenth century most vowed women were cloistered nuns living the contemplative life.[42] With the nineteenth century a vast expansion took place of sisterhoods engaged in active apostolates of teaching, caring for the sick, social works of charity, and the missions. Their routine of prayer and manner of dress was similar to that of cloistered nuns, but their lives, far from being devoted to contemplation, were ones of intense active service.

Pius XII initiated efforts to update many aspects of religious life. Since Vatican II the incongruity of active ministries with the pattern of life and dress of nuns has become so apparent that the sisterhoods are in considerable confusion about their identity. They suffer from a great decline of vocations and many not very successful "experiments" in their lifestyle.[43]

It is too early to know definitely how the active sisterhoods are

42. While women have always exercised active ministries in the church, such ministry was not thought compatible with canonical religious life, i.e., the cloistered, contemplative life of nuns. After the Council of Trent this distinction was enforced by the decree *Cura Pastoralis* of Pius V in 1566, issued to reform the existing religious life of women much criticized by the Protestant Reformers. Consequently, the communities of women who wished to engage in the active ministry, such as the Daughters of Charity founded by St. Vincent de Paul, were not, canonically speaking, "religious" until the decree *Quam justo* of Benedict XIV in 1749 gave full canonical recognition as religious to active communities of women. Following the French Revolution these communities expanded remarkably, but their decline in vocations began in France as early as 1930. See Michel Dortel Claudot, article, "Vie consacrée," *Dictionnaire de spiritualité,* fasc. 104, cols. 663–703. For an incisive (but debatable) analysis of the causes of decline in the United States, see Elizabeth McDonough, O.P., "Beyond the Liberal Model: Quo Vadis?" *Review for Religious* 50 (1991): 866–81.

43. On the changes in the Catholic sisterhoods see Elizabeth Kolmer, A.S.C., *Religious Women in the United States: A Survey of the Influential Literature from 1950–1983,* Consecrated Life Series, no. 4 (Wilmington, DE: Michael Glazier, 1984).

going to solve this identity crisis in a creative way that church authorities can approve in view of the good of the church as a whole. My own guess is that these active sisterhoods may well be transformed into "secular institutes," i.e., a form of consecrated life canonically approved by the church but distinct from that of the religious orders in that members of such institutes adopt the lifestyle of the Christian laity in order to act as a leaven in the world.[44] Such secular institutes seem especially adapted to the needs of the church at this time, although only a few of them such as Opus Dei (which is technically a special case) seem as yet notably successful.[45]

In my opinion, therefore, the answer to this objection is that, as I have already said, men religious, though they witness to the kingdom by the observance of their vows, do not as such *symbolize* Christ and Mary as do priests and consecrated virgins in the church. They simply manifest the need of every Christian to seek Christian perfection by penance and good works and to prepare for the coming of the Lord. This holds true also, it seems to me, for the active sisterhoods. Although they took over from the nuns many customs that designated them as "brides of Christ," etc., these reflected the ambiguous identity of which I have spoken, which now requires to be clarified.

Certainly every woman, religious or not, can in a private way understood herself as a bride of Christ. Indeed some men (e.g., John of the Cross) have used that language even of themselves,

44. "Secular institutes are not religious communities but they carry with them in the world a profession of the evangelical counsels which is genuine and complete, and recognized as such by the Church" (Vatican II, *Perfectae Caritatis*, no. 11). The following sections from *The Code of Canon Law* apply: "In itself the state of consecrated life is neither clerical or lay" (Canon 588, no. 1); "A secular institute is an institute of consecrated life in which Christ's faithful, living in the world, strive for the perfection of charity and endeavor to contribute to the sanctification of the world, especially from within" (Canon 710); "Without prejudice to the law concerning institutes of consecrated life, consecration as a member of a secular institute does not change the member's canonical status among the people of God, be it lay or clerical" (Canon 711).

45. See Armando Oberti, "I fondamenti della 'consacrazione' negli istituti secolari: La Secolaritá consecrata nel Magistero pontificio," *Vita Consecrata* 29 (July–Aug. 1993): 457–67.

since in the language of analogy the soul is feminine in relation to God. But such usages (like references of some medieval writers to God and even to Christ as feminine) are personal, they have not been publicly adopted by the church.[46]

Objections can also be raised at a number of points as to my argument's historical foundations.[47] Since there were no cloistered nuns in the early church, how can one believe this symbolism really has a permanent and unchanging value in the church? Certainly, the priesthood and consecrated virginity have undergone and will continue to undergo a historical development in the church, but this development has not been shaped only by explicit commands of Jesus or official acts of popes and councils. It has also been powerfully molded by the symbol-system provided by the Bible and organically elaborated in the church's tradition, just as in the development of the doctrine of the Petrine Office, scattered stories and references in the New Testament to the leadership of Peter among the Twelve took on a symbolic character and provided a model that shaped and regulated the papal institution.[48]

The same is true, I believe, of the priesthood and consecrated virginity. What these have become in the church has not been determined simply by some specific acts of institution recorded in the historical data available to us. Under the guidance of the Holy Spirit the meaning of model persons and significant events of New Testament times, in the context of Old Testament traditions, has been explicated, unified, and institutionalized from elements that were implicit or dispersed. These institutionalized forms are still open to many nonessential modifications but they are grounded in a permanent core of meaning.

I have tried to show what this enduring significance of the priesthood is and why the gender differentiation that it requires should not detract from the dignity of women in the church. When

---

46. See Sister Ritamary Bradley, "Patristic Background of the Motherhood Similitude in Julian of Norwich," *Christian Scholar's Review* 8 (1978): 101–13.

47. For the history of the development of the priesthood see Osborne, *Priesthood: A History;* Dunn, *Priesthood: A Re-Examination;* and Brown, *Priest and Bishop.*

48. See Raymond E. Brown, et al., eds., *Peter in the New Testament.*

rightly understood and practiced, this complementary equality will greatly enhance women's personal dignity in its own reciprocal symbolism.

Sex and Spirituality

Sex and Sanctification

My discussion of priesthood and consecrated virginity would not be complete unless I related these to the role of married couples who make up the greater part of the church. In my last chapter, I already considered the role of man as father and woman as mother, but I need now to speak of the couple as such.

Following the teaching of St. Paul the church has always maintained the superiority of celibacy for the sake of the kingdom to marriage, not indeed as a comparison of good to bad, but of the better to the truly good. Vatican II, however, without repudiating this traditional position, in deference to the allergy of our culture to any talk of inequality, even functional inequality, avoided making this odious comparison, and contented itself with praising both states of life and asserting the freedom of the Christian to choose between them.[49]

Nevertheless, I will try to confront this comparison frankly. My thesis on this point is that in the creation we were made male and female in order to form the family community, which is the basis of the total community. If there had been no sin, all persons would have married because our sexuality is designed by God to help us

49. Vatican II, *Lumen Gentium*, no. 44, explains how by religious vows a baptized Christian is "more intimately consecrated to divine service," and in *Presbyterorum Ordinis*, no. 16, it says: "With respect to the priestly life, the Church has always held in especially high regard perfect and perpetual continence on behalf of the kingdom of heaven." But in *Gaudium et Spes*, no. 48, it also gives high praise to the sanctity of the married state, without however, using such terms as "more intimately consecrated" or of "especially high regard," which gently imply a comparison. See also Paul VI's encyclical, "On Priestly Celibacy" *(Sacerdotalis Coelibatus)*, June 24, 1967, no. 95 (in Flannery, ed., *Vatican II Postconciliar Documents*, pp. 285–317).

learn to love unselfishly.[50] Through the unselfish love of the couple for each other and for their children they are taught by God to love him more profoundly.

Since marriage was designed by God to sanctify men and women, for them to have remained celibate before sin came into the world would have deprived them of one of the chief means to come to know and love God, i.e., it would have been a sinful neglect of God's gift of fruitful sexuality.

Sex and Asceticism

In fact, however, we live in a sinful world in which the evil desire for personal autonomy, alienated from the guidance of God by which we are led to our true happiness with him, has converted the good things of creation and especially the best things into temptations to further sin and alienation. Among these distortions one of the most powerful is the perversion of sexuality, intended by God to teach us self-giving, into a snare of selfish satisfaction and domination over others. Christ has come to free us from all forms of sin, including this addictive enslavement to the selfish and exploitative use of sex and to restore sex to its original orientation toward God.[51] This restoration, however, will not be complete un-

50. St. Thomas Aquinas, citing St. Augustine, says, "Therefore, the fact that [sexual] continence [before the Fall] was not praiseworthy, but in our time is praised, is not because of its infertility, but because of its freedom from disordered desire, since then [before the Fall] it was without that [disordered] desire"—but sex, because the human body was then in a purer and more sensitive condition, was more intensely pleasurable (*ST* I, q. 98, a. 2, ad 3). And see *ST* III, q. 99, a. 2, ad 3, for Aquinas's response to the objection that before the Fall all humans except Eve might have been male and therefore more perfect(!) since Eve could have lived to produce all human beings. He answers: "Children would have been born living with animal life to which it is proper to generate just as to eat food. Hence it would have been proper for all to generate just as did the First Parents. From which it seems to follow that as many females as males would have been born." Since for Aquinas, marriage when lived according to reason and faith is meritorious (Suppl. q. 41, a. 4), and this implies an increase in charity, it is clear that he would agree with Vatican II's praise of conjugal love in *Gaudium et Spes,* no. 49.

51. Thus to write of the Catholic attitude toward sex as "negative" is as wrong as to claim that the Catholic attitude toward alcoholic beverages is "negative" just because Catholics deplore drunkenness. What is condemned is a misuse of a good thing.

til the Kingdom of God has come in its fullness. Even in marriage sanctified by the sacrament of matrimony, the temptation to make an idol of sexual pleasure and domination must still be confronted.

This means that married couples, although they are sanctified by their marriage and by the marital act itself when it is motivated by a faithful love open to the transmission of life, need nevertheless, like every Christian, to practice an asceticism with regard to marital pleasures. They need, "to abstain for a time for the sake of prayer" (Cor 7:5) and for responsible family planning, just as they need to fast and do other forms of penance.[52] Thus marital spirituality centers in the fulfillment of the covenant between man and wife, which sacramentally represents the covenant of Christ and his church (Eph 5:21, 32). Their marriage constitutes the domestic church and they beget and educate children for the building up of the church as a whole. The man is sanctified by being a faithful husband and caring father, the woman by being a faithful wife and caring mother.

These spousal roles will be differently stylized in different cultures, but their essential structure needs to be maintained in every culture if their God-given purpose is to be fulfilled. According to the economy and culture, the activity of both man and woman inside and outside the home will vary, but the essential family structure and the rights of children for care have a priority based on the right of the child to be helped to attain maturity.

Nevertheless, married life in the church, caught as it is in the

---

52. In the context of the text quoted, St. Paul was warning against the excessive asceticism that some married persons in Corinth were attempting, but this also implies that he approved the more prudent sexual abstinence of others. This topic has been well analyzed by William D. Virtue in his as yet unpublished dissertation, "Absence and Desire in Christian Married Love," (Licentiate in Sacred Theology diss., Pontifical John Paul II Institute for Studies in Marriage and Family, Washington, D.C., 1990). He concludes, "Through abstinence Christian married persons are truly perfected in love by an increase of desire. This desire is directed toward one another and in prayer transposed toward God. Spouses who grow together in the love of God experience also a perfection of their marital love . . . *thus Christian Matrimony is a sign of the love of Christ and the Church not only under the form of union but also in the cross of separation*" (p. 102).

tension between a sinful world and the restoration of the original order of creation, is for all its rewards and its sanctifying power, full of difficulties. St. Paul, after recommending celibacy to the unmarried young men of Corinth, says very soberly to them: "If you marry, however, you do not sin, nor does an unmarried woman if she marries; but such people will experience affliction in their earthly life, and I would like to spare you that. I tell you, brothers, the time is running out. . . . For the world in its present form is passing away" (1 Cor 7:28–29, 31b)."[53]

Among these risks of marriage is that a couple will become so absorbed in family life that they will forget that this life is passing away, and that in eternal life there is, as Jesus said, "no giving in marriage" (Mt 22:30), i.e., sexual and parental love will be transcended in the eternal life of the community of the Trinity.[54] So that married couples may be convincingly reminded of this hope in a world that seems to deny it, there need to be in the church those "wise virgins," as Jesus called them, who by their whole manner of life demonstrate to us the eschatological dimension of Christian faith.[55]

53. On this text see Conzelmann's commentary. He denies this text is derived from Stoicism: "Paul's advice is not to withdraw into the safe and unrestricted realms of the inner life, but to maintain freedom in the midst of involvement. Eschatology really determines the conduct of life, whereas Stoic metaphysics is merely an expression of an attitude to the world" (p. 133).

54. "At the resurrection they neither marry nor are given in marriage but are like the angels in heaven" (Mt 22:30). "So also is the resurrection. It [the body] is sown corruptible; it is raised incorruptible. It is sown dishonorable; it is raised glorious; It is sown weak; it is raised powerful. It is sown a natural body; it is raised a spiritual body. If there is a natural body, there is also a spiritual one" (1 Cor 15:42–44). These texts should not be understood to deny the physical reality of the resurrected body. Jesus, agreed with the Pharisees, who believed, against the Sadducees, in both angels and bodily resurrection, but the Pharisees probably thought of angels as corporeal not as pure spirits. As for St. Paul, he uses the term "spiritual" as synonymous with "incorruptible," "honorable," and "powerful," not with "immaterial." On this see Conzelmann, *1 Corinthians*, 282–83, who, citing E. Schweitzer, says that for Paul a "spiritual body" is still a body but one "determined" by spirit. This agrees with Aquinas's explanation of the text, *ST* III, q. 54, a.1, ad. 2.

55. See K. P. Donfried, "The Allegory of the Ten Virgins as a Summary of Matthean Theology," *Journal of Biblical Literature* 93 (1974): 415–28.

Celibacy and Marriage

This witness is made explicit in those who live the vowed celibate life, and in a particular way in the consecrated virgin. In another mode it is made manifest by the representation of Christ in the church by the ordained priests, ministers of the sacraments, above all as they act *in persona Christi* in leading the celebration of the Eucharist, invested in the white linen of their priestly celibacy.[56] Thus married spirituality, which restores the order of creation, is complemented and provided with a model by the priest and consecrated virgin, representing Jesus and Mary still present to the church as New Adam and New Eve.

The Domestic and the Public

Does all this mean that woman's world is confined to the private and domestic, while public life is only open to men? St. Thomas Aquinas explained the text of St. Paul about women keeping silence in church by means of this distinction and, as we have seen, it seemed obvious in the days of St. Paul and of St. Thomas Aqui-

---

56. This symbol of virgin white garments (see Rv 7:9; 14:4) in the Bible refers to the refusal of the "fornication" of idolatry (Rv 2:14–15, 20–22), but has been used liturgically in the investiture with the alb as appropriate to the priest who is ritually pure for the offering of the true sacrifice to the true God. Christ himself is similarly vested (Rv 1:13; cf. Dn 10:5). The following works are helpful works on the Christian meaning of celibacy: Max Thurian, *Marriage and Celibacy* (London: SCM Press, 1959); Edward Schillebeeckx, *Celibacy* (New York: Sheed and Ward, 1967); Lucien Legrand, *The Biblical Doctrine of Celibacy* (New York: Sheed and Ward, 1963); Eugene H. Maly, "Celibacy," *The Bible Today* 34 (Feb. 1968): 2392–2400; Karl Rahner, "The Celibacy of the Secular Priest Today," *The Furrow* Feb. 1968: 59–72, and included in his book *Servants of the Lord* (New York: Herder and Herder, 1968), 149–72; Jerome D. Quinn, "Celibacy and the Ministry in Scripture," *The Bible Today* 46 (Feb. 1970): 3163–3175; George Wesley Buchanan, "Jesus and Other Monks of New Testament Times," *Religion in Life* 48 (1979): 136–42; Peter Brown, *The Body and Society: Men, Women, and Sexual Renunciation in Early Christianity* (New York: Columbia University Press, 1988); Gary Anderson, "Celibacy or Consummation in the Garden? Reflections on Early Jewish and Christian Interpretations of the Garden of Eden," *Harvard Theological Review* 82 (1989): 124–48. Buchanan shows that the ancient Jews thought there was intercourse in the Garden of Eden, although *Jubilees* thought of the Garden as the Temple and therefore subject to levitical rules of abstinence, this was followed by some Christians, such as St. Ephraem of Nisbis.

nas and indeed in most historic cultures.[57] Mothers of many children whose life expectancy does not far exceed their child-bearing years necessarily live their lives within the domestic circle, while the father's natural role as provider and protector tends to draw him into public life.

In our culture, however, where an abundant economy, regulation of birth, and a longer life expectancy have opened education and a variety of work opportunities to both sexes, there is no reason that either women or men need to confine their energies to the home. This change in our cultural situation is in itself a positive one and has been so recognized by Pope John Paul II.[58]

Is this acceptance of the entry of women, and especially of married women and mothers, into public life inconsistent with the theses I have been arguing? It is not, if we understand the traditional notion that motherhood is the supreme achievement of woman as true only in the sense that it is her supreme achievement precisely as woman, but not as person. The same should equally be said of man, that his supreme achievement as a man, but not as a person, is fatherhood. St. Paul's commendation of celibacy[59] shows that as persons both women and men have a destiny that expands beyond the family to participation in the wider society and ultimately the community of the Trinity. Thus in the plan of God, domestic life was never intended to constrict the life of either woman or man, but to prepare them for a wider and richer life.

57. See Aquinas's comments on Paul's texts: *Super 1 Cor.*, chap. 14: lect. 7, nos. 879–80 (a *reportatio*). He interpets v. 37 to mean that this admonition is "a command of the Lord." *Super 1 Tim.*, chap. 2, lect. 3, no. 80; *Super Tit.*, chap. 2, lect. 1, no. 53; *ST* II–II, q. 177. a. 2; *ST* III, q. 55, a. 1, ad 3; *ST* III q. 67, a. 4, ad 1; *ST* Suppl. q. 39, a. 1.; and IV Sent. dist. 25, q. 1, qla. 1, ad 4.

58. In *Mulieris Dignitatem*, no. 31, John Paul II calls on the church to thank women of every vocation for their work in the church and the world and for "women who watch over the human person in the family, which is the fundamental sign of the human community; for women who work professionally and who at times are burdened with great social responsibility . . . as they assume, together with men, a common responsibility for the destiny of humanity according to daily necessities and according to the definite destiny which the human family has in God himself, in the bosom of the ineffable Trinity."

59. 1 Cor 7:8–9, 25–38. On the obscurities of this passage see Conzelmann, *1 Corinthians*, 130–36. He believes the passage refers not to a father and daughter but to a fiance and his betrothed in a real (not spiritual) betrothal.

The fact that, in the cultures of the past and still to a significant degree in our own culture, there has been a bitter conflict between the responsibilities of parenthood and wider participation in public life is due to our fallen condition in which the curses of Genesis 3:15–19—fruitless toil for the man and the burden of pregnancy for the woman—distort the human lot and narrow its possibilities.[60] In redeemed society parenthood can become a preparation both for women and for men to share in the work and leisure of the larger society. Thus once again the subordination of functional to personal equality for which I have been arguing provides a resolution to an apparent contradiction.

Women and Worship

Women's Participation in Liturgy

A matter closely related to the contemplative vocation of women in the church, is the role of women in worship. The liturgy provides in symbolic form the Christian community with the pattern of its own structure and life.[61] If we deny to women the role of presiding at the altar, do we not seem to deny their personal equality in the church by omitting them from the liturgical paradigm of its life?[62] This I believe motivates some of the demands

60. On the significance of these curses see John Paul II, *Mulieris Dignitatem,* no. 10.

61. "The liturgy is the summit toward which the activity of the Church is directed; at the same time it is the fountain from which all her power flows. . . . The liturgy in its turn inspires the faithful to become 'of one heart in love' [Postcommunion of Easter Vigil] when they have tasted to their full of the paschal mysteries; it prays that 'they may grasp by deed what they hold by creed' [Collect of Tuesday, Easter Week]" (Vatican II, *Sacrosanctum Concilium,* no. 10).

62. Elisabeth Schüssler-Fiorenza, "To Console or Challenge," argues that "sacramental grace is present in every act of women ministers that reconciles people with God and mediates God's grace to the people. . . . This happens for example when persons confess their sins to women or when women ministers break bread in community. One could argue that these sacramental acts of women ministers lack the *public* dimension of church insofar as they lack juridical legitimization through ordination. This argument overlooks, however, that the denial of juridical ordination of women to the priesthood is engendered by the structural sin of patriarchal sexism. Since the symbolic sin of sexism destroys the universal character of the sacrament, one can argue to the contrary that women's sacramental ministry

for greater participation by women in the liturgy. More seriously, it has raised the question of the possibility of women deacons.

I would argue that women should be given a place in the liturgy. True, we must take seriously the text of 1 Corinthians 14:33b–35: "As in all the churches of the saints, women should keep silent in the churches, for they are not allowed to speak, but should be subordinate as the law says. But if they want to learn anything, they should ask their husbands at home. For it is improper for a woman to speak in church." Seas of exegetical ink have been spilled over that troublesome Pauline dictum.[63] In view of my general analysis, I believe that Paul's concern was not to silence women altogether but to maintain the role of the husband as head of the family. Paul acknowledged that women have prophetic gifts (1 Cor 11:4), and he did not want such gifts suppressed (1 Thes 5:19). In the Corinthian situation, however, the exercise of prophetic gifts by wives in the church assembly was shaming their husbands, whose proper office as heads and therefore public representatives of their families, seemed (according to the customs of the times) usurped. Consequently Paul ordered that women should restrain

symbolizes (i.e. sacramentalizes) fully the sacramental grace of the church insofar as 'Christ's deed and vitality of the Church' is not distorted by sexist symbolism." This line of argument would seem to conclude that at present the sacraments performed by ordained males are invalid and those performed by unordained females are valid! Why then ordain women?

63. See Chapter III note 70 above, and note 34 above. On the text's commanding women to be silent, a suggestion, similar to the one I have adopted, is that of Robert J. Karris, "Women in the Pauline Assembly: To Prophesy, but Not to Speak?" in *Women Priests: A Catholic Commentary,* ed. Leonard and Arlene Swidler, 205–8, who tries to resolve the seeming contradiction in Paul of which McKenzie complained. Karris thinks that *lalein* (speak) probably means "ask questions" in 1 Cor 14:34–45, i.e., women are not forbidden to speak but to interrupt the preacher, while *didaskein* (teach) in 1 Tm 2:12 from the special context may mean they are forbidden "to teach *falsely,*" not forbidden to teach at all. This solution may be questioned, but at least it seeks to understand Paul, not to dismiss him. As regards another seemingly antifeminist text, J. Winandy, O.S.B., "Une curieux *casus pendens:* 1 Corinthians 11:10 et son interpretation," *New Testament Studies* 38 (Oct. 1992): 621–29, argues that the puzzling phrase "because of the angels" probably means "because of the apostles," i.e. the messengers from other churches who may be shocked by the prophetesses uncovering their hair contrary to the custom of these other churches (cf. Rv 1:20 ff. where "angels" probably are the heads of the various churches).

their prophecies in the public assembly, and permit their husbands to act as their representatives in the community discussions. There were evidently other situations in which they were free to exercise these gifts even in the public assemblies.

Thus we can draw from Paul's judgment the principle that not all gifts need explicit manifestation in the liturgy, but can find appropriate expression elsewhere. Hence it does not follow that if women do not have special roles in the liturgy, they are not recognized in the church, or that they are not participating in the liturgy. After all, most of the males in the congregation do not have special roles either. In past times the presence of Sisters in habit at the Eucharist did give a public recognition to their ecclesial role, although they did not enter the sanctuary. Today, since Sisters are seldom present in habit or as a recognizable group, and since the general cultural climate looks for some expression of the personal equality of women, it does seem that we need some special liturgical roles for women.

In some places today altar girls are permitted, while women acting as lectors, Eucharist ministers, and leaders of song are common throughout the United States. In some places also permission is given by the bishop for women to preach, provided they do not give the homily. Feminists regard these as mere token concessions, and in my opinion, although in some cases they may be pastorally justifiable, they are not very satisfactory from a liturgical point of view. They have no special meaning except tokenism and seem to be either a reluctant concession or an edging up to ordination. What is needed are roles for women that manifest their motherhood just, as we have seen, the priests' role manifests his fatherhood.

Diaconate and Women

Consequently the question of ordination to the diaconate is a serious one. I do not believe that a strong case can be made for this from tradition.[64] It is true that there were "deaconesses" in

64. See Gryson, *Ministry of Women in the Early Church*, M.-J. Aubert, *Des*

the early church, but their functions were limited to preparing women candidates for baptism by catechizing them and attending them when they were baptized nude. It seems to be true also that in some places they were instituted in office with ceremonies that resembled those of the ordination of deacons, and what is perhaps more significant were seated in the *presbyterium* with priests. Yet there are other examples in history where the sacraments were *imitated* in the creation of rituals (e.g. the anointing of kings and queens).[65] How this is to be theologically understood remains a matter of speculation. Perhaps it was not until the scholastics clearly developed the principle that "sacred orders" in the strict sense were all, even the diaconate, ordered to the Eucharist, that a theological reason emerged why the "ordination" of deaconesses was probably a sacramental not a sacrament.

The opening of ordination to the diaconate to women would be justified only if we become clear about the nature of the diaconate itself. The reestablishment by Vatican II of permanent deacons in the church has raised many questions on this score, since exegetes are not agreed that the basic scriptural text traditionally used to explain their origin and function in Acts 6:1–7 refers to deacons rather than presbyters.[66] Moreover in the actual practice

---

Femmes Diacres: Un nouveau chemin pour l'Église (Paris: Beauchesne, 1986), and Sister Marie Walter Flood, O.P., "The Place of Women in the Ministerial Offices of the Church as Witnessed by Ecclesiastical Tradition and Rites of Ordination" (Ph.D. diss., University of Toronto, 1976), who believe this was a true sacrament. A. G. Martimort, *Deaconesses: An Historical Study* (San Francisco: Ignatius Press, 1986), holds the opposite opinion. See also the articles by Manfred Hauke and Bruno Kleinheyer in *The Church and Women*, 115–40. On the movement for reestablishment of this office see Virginia Kaib Ratigan and Arlene Anderson Swidler, eds., *A New Phoebe: Perspectives on Roman Catholic Women and the Permanent Diaconate* (Kansas City, MO: Sheed and Ward, 1990).

65. See *New Catholic Encyclopedia* (1967), s.v. "Anointing," by Jean Gaudemet, and Gerard Austin, O.P., *Anointing with the Spirit: the Rite of Confirmation: The Use of Oil and Chrism* (New York: Pueblo Publishing Co, 1985), 97–122. On the theories about the sacramental character of the anointing of the Byzantine and Russian emperors see Martin Jugie, S.J., *Theologia dogmatica christianorum orientalium ab ecclesia catholica dissidentium* (Paris: Letouzey et Ane, 1926–35), vol. 3, pp. 151–62.

66. See Galot, *Theology of the Priesthood*, 160–64. He concludes that the office conferred was that of presbyter (not yet clearly distinguished from bishop),

of the church for centuries the deacon has been simply a liturgical assistant of the priest the meaning of whose role is quite obscure. I can here only state an opinion. Whatever is to be said about the historical significance of Acts 6:1–7, it does seem to provide a solid reason why in addition to the presbyteral role, there needs to be in the church ordained ministers whose function is the supervision of the church's *corporal works of mercy:* "It is not right for us [the Twelve] to neglect the word of God to serve at table" (6:2b).[67] Jesus prepared his audiences to hear his preaching by works of charity, healing, and feeding the multitude. It is this aspect of ministry that is especially celebrated (along with their martyrdom) in the feasts of Ss. Stephen, Vincent, and Lawrence.[68] The role of preaching and administering some sacraments is perhaps a practical accommodation rather than proper to the diaconate.[69]

---

not deacon, and the "table-service" in question was eucharistic. To me the arguments of exegetes against the traditional opinion do not seem conclusive (see next note).

67. Exegetes doubt this text about the Seven refers to deacons (in the modern sense) because it does not use the word *diaconos*, it seems to gloss over deeper reasons for the split between the Hebraic and Hellenist Christians than "table-waiting," and it depicts two of those "ordained" (Stephen and Philip) not as table-waiters but as evangelists. Hence, André Lemaire, "The Ministries in the New Testament," says that the majority of scholars deny that Seven were deacons rather than presbyters. In his *Les ministères aux origines de l'Église* (Paris, 1971), 49–58, Lemaire argues that the "tables" refer not to the Eucharist or love-feasts connected with it, as most exegetes think, but to money-exchange tables for the distribution of alms. Jacques Dupont, after relating and agreeing with the majority opinion, adds, "Si c'est bien ainsi que les choses se sont pensées, on comprehend sans trop de peine que Luc avait reculé devint l'image d'un éclatement de la communauté presenter les Sept comme les préposés des services caritatifs d'une communauté unitaire, des *sortes de diacres avant la lettre*" (Jacques Dupont, *Nouvelles études sur les Actes des Apôtre*, Lectio Divina 118 [Paris: Cerf, 1984], 154, emphasis added; cf. pp. 151–57). It should be noted that the interpretation of this text as the origin of the diaconate goes back to St. Irenaeus in the second century, *Adversus haeresis*, 3:2, 10 and 4:15, 1 and is retained in the revised Latin rite of ordination.

68. On the rather obscure history of the diaconate see Edward D. Hardy, "Deacons in History and Practice," in *The Diaconate Now*, ed. Richard T. Nolan (Washington/Cleveland: Corpus Books, 1968), 37–56, and James Monroe Barnett, *The Diaconate: A Full and Equal Order* (New York: Seabury, 1981), and in a more popular vein, Lynn C. Sherman, *The Diaconate in the Church* (Staten Island, NY: Alba House, 1991), 5–26.

69. According to George Florovsky, "The Problem of the Diaconate in the Orthodox Church," in *The Diaconate Now*, ed. Nolan, 81–99, the Eastern tradition

The deacon's actions in the liturgy were perhaps intended to link symbolically the church's care of the poor with its offering of the Eucharist.

It could be argued, therefore, that a woman deacon might prepare the gifts at the Eucharist, symbolizing the church in her nurturing motherhood, as Mary prepared Jesus for the presentation in the Temple, invited him to perform his first miracle at the banquet of Cana, and stood at his side on Calvary.[70] The objection to this argument, however, would be that the close involvement of a woman in the actual offering of the Eucharist has always been felt in the past to obscure the celibate status of the priest,[71] which has been supported by the distinction of the presbyterium from the nave of the church and by the exclusive employment of males as subsidiary ministers.[72] It is the *congregation* that is the feminine

---

puts the primary emphasis on the liturgical function of the deacon not on the administrative or charitable functions. He believes that musical considerations have led to giving the deacon an undue liturgical prominence.

70. Of course, women, especially nuns and religious sisters, have often been entrusted with sewing the altar linens, baking the altar breads, and acting as sacristans. These were not understood as menial tasks, but as acts of eucharistic devotion patterned on the ministry of Martha to Jesus. In an interesting article, A. M. Tortras, "Women Priests or Women Deacons," *Theology Digest* 29 (1981): 245, notes that in the *Didiscalia*, the deaconesses is a symbol of Holy Spirit and that the magisterial document *Ad Gentes*, no. 16 argues that those who do a deacon's job should be ordained deacons. He also hopes this would prepare people for women priests.

71. To our literal minded contemporaries the idea that the presence of women in the sanctuary imperils priestly chastity seems absurd and insulting to both women and priests. What is involved, however, is not really moral risks, but a symbolic separation of man and woman to remind us ritually that in the liturgy we transcend the affairs of time, typified by the sexual relationship with its connotations of birth and death, and enter into the eternal. Eastern liturgical practice which veils the altar with the iconastasis is also alien to us and seems an exclusion of the laity, rather than as a revelation to them of mystery. Should we accommodate the "modern mentality" or does this "modern mentality" especially need the illumination of such symbols of transcendence? Why are so many today seeking in the occult and exotic the mysteries they no longer find in Christian worship?

72. It has been charged that this exclusion is based on the concern in the Old Law which treated menstruants as ritually unclean (Lv 15:19–30). Thus Elizabeth Dodson Gray, *Patriarchy as a Conceptual Trap,* says of Judaism, "When the holy space of a religion is sacred for male sexuality (as in the making of the covenant upon the male phallus in circumcision), and sacred for blood-sacrifice presided over by males; and when that same holy space is contaminated by female blood and female fertility (as in menstruating and giving birth), we are dealing with a male

church, the Bride of Christ, not some particular woman minister, and this fact is confused by the presence of a woman deacon. I would say the same for other female auxiliary ministers in the sanctuary such as altar girls, although these are now permitted.

One might say, of course, that since the congregation is made up of both men and women, its feminine symbolism is not at all clear. But it is as a *whole* that the people stand for Mother Church. When considered in its members, male as well as female, these are Mother Church's children. Thus a symbolic analysis of the liturgical structure seems to lead to the conclusion that nothing much is gained by a female diaconate.

We might, however, revive an opinion of St. Thomas Aquinas, which has not generally been followed by sacramental theologians. Aquinas explained the so-called minor orders abolished by Vatican II, not as mere "ecclesiastical institutions" as the acolytate and lectorate are now titled (but oddly enough still restricted only to males), but as subdivisions of the sacramental order of the diaconate.[73]

Thus the former minor orders, according to Aquinas, were real "orders" and yet distinguished from the diaconate only by an action of the church. The Eastern church seems to have accepted a similar line of thought, explaining the anointing of the Emperor either as a form of confirmation or of the diaconate. If this line is followed, then, instead of "instituting" acolytes and lectors,[74] the church could ordain them and also install other officials, such as

---

fertility cult, no matter what its other lofty spiritual insights may be" (p. 26). This misses the point that for Judaism blood was the principle of life, but bodily emissions were associated with corruption and death, whether these be female menstrual blood or male seminal emissions. (Lv 1–14, 31–33). The Christian exclusion of women from the sanctuary was not because they were unclean (since they too were made holy by baptism and the Eucharist) but to avoid suspicions (endemic to cultures where the segregation of the sexes in public places was customary) of a celibate clergy which mingles too easily with women.

73. *ST* Suppl. q. 37, a. 2, ad 2. This opinion was abandoned by Cajetan, Soto, and Vasquez. Some, however, thought it was affirmed by Trent, Sess. 23, can. 2 and 3, DS nos. 1772–73.

74. Paul VI suppressed the sub-diaconate and minor orders by a *Motu Proprio Ministeria Quaedam*, Aug. 15, 1972, but retained the ministries of lector and acolyte to be conferred not by "ordination" but by "institution."

the director of song, by a genuinely sacramental ordination. In that case women might be ordained to some appropriate liturgical offices in the church, such as distributors of the Eucharist, lectors, or leaders of song, without being deacons in the ordinary sense. On the whole I would conclude that the public participation of women in the church can be publicly recognized more easily than by compromising liturgical manipulations that lack grounding in tradition and that appear as mere tokenism as long as the mistaken notion that women are personally equal to men only if they can be ordained is encouraged. What really is needed is to make sure that the immense contribution of women to the life of the church is publicly commended by requiring that they be consulted on all important matters of church policy, and that their prophetic role in the church be highlighted.[75]

75. "The church gives thanks for all the manifestations of the feminine 'genius' which have appeared in the course of history in the midst of all peoples and nations; she gives thanks for all the charisms which the Holy Spirit distributes to women in the history of the people of God, for all the victories which she owes to their faith, hope, and charity: She gives thanks for all the fruits of feminine holiness. The church asks at the same time that these invaluable 'manifestations of the Spirit' (Cf. 1 Cor 12:4 ff.) which with great generosity are poured forth upon the 'daughters' of the eternal Jerusalem, may be attentively recognized and appreciated so that they may return for the common good of the church and of humanity; especially in our times" John Paul II, *Mulieris Dignitatem*, no. 31.

Conclusion: Justice in the Church

Let me now summarize the fundamental argument of this book. The church cannot preach justice unless she practices it. Justice in the church, however, cannot be evaluated by the standards of our so-called democratic way of life, which is influenced more by the agnostic scientism and romanticism of Enlightenment humanism than by the Gospel. In order to serve our times according to the "signs of the times" we need to distinguish clearly the two notions of justice so as to establish their proper relation.

The Christian view of justice does not confuse the personal equality due to all members of the church and of society because they are created in God's image with the necessarily hierarchical inequality of gifts, offices, and kinds of status required for a community to achieve the common good of its members and to permit the maximum participation by all. Yet this inequality of function and status must always be in the service of personal equality, and must never override that more fundamental equality. The Christian in whatever functional status must imitate Christ who came not to be served but to serve. Consequently, it is not unjust but the realization of true justice that the church has a hierarchical structure, and that only persons possessing the qualifications for an office, even when this qualification is one of gender, are admitted to it.

The actual structure of offices in the church cannot be reduced to the naturally determined offices of the family in which the husband is the natural head, nor to the state in which nature does not determine that any one form of government is best, provided only that it aim at the common good. It is paramount to recognize, however, that an important feature of the common good without which full justice is not possible is the principle of subsidiarity and participation by all its members in decision-making.

Vatican II, echoing the Council of Trent, but with due regard to the historical studies of recent times, says,

Christ whom the Father sanctified and sent into the world (Jn 10:36) has, through his apostles, made their successors, the bishops, partakers of His consecration and His mission. These in their turn have legitimately handed on to different individuals in the Church various degrees of participation in this ministry. Thus the divinely established ecclesiastical ministry is exercised on different levels by those who from antiquity have been called, bishops, priests, and deacons.[1]

Thus Christ in instituting the church gave it an essential and permanent structure, including a priesthood and episcopacy, with the successor of St. Peter as head of the college of bishops.[2] While the church as a whole shares in Christ's priesthood, only the priest sacramentally ordained in the Holy Spirit represents the presence and action of Christ as priest and mediator in the church leading the church in the worship of the Father. For that reason this office of priesthood, which bishops receive in its fullness,[3] can be conferred only on males, because as I have tried to show, maleness is essential to Christ's revelation of the nature of God as Father, Son, and Holy Spirit.

This exclusion of women from this office in the church is not a denial of personal equality because males are also excluded from

1. Vatican II, *Lumen Gentium*, no. 28; Trent, DS nos. 1773, 1776.
2. The Council of Trent defined that holy orders are "truly and properly a sacrament instituted by the Christ the Lord" (DS 1773) and that there is in the Catholic church "a hierarchy, divinely instituted, consisting of bishops, presbyters, and ministers" (DS 1777). Vatican I defined that the Petrine office was instituted by Christ (DS 3055). Vatican II recapitulated these teachings, *Lumen Gentium*, chap. 3, nos. 18–29. Theories about the historical development of this structure, consistent with the somewhat fragmentary biblical and patristic data, are required for honest apologetics, but faith and theology must recognize the force of these conciliar definitions.
3. Vatican II, *Lumen Gentium*, no. 26.

a complementary role in the church fulfilled by consecrated virgins, living a contemplative life superior even to the life of ministry. These contemplative women make present to the church the role of Mary as New Eve, Mother of the church complementary to that of Jesus as New Adam and Father of all the redeemed.

Thus the tradition of the church in ordaining only men, although it has often been expressed in ways that implied personal inferiority of women, does not rest on that erroneous assumption, but on the revealed, Christian understanding of why God created us male and female, a relationship that is so fundamental to our human experience that God has also used it in the Incarnation, the Bible, and the sacraments to reveal symbolically the Trinitarian Mystery and his love for us.

Married couples also, through the sacrament of matrimony, manifest the marriage covenant of Christ with his church. This witness, however, was never intended to confine either woman or man to a purely domestic or private life, but to prepare both for full participation in the life of the total society. Yet in a sinful world, they need the reminder of the eschatological realities of which their marriage is only a sacramental sign, a reality lived by the consecrated virgin, and in less symbolic ways by all who vow themselves to celibacy for the kingdom.

Finally, celibates also need the example of the married in order to realize that the celibates' love of God must be fruitful for the church, and not merely a sterile personal perfection or one-to-one relation to God. The celibate man must be a spiritual father, the celibate woman a spiritual mother. In the same way Christian men and women acting in society outside the domestic circle, must enhance their service of society with the gifts of their masculinity and femininity, their spiritual fatherhood and motherhood.[4] Single persons preparing for marriage must live chastely so that their marriages may be faithful. Those choosing not to marry or disabled from marrying must also as chaste celibates realize their sex-

4. See John Paul II, *Mulieris Dignitatem*, nos. 20–22.

uality by a spiritual fatherhood and motherhood in support of families and in serving society as a whole.

The economy of the church, which I have tried to sketch, and which seems to me exemplified in the Scriptures and in the church's tradition, although we have never yet realized it in its fullness, thus provides not only for justice, but a justice that flourishes in love. Alas, instead of working to renew the church in the light of the teachings of Vatican II, we so often stray into blind alleys in search of a utopian justice alien to the Christian vision of the justice of the Kingdom, which as St. Paul says, "begins and ends in faith" (Rm 1:17).

Some Current Objections

Soon after the appearance of *Inter Insigniores* in 1976[1] Leonard and Arlene Swidler, *Women Priests: A Catholic Commentary on the Vatican Declaration*,[2] collected some forty-six criticisms of the document by American theologians.[3] With one exception (that by Thomas P. Rausch), these

1. Sacred Congregation for the Doctrine of the Faith, "Declaration on the Question of the Admission of Women to Ministerial Priesthood," *Inter Insigniores* (Oct. 15, 1976; *AAS* 69 [1977]: 89–116).

2. Leonard and Arlene Swidler, eds., *Women Priests: A Catholic Commentary*. For good overview see Leonard Swidler, "Prolegomena," pp. 3–18. The Vatican Declaration is given on pp. 37–52, and the official "Commentary" in appendix 1, pp. 319–37. Appendix 2 contains the "Pontifical Biblical Commission's report, "Can Women Be Priests?" (pp. 338–46). See also Anne Marie Gardiner, S.S.N.D., ed., *Women and Catholic Priesthood, An Expanded Vision: Proceedings of the Detroit Ordination Conference, 1975* (New York: Paulist, 1976).

3. For some other interesting comments on the topic pro and con see: Paul F. Palmer, S.J., "The Authenticity of Christian Ministry," *Communio* 3 (1976): 272–78; Bernard Lambert, *Can the Catholic Church Admit Women to Priestly Ordination?* (Boston: Daughters of St. Paul, 1977); "Letter to the Apostolic Delegate," by the theologians of the Jesuit School of Theology in Berkeley, *Origins* 6 (Apr. 7, 1977): 661–64, with reply by J. Jadot (p. 665); M. Slusser, "Fathers and Priestesses: Footnotes to the Roman Declaration," *Worship* (Sept. 1977), pp. 434–46; Carroll Stuhlmueller, C.P., "Leadership: Secular Gift Transformed by Revelation, in *Women Priests: A Catholic Commentary*, 307–9, and in Stuhlmueller, ed., *Women and Priesthood: A Call to Dialogue from the Faculty of the Catholic Theological Union at Chicago* (Collegeville, MI: The Liturgical Press, 1978); John R. Donahue, S.J., "Women, Priesthood and the Vatican," *America* 136 (1977): 285–89; David Burrell, "The Vatican Declaration: Another View," *America* 136 (1977): 289–92; Catholic Theological Society of America, *A Report on the Status of Women in Church and Society: Considered in Light of the Question of Women's Ordination* (Mahwah, NJ: Darlington Seminary, 1978); David M. Maloney, *The Church Cannot Ordain Women to the Priesthood* (Chicago: Franciscan Herald Press, 1978); Robert L. Kinast, "The Ordination of Women: Acceptable Doctrinal Development?" *Review for Religious* 37 (1978): 905–19, applying Newman's criteria of doctrinal development; Catholic Biblical Association, "Women and Priestly Ministry: the New Testament Evidence," *Catholic Biblical Quarterly* 41 (1979): 608–13; Janice G. Raymond, ed., *The Trans-sexual Empire* (Beacon Press, 1979); Jerome D. Quinn, "New Testament Data on Ordination," *America* 143 (1980): 306–7, answered by Madelaine Boucher, "New Data on Ordination: A Rejoinder,"

were almost unqualifiedly negative in tone.⁴ As the Swidlers' collection developed these major problems, they can be reduced to four main areas:⁵

First are questions about the authority of the document. *Inter Insigniores* was only a document of a Roman Congregation, although commissioned and approved *in forma communi* by the pope, and it concluded with a rather cautious formula that it "judges it necessary to recall that

America 143 (1980): 303–4; Stephen Long, "The Metaphysics of Gender and Sacramental Priesthood," *Louvain Studies* 10 (1984): 41–59; Joan Chittister, *Winds of Change: Women Challenge Church* (Kansas City, MO: Sheed and Ward, 1986); David Power, O.M.I, "Representing Christ in Community and Sacrament," in *Being a Priest Today* ed. Donald J. Goergen, O.P. (Collegeville, MN: The Liturgical Press, 1992), 97–123; Johanna Schiessl, "The Priesthood of Women," *Theology Digest* 41 (1994): 141–45; and Fergus Kerr, O.P., "Discipleship of Equals or Nuptial Mystery," *New Blackfriars* 75 (1994): 344–54.

4. A number of women, however, none of whom are represented in *Woman Priests,* published articles which argued that *Inter Insigniores* was sound and by no means anti-woman, e.g., Edith Black, "Why Women Cannot Be Ordained: Biblical Argument," *Homiletic and Pastoral Review* 80 (1980): 21–31; Marie M. Brown, "The Fallacy of the Fempriest," *Homiletic and Pastoral Review* 82 (1981): 18–25; Joyce A. Little, "Women and Ordination," *Faith and Reason* 13 (1987): 266–82; Mary F. Rousseau, "The Ordination of Women: A Philosopher's Viewpoint," *The Way* 21 (1981): 211–24, and "Real Fems Don't Go to Church," *Catholicism in Crisis* 2 (Feb. 1984): 17–22; "Pope John Paul II's Letter on the Dignity and Vocation of Women: The Call To *Communio*," *Communio* 16 (1989): 212–32. See also citations to Sara Butler in note 13 below. Donald J. Keefe, S.J., "Sacramental Sexuality and the Ordination of Women," *Communio* 5 (1978): 228–51 "The Sacrament of the Good Creation: Prolegomena to the Discussion of Ordination," *Faith and Reason* 9 (1983): 128–41 "Gender, History and Liturgy in the Catholic Church," *Review for Religious* 46 (1987): 866–81, and "The Present Situation of Eucharistic Theology," *Faith and Reason* 14 (1988): 255–322, has also supported the magisterial position on the basis of his own studies of the relation of the sacraments to the doctrine of creation and salvation history.

5. Joseph A. DiNoia, O.P., "Women's Ordination: Can the Debate Be Revived?" *New Blackfriars* 59 (1978): 488–97, gives an objective analysis of the theological issues, and points out that a major problem is that the Bible gives no explicit explanation of the tradition (p. 495). Alberic Stacpoole, O.S.B., "Ordination of Women: Two Traditions," *Month,* 2nd n.s. 18 (1985): 15–23, is a good history of the Anglican and Catholic controversies; while Arlene A. Swidler, complains that the work of the Anglican commission on women's ordination has been ignored by Catholics, "Ecumenism and the Lack Thereof," in *Women Priests: A Catholic Commentary,* 65–69. For another survey see Sandra M. Schneiders, I.H.M., "Theological Trends: Ministry and Ordination II," *The Way* 21 (1981): 137–49. See also Eric Meyer, C.P., "Are There Theological Reasons Why the Church Should Not Ordain Women Priests?" *Review for Religious* 34 (1975): 957–67; John R. Breslin, "Let My Sisters Go," *America* 131 (1979): 333–34, who reviews the works of van der Meer and George A. Tavard; and Peter Hebbelthwaite's writings on the work of Peter Hünermann in *Theologische Quartalschrift* 3 (1993) and *The Tablet* 248 (1994): 332, show the progress of the debate.

the church, in fidelity to the example of the Lord, does not consider herself authorized to admit women to priestly ordination."[6] But John Paul II's *Ordinatio Sacerdotalis* of 1994,[7] concludes:

6. On the authority of *Inter Insigniores* see Karl Rahner, "Priestertum der Frau?" Rahner was the director of Haye van der Meer, *Women Priests in the Catholic Church: A Theological-Historical Investigation,* still the most thorough defense of women's ordination, but it should be noted that according to Helmut Moll, in *The Church and Women,* 162 n. 1, Haye van der Meer has now retracted the thesis of his very influential work in favor of women's ordination. Rahner considered the question still too immature for a definitive decision, especially in view of the difficulty of the historical conditioning of Jesus' actions in choosing the apostles. Francis G. Morrisey, "The Juridical Significance of the Declaration," in *Women Priests: A Catholic Commentary,* 19–22, and Francine Cardman, "Non-Conclusive Arguments: Therefore, Non-Conclusion?" in ibid., 92–98, charge that the declaration was voluntaristic and fideistic and ignored the newer views that change in the church begins with practice, which in the case of ministry by women is already taking place. Mary Ellen Sheehan, "Important Clarifications on Argument and Authority," in ibid., 239–43, asks whether the official commentary, based as it is on arguments of convenience, has any theological authority. Anne Carr, "Authentic Theology in Service of the Church," in ibid., 221–26, seems to me to take an extreme position when she says, "The theological position maintained by the ordinary magisterium is as authoritative as the power of theological argumentation which supports it" (p. 222), and argues that *Inter Insigniores* is not authentic because: (1) it was not the result of mature theological dialogue; (2) it makes no reference to the report of the Pontifical Biblical Commission which concluded that the biblical evidence is inconclusive; (3) the "tradition" on which it rests its case arose from the notion of female inferiority; (4) it makes no use of findings of modern human sciences; and (5) it takes no account of our contemporary experience. Carr thus reduces the authority of the ordinary magisterium to that of theological expertise, a position difficult to reconcile with Vatican II, *Lumen Gentium,* no. 25, which says that even the ordinary teaching of the papal magisterium requires submission of mind and will. As Sullivan in his article says, this submission "does not mean that one must agree that the arguments given for this judgment are convincing" (p. 768); hence its authority does not rest on theological arguments but on our faith in the Holy Spirit's guidance of the church through its legitimate pastors. See also Bernhard Häring, "Living with the Pope's 'No'," *The Tablet* 248 (1994): 736.

7. Cited in Chapter I note 1 above. The editors of *The Tablet* requested Francis Sullivan, S.J., a recognized specialist on the authority of various kinds of magisterial teaching to evaluate this document. In an article "New Claims for the Pope," *The Tablet* 248 (1994): 767–69, he draws the following conclusions: (1) *Ordinatio Sacerdotalis* is authoritative teaching not merely disciplinary; (2) it requires assent of the mind; (3) it is not proposed as a dogma of faith and hence is in principle reformable; (4) it seems to be stronger than an encyclical or other such teaching belonging to the third class of teaching mentioned in the oath of fidelity now required of some church office-holders, which requires a religious submission of will and intellect; (5) it seems to pertain to the second class of teaching, which is the "definitive" and pertains to the secondary object of faith as "required for the safeguarding or exposition of what is contained in the deposit of faith," which requires "unconditional assent," but is not as such divinely revealed, although according to

Wherefore, in order that all doubt may be removed regarding a matter of great importance, a matter which pertains to the church's divine constitution itself, in virtue of my ministry of confirming the brethren (cf. Lk 22:32) I declare that the church has no authority whatsoever to confer priestly ordination on women and that this judgment is to be definitively held by all the church's faithful (no. 4).

This statement seems to indicate that the pope intends to exercise his apostolic authority ("in virtue of my ministry of confirming my brethren"), to do so in a definitive manner ("to be held definitively by all the church's faithful"), and about a matter of faith and morals ("a matter which pertains to the church's divine constitution itself"). Hence, it is difficult not to see in this what the "The Instruction on the Ecclesial Vocation of the Theologian"[8] characterizes as follows: "When the magisterium proposes 'in a definitive way' truths concerning faith and morals, which even if not directly revealed are nevertheless strictly and intimately connected with revelation, these must be firmly accepted and held" (no. 23).

The second major area of criticism of *Inter Insigniores* was its arguments and those of its official commentary drawn from Scripture. The critics, relying chiefly on historical-critical exegesis, questioned whether it is possible to prove from the Bible that Jesus willed to exclude women from priesthood, or even that he willed there should be a priesthood, or a form of sacramental ordination by which it was conferred. Rather the historical evidence, it was alleged, shows the priesthood as a gradual development subject to change by the consensus of the Christian community, and hence to the admission of women to priesthood in conformity with our contemporary ethics. Biblical guidance, therefore, cannot be sought in the historical customs of the early church, but only in Jesus' inclusive call to discipleship of all people without sexual or ethnic or social discrimination.

---

a statement of Cardinal Ratzinger it is "irreformable" yet does not involve papal infallibility; (6) it is not clear that it is yet an act of the *universal* ordinary magisterium, because the bishops have not yet concurred on its definitive character; (7) it seems without precedent for a pope to claim that an exercise of the *ordinary* magisterium can be "definitive" in the sense of "irreformable" and requiring "unconditional assent." For further discussion see Appendix 3, below. For the witness of the Orthodox churches on this question as a *traditio divina* see "Conclusion of the Inter-Orthodox Consultation on Women and the Question of Ordination, (Rhodes, Oct. 30–Nov. 7, 1988)," *Ecumenical Trends* 18 (1989): 36–42. This consultation included representatives of fourteen autocephalus churches and fifty theologians, eighteen of whom were women). Also see Thomas Hopko, ed., *Women and the Priesthood,* and Michael A. Fahey "Eastern Orthodoxy and the Ordination of Women," in *Women Priests: A Catholic Commentary,* 107–13.

8. Sacred Congregation for the Doctrine of the Faith, "Instruction on the Ecclesial Vocation of the Theologian," *Origins* 20 (July 5, 1990): 117–27.

The third criticism of *Inter Insigniores* raised by critics in the Swidlers' collection concerned the argument from tradition, which was generally considered to be the fundamental one in the "Declaration." The critics were not persuaded by this argument because they believed it was not based on the "will of Christ" but on the concept of the inferiority and subordination of women prevalent in Jewish, pagan, and medieval culture, like the concept of the naturalness of slavery, both of which concepts Vatican II and even this very "Declaration" have repudiated. This major criticism was backed by various kinds of historical data to show the sources of this erroneous understanding of gender and its inconsistency with certain incidents in the life of Jesus, and the early and medieval church.

The fourth problem area was the appeal of the magisterium to the notion that a priest must be male in order to act *in persona Christi*, as an image of Christ. Here several questions were raised. Can so important a matter of justice rest on mere "symbolism," especially sexual symbolism of so primitive and dualistic a type? Is not symbolism inherently polyvalent and constantly shifting with the culture?[9] Is not the priest the rep-

---

9. Many of the contributors to *Women Priests: A Catholic Commentary* attacked the symbolism argument of the official commentary on *Inter Insigniores*. Thus Sidney Callahan, "Misunderstanding of Sexuality and Resistance to Women Priests," 291–94, claims it exaggerated the theological importance of a primitive dichotomy. Michael A. Fahey "Eastern Orthodoxy and the Ordination of Women," 107–13, while pleading for "flexibility" explains the support for this symbolism in the Orthodox churches. Dorothy Irvin, "'Omnia Analogia Claudet'," 271–77, argues the polyvalence of symbolism and criticizes the declaration's interpretation of biblical symbols, especially the Song of Songs, which is simply love songs, perhaps composed by women. Carol Stuhlmueller, C.P., "Bridegroom: a Biblical Symbol of Union, Not Separation," 278–83 says that Christ is called a bridegroom to signify the union of Christ with the church, not the exclusion of women from full participation in the church. Sonya A. Quitsland, "In the Image of Christ," 260–70, argues that since woman was created in the image of God, she can also image Christ, that we should avoid literalism in symbolic interpretation and leave symbols open to the future, and, finally, that Christ was male only to be a servant not a master. Pauline Turner and Bernard Cooke, "Women Can Have a Natural Resemblance to Christ," 258–59, argue that the resemblance to Christ is in the gift of self, best symbolized not by man or woman, but by their relationship. Elsewhere, some writers have been more sympathetic to the argument from symbolism; see Quigley, "Male and Female Symbolism in Catholic Faith," *Homiletic and Pastoral Review* 87 (1987): 27–32 and 50–53; and John Garvey, "Gender and Religious Symbols," *Commonweal* 115 (1988): 615–16, and "Women's Ordination: Another Go at the Arguments," *Commonweal* 117 (1990): 40–41. To my mind the most stimulating contribution is that of James P. Grace, "Symbol and Priesthood," *America* 153 (1985): 233–35, who makes use of Charles S. Peirce's theory of three levels of symbolization, and says that the declaration neglects the third aspect of a symbol by which it effectively causes change. I would reply, however, that the declaration certainly sees the sacraments as *effective* signs.

resentative of the Christian community of both sexes, rather than the male Christ? To be a representative of the people, need the priest be an "image" of Christ? And if so is this likeness one of gender, or rather of faith, love, and compassion? Is it not much more significant that the Son assumed human nature to redeem both women and men than that he assumed masculinity? How do we determine what is of the unchanging "substance" of the sacraments, which in fact have historically been changed in so many ways?[10]

The numerous critiques that have appeared since the Swidlers' commentary have covered much the same grounds, so it is reasonable to suppose that the major theological problems which the "Declaration" raises have already been mapped out and were known to John Paul II, before he made his recent "definitive" pronouncement. It seems to me that the chief questions that make this pronouncement hard to accept for many theologians reduce to two: Does the traditional formula according to which a priest acts *in persona Christi* exclude women's ordination? Is this traditional exclusion of women from ordination really a *traditio divina*?

Some readers of my book in manuscript have, therefore, suggested that I address in this appendix these two issues more directly as they have been formulated by some recent articles.

The Traditional Meaning of in persona Christi

Fr. Edward J. Kilmartin, S.J., in "Apostolic Office: Sacrament of Christ,"[11] denies that the traditional phrase *in persona Christi et ecclesiae* means that the priest *directly* represents Christ, and contends instead that the priest directly represents the church, and only indirectly Christ.[12] Since

10. Paul J. LeBlanc, "Substantive Changes in Sacraments?" in *Women Priests: A Catholic Commentary*, 216–20, gives many examples of changes in the sacraments and asks whether ordaining women is any more "substantive" than were these changes.

11. *Theological Studies* 36 (1975): 243–64. See also Kilmartin, "Bishop and Presbyter as Representatives of the Church and Christ," in *Women Priests: A Catholic Commentary*, 295–302, in which he argues that *Inter Insigniores* is based on scholastic theology and its "concept of the priest functioning as an index of Christ in the Eucharist is in complete isolation from his index function as confessing believer and representative of pastoral office of the apostolic Church" (p. 299). Bernard Cooke and Pauline Turner, "Women in the Sacramental Priesthood," in *Women Priests: A Catholic Commentary*, 258, give a similar criticism.

12. Kilmartin says, "The apostolic office is *sacramentum* of the Church united in faith and love, which in turn as *res* is also *sacramentum* of Christ and the Spirit, the *res tantum*. In this way apostolic office is correctly ordered to the Church, sacrament of Christ, and to Christ, sacrament of God" ("Apostolic Office," 260). For Augustine and Aquinas (cf. ST III, q. 66, etc.), however, the *res tantum* of a sacrament is the special grace that Christ confers, and Christ is the *res et sacra-*

a woman can represent the church just as well as a man, she can be ordained. This argument is also adopted by Mary Schaefer.[13]

Going even beyond Kilmartin, Dennis Michael Ferrara in "Representation or Self-Effacement: The Axiom *In Persona Christi* in St. Thomas and the Magisterium"[14] claims that the phrase *in persona Christi*, though it can mean that a priest presiding at the Eucharist or other sacraments is a "representative" of Christ—like Christ's ambassador, John the Baptist—it does not imply that a priest is in any way a "representation" of Christ. Hence, argues Ferrara, since no "representation" or likeness to Christ is required, Christ's maleness is not relevant, and a woman can fill the role of "representative" or ambassador just as well as a man. Ferrara, admits that in a few texts St. Thomas Aquinas seems to use *in persona Christi* in a representational sense, but dismisses these as marginal, claiming that Aquinas generally uses the phrase to refer not to the priest's ministerial sacramental role, but to pastoral governance, or "regitive-hierarchical" power in which symbolism (representation) is irrelevant. Furthermore, Ferrara tries to show that Aquinas, in spite of his notorious acceptance of Aristotle's views on female inferiority, surprisingly clears the way for women's ordination by insisting that the priest's sacramental causality is purely instrumental and hence "apophatic" (negative) and ministerial, not a dramatic representation. This is clearly evident, Ferrara says, from the rite of the supreme sacrament, the Eucharist, in which,

---

mentum, i.e., the external sacramental sign *directly* signifies Christ and *indirectly* (Kilmartin's term, but better *mediately*) through Christ signifies some special grace. Applied to priesthood, this would seem to mean that the priest by reason of the priestly "character" immediately signifies Christ the Head (*ST* III q. 63, a. 3, ad 2) and Christ signifies the church, i.e., the head signifies the body of which it is the head.

13. Mary Schaefer, "Ordaining Women," with response by Sara Butler, *Worship* 63 (1989): 467–73. Schaefer wrote in answer to an earlier article by Butler, "Second Thoughts on Ordaining Women," *Worship* 63 (1989): 157–65. The debate was continued by Bishop Kenneth Untener, "The Ordination of Women: Can the Horizons Widen?" *Worship* 65 (1991): 50–59), and was answered in the same issue of *Worship* by Bishop John R. Sheets (pp. 451–61), Charles R. Meyer (pp. 256–62), and Sara Butler (pp. 263–68). Butler later published, "The Priest as Sacrament of Christ the Bridegroom," *Worship* 66 (1992): 498–517, to which Elisabeth Picken responded in "Christ is Bridegroom: The Priest Must be Male," *Worship* 67 (1993): 269–79. Butler was editor of the *CTSA Research Report: Women in Church and Society* (Mahwah, NJ: Darlington Seminary, 1978), which urged women's ordination, but now supports the magisterial position, according to her "Second Thoughts."

14. *Theological Studies* 55 (1994): 195–224. One might wonder why the author calls this a theological "axiom," i.e. a first principle? Is it not a theological conclusion derived from a principle, namely, the article of faith that Christ, true God and true Man, has offered himself for us (i.e., is our priest)?

according to Aquinas, the priest for validity need do nothing but simply narrate the words of Christ, an event of the past in which the priest has personally taken no part: "And the point I am making is that in the formal constitution of the sign the priest's role is not representational but apophatic; in the quotation of Christ's words of institution by way of anamnesis, the 'I' of the priest steps aside in order to let the 'I' of Christ appear, the *persona* of the priestly narrator *gives way visibly* to the *persona* of Christ."[15]

In replying to Kilmartin's and Ferrara's arguments, I note first that for his interpretation of the traditional phrase *in persona Christi capitis et in persona ecclesiae* Ferrara relies largely on the careful historical study of Bernard Dominique Marliangeas, *Clés pour une théologie du ministère in persona Christi, in persona ecclesiae,* with an important supporting preface by the noted ecclesiologist Cardinal Yves Congar.[16] Yet this work,

15. Ferrara, "Representation or Self-Effacement," 213. Some argue that the priest acts *in persona Christi* because in consecrating the Eucharist he says, "This is *my* Body," "This is *my* Blood." Others object to this by citing two important facts: First, the anaphorai of the *didache* and the Syrian rite of Addai and Mari do not contain these words. Second, the Orthodox churches, although their anaphorai do include these words, attribute the consecration not to them but to the *epiclesis* or invocation of the Holy Spirit. In reply it should be noted that it is not certain the thanksgiving prayer of the *Didache* was a eucharistic anaphora. Even if it was, the same can be said of it as F. Macomber says of the Anaphora of Addai and Mari: "There may be no formal Institution Narrative and no independent *anamnesis* as a separate section of the anaphora, but it cannot be denied that the substance of both such elements is clearly present in the anaphora in such a way as to suggest that it is of primary importance in determining the nature of what is being done. Botte . . . in his examination of the *anamnesis* of Hippolytus draws attention to three elements: a recollection of the Institution, the enumeration of the saving mysteries, and a prayer of offering. All three elements are present in the Anaphora of Addai and Mari. The distinctive feature is that they are mentioned indirectly in the course of setting the intercessions within the context of the eucharistic celebration, and that they are not put together to form an *anamnesis* as a distinct section with the anaphora" (F. Macomber, "The Ancient Form of the Anaphora of the Apostles," in *East of Byzantium: Syria and Armenia in the Formative Period,* ed. Nina G. Garsoian, T. F. Mathews, and Robert W. Thomson [Washington, DC: Dumbarton Oaks Center for Byzantine Studies, 1982], 73–88). See also A. Gelston, *The Eucharistic Prayer of Addai and Mari* (Oxford: Clarendon Press, 1992). As for the question of the *epiclesis,* it seems generally admitted today that all the traditional eucharistic prayers in some manner invoke the Holy Spirit in the celebration of all the sacraments and that this invocation is joined with the prayer of Christ who acts always through his Holy Spirit. Thus the *in persona Christi,* while it is made explicit by the "words of institution" and hence these are found in almost all forms of the eucharistic anaphora, does not depend on these words as such, but on the three elements enumerated by Dom Botte.

16. (Paris: Beauchesne, 1978). See also Leo Scheffczyk, "Die Christusrepräsentation als Wesenmoment des Priesteramtes," *Catholica* 27 (1973): 293–311. I am grateful to Brother J. Reid Perkins-Buzo, O.P., for his research on this topic.

far from supporting Ferrara's argument, refutes it. Marliangeas shows that historically *in persona Christi* never meant that the priest acts as a mere "delegate" (representative) of the church, but only that he is "chosen" from among its members to be ordained by a bishop in the apostolic succession so as to be able to act as an instrument of Christ whom he represents as a sacramental instrument. Congar calls attention with approval to the teaching of the Eastern church that the priest is an "icon" or image of Christ whom he makes symbolically present.

For Ferrara, however, the fact, emphasized by Aquinas, that the ministerial priest plays a merely instrumental role in total subordination to Christ's principal causality, is the very reason that priesthood is "apophatic" and cannot be representational. It is also the reason that his sacramental role is so contrasted to his "regitive-hierarchical role." In the former, the priest is humbly transparent to Christ, in the latter he occupies an office of power and prestige.

This interpretation is a reversal of Aquinas's thought, as is evident from the texts collected in Marliangeas's book. For Aquinas, as for Vatican II, there can be no opposition between the priest's "regitive-hierarchical role" as pastor, his role as a preacher and teacher of the Gospel, and his role in the sacraments, precisely because all these priestly roles are exercised *in persona Christi* as instruments of Christ. Nor is there any contradiction between being a representative of Christ as his instrument and representing Christ himself. A sacrament is an instrument of Christ which causes what it signifies, and it signifies by *representing*—of course in an analogous, symbolic way, not literally—both Christ, who is the principal agent of whom the priest is a minister, and the grace which it effects.

The act of baptism, for example, represents both the grace of cleansing from sin and the Christ who washes us from sin in his blood.[17] Moreover,

17. A number of authors fault *Inter Insigniores* for seeming to ignore the dignity of the baptized laity as images of Christ. Thus Robert W. Hovda, *Women Priests: A Catholic Commentary,* 251–52, argues that the Rites of Initiation "are the most obvious indication of where faith stands on the issue of identification with Christ," and that the "ministries of presbyter and bishop are minor compared with baptism." Denise C. Hogan, "Reflections on Discipleship," ibid., 284–90, argues that "discipleship" not gender should be the criterion for ordination. Jean M. Higgins, "Fidelity in History" ibid., 85–91, points out that in spite of the early church's sexist attitudes it allowed women to baptize. In any case, she says, the fact that early canon law opposed women's ordination is no criterion now. Eric Doyle, "The Question of Women Priests and the Argument *In Persona Christi,*" *Irish Theological Quarterly* 50 (1984): 212–21, also argues that since women can confer baptism they must be able to act *in persona Christi;* see also Doyle's "God and the Feminine," *Clergy Review* 56 (1971): 861–67. J. Massyngberde Ford, "The 'Ordination' of Queens," in *Women Priests: A Catholic Commentary,* 303–9, suggests that women should be made cardinals and discusses the anointing of

a symbol is not an arbitrary sign, but renders present (re-presents) the reality symbolized by a kind of identification of sign and signified. It is in this sense that the Eucharist is an *anamnesis* (commemoration) enabling priest and congregation to participate here and now in the unrepeatable act of Christ, not a mere historical narration of that event as past.[18]

Because the sacraments are effective symbols which are used by Christ as his instruments, they must be understood in terms of Christ who as the One Priest is their principal cause. Christ is the Mediator who, on the one hand, as Son of God offers himself to the church as the life-empowering gift of the Father and, on the other, through his incarnation as one of us and Head of the church which is his Body, offers himself along with us to the Father. While it is true, as these critics of *Inter Insigniores* insist, that the priest can act *in persona Christi* only because he is a minister of the church, it is equally and even more fundamentally true that he can act in *persona ecclesiae* only because the church has first been created by Christ and given its life by him through the apostolic preaching, governance, and sacramental action of priests as *his* ministers.

Thus to argue that women can be ordained since Christ's gender is irrelevant to acting *in persona Christi,* because the priest represents the church rather than Christ (as Kilmartin argues), or because the priest does not represent Christ at all but is merely his representative (as Ferrara argues) cannot be supported from the text of Aquinas, and in fact is without solid theological foundation. Of course the failure of these arguments for

---

queens which resembles an ordination. Helen M. Wright, "Diversity in Roles and Solidarity in Christ," *Women Priests: A Catholic Commentary,* 244–48, points out that Christ offers himself for all of humanity, not just for males, and as Divine Person not as a male. E. Ann Matter, "Innocent III and the Keys to the Kingdom of Heaven," *Women Priests: A Catholic Commentary,* 145–51, rejects arguments based on the concept of Mary as the New Eve, because Eve's sin is used to subordinate women. These authors do not explain why they are not satisfied with the traditional answers to these difficulties: the reason even an atheist can confer baptism is because it is *necessary* in a way no other sacrament is; the priest is a servant of the baptized not their rival in dignity; the priest represents Christ not just as true God but as the New Adam, spiritual father of both his male and female children; priesthood should not be confused with other offices such as being a cardinal or a queen; the New Eve *cancels* the subordination of women resulting from Eve's sin.

18. The biblical exegete Jerome Murphy-O'Connor, commenting on St. Paul's tradition of the eucharistic words of institution, which Ferrara argues are simply a recital of a past event, says that "authentic remembrance is concerned with the past only insofar as it is constitutive of the present and a summons to the future. What he [Paul] desires to evoke is the active remembrance of total commitment to Christ which makes the past real in the present, thus releasing a power capable of shaping the future" (*1 Corinthians* [Wilmington, DE: Michael Glazier, 1979], 112).

women's ordination does not settle the debate, but they enable us to focus on the real question, which can be formulated as follows: Since the priest acts both *in persona Christi et ecclesiae,* but most fundamentally *in persona Christi,* is Christ's maleness essential to the symbolism of the sacraments in which the priest ministers as Christ's iconic instrument?[19]

Tradition and the Non-Ordination of Women

Hervé Legrand, O.P., in "*Traditio perpetua servata?* The Non-ordination of Women: Tradition or Simply an Historical Fact?"[20] seems to agree with the contention of Kilmartin and Ferrara that the priest acts *in persona Christi* only because he acts *in persona ecclesiae.*[21] But since the position of *Inter Insigniores* does not rest primarily on this point, but rather on the fact that the church has never ordained women, it is this historic fact that Legrand examines. He admits that there is a very ancient tradition against women's ordination, but is it "a *traditio divina*"? He states the criteria that need to be met: "The non-ordination of women is part of the Tradition only if such a tradition has a foundation in Scripture itself or, at least, in the apostolic period. One must be able to connect it to the will of Christ which would be known, at the very least, by these two means."[22]

Legrand and Ferrara are both of the opinion that the magisterium contradicts itself when on the one hand, because of its present defense of the equality of the sexes, it rejects the old arguments against women's ordination based on the theory of women's subordination to men, yet on the other hand, it appeals to a "tradition" which was in fact based on that very same theory.[23] Thus Ferrara writes that the "theological tradition

19. As for the objection that if it were theologically significant that the Word took male rather than female flesh, then according to the patristic dictum that "what is not assumed is not redeemed" women would not be redeemed, see Chapter III note 71 above.

20. *Worship* 65 (1991): 482–508.

21. Legrand had argued in a previous article, "The Presidency of the Eucharist in the Ancient Church," much as did Kilmartin, that the priest acts directly *in persona ecclesiae* only because he is head of the community. But it is necessary also to see that although it is the one who presides over the community that presides over the Eucharist, to preside legitimately over the Christian community requires apostolic authorization which is conveyed only by ordination. This is the point that the exegete Pierre Grelot so thoroughly documents in his, *Église et Ministères.* See also Legrand, "View on the Ordination of Women, *Origins* 6 (Jan. 6, 1977): 467.

22. "*Traditio perpetua servata,*" 482.

23. R. A. Norris, Jr., "The Ordination of Women and the 'Maleness' of Christ," *Anglican Theological Review,* Supplementary Series, no. 6 (June 1976): 69–80, had already claimed that the *in persona Christi* was novel, and that the tradition really rested on the notion of female submission. His article seems to have influenced many Catholic writers.

prior to Vatican II knows only one intrinsic argument against the ordination of women, the 'faulty' argument from women's inferior status, an argument linked . . . to the priest's hierarchical rather than sacramental role."[24]

Richard Viladesau, in an especially well-crafted article, "Could Jesus Have Ordained Women: Reflections on *Mulieris Dignitatem*,"[25] agrees on the contradictory character of John Paul II's position and further shows that the pope's historical argument for this tradition rests on the following series of assumptions, which have been thoroughly undermined by modern historical scholarship: that Jesus completely transcended the mentality of his times as regards women; yet he only chose men for his Twelve apostles, with the purpose of freely excluding women. That he did so without regard to the customs of his time, and made them priests, whom he commanded to celebrate the Eucharist. That he did so with the purpose of revealing a timeless truth about gender roles. That today's priesthood is identical with that of the Twelve.

Like Viladesau, Legrand refers to biblical scholars who say that Jesus, who limited his own mission to Israel, chose men as the Twelve only in order to symbolize Israel's twelve tribes.[26] Hence, once the Gospel was

---

24. "Representation or Self-Effacement," 718. Note how Ferrara again tries to oppose the "hierarchical" role of the priest to his sacramental role.

25. *Thought* 67 (1992): 5–20.

26. Critics often fault *Inter Insigniores* for arguing from the will of Christ to institute the church and its sacraments and for claiming that the bishops are the successors of the Twelve Apostles, claiming this has been undermined by modern biblical scholarship (see Chapter III note 32 above). Yet here is the nuanced conclusion of Raymond E. Brown, *Responses to 101 Questions on the Bible* (New York: Paulist, 1990), an exegete whose commitment to the historical-critical method is unimpeachable: "The church is no mere human institution, nor was its origin simply the result of a perceptive idea on the part of Jesus' followers. They understood their calling believers together into a community was a direct continuation of what Jesus had done when he called them together and sent them out to continue his work. For that reason I insist on retaining the notion that Christ founded the church" (p. 106); and, he continues, "institution by Christ means that those actions we call sacraments are specifications and applications of a power that during his ministry and after his resurrection Jesus Christ gave to his church in and through the apostles—a power containing what was necessary to make God's rule or kingdom triumph over evil by sanctifying the lives of people from birth to death. The sacraments, we are saying, are not inventions of the church but are part of Christ's plan. I find no conflict between a modern biblical approach and 'institution by Christ' so understood" (p. 107); and, finally he notes, "By the last third of the [first] century and perhaps even slightly earlier, we find the name 'bishops' for those who played a role of leadership in some communities. In the earlier stage there were plural bishops or overseers in an individual community; in the later there was the custom of having only one bishop per community. Therefore, one may very correctly say that the bishops took over the pastoral care of communities

extended to the Gentiles, the gender of the Twelve was no longer ecclesiologically relevant.[27] Jesus himself, Legrand thinks, taught what feminist

---

founded by the apostolic evangelization and thus were successors of the apostles. . . . Apostolic succession concerns the fact that the bishops eventually took over the pastoral tasks of the apostles; it does not involve *how* the early bishops were chosen or appointed. We know little about that, not even being certain there was a formal action designating them. . . . Eventually, of course, the church developed a regularized pattern of selection and ordination of bishops, and from the third century on that was universally followed" (p. 120; see also note). The distinguished French exegete, Pierre Grelot, *Église et Ministères*, comes to a similar conclusion.

27. The claim of *Inter Insigniores* that Jesus ordained the Twelve male apostles and that the bishops are their successors, attacked by Legrand and also by Ida Raming, "'The Twelve Apostles were Men,'" *Theology Digest* 29 (1981): 21–25, is central to the criticism of many of the writers in *Women Priests: A Catholic Commentary*. Elisabeth Schüssler-Fiorenza, "The Apostleship of Women in Early Christianity" (pp. 135–40), points out that only Luke calls the Twelve "apostles" but elsewhere in the New Testament others than the "Twelve" are called "apostles"; that it is applied in the New Testament to witnesses of Jesus' ministry and resurrection, including women, or to those having the missionary charism, including a woman Junia (Rom 16:7) or to apostles of churches—Phoebe at Cenchrae is called a *diakonos* (Rom 16:1). That the text of Rom 16:7 really does speak of a woman, Junia and not a male apostle is argued at length by Bernadette Brooten, "Junia . . . Outstanding Among the Apostles, (Romans 16:7)." Schüssler-Fiorenza, "The Twelve" (pp. 114–22), adds that the church has ordained deaconesses without seeking to justify this action by proving this to be the will of Christ. Why not then ordain women priests, even if the will of Christ is unknown? Sandra M. Schneiders, "Did Jesus Exclude Women from Priesthood? (pp. 227–33), claims that the Twelve were not priests, but had only the function of representing redeemed Israel, and therefore their choice does not indicate the will of Christ for the future church: Jesus chose only Jews as the Twelve, and aren't ethnic differences more significant than gender? Yet the church departed from Christ's will and chose gentiles as apostles, so why can't it now choose women as priests? Furthermore, how can we decide what elements of Jesus' teaching still bind us, when the Pontifical Biblical Commission admits that the biblical evidence on ordination is inconclusive, and there is no consensus among theologians nor the faithful? Clearly the church did not require a special revelation to admit women to baptism, nor was it limited by Christ's will when formerly it reserved the eucharistic chalice to the clergy, nor in its recent permission for alcoholic priests to use grape-juice not wine. Mary Rose D'Angelo, "Women and the Earliest Church: Reflecting on the Problématique of Christ and Culture" (pp. 191–201), also rejects the argument from the Twelve, because Jesus was conditioned by the culture of his times, and Paul became even more conformed to it. While the New Testament furnishes no conclusive evidence about what Jesus' thought about women and ordination, he did treat women as equals within the limits of his culture, so we can also extend this to our present situation of complete gender equality. J. Massyngberde Ford, "Women Leaders in the New Testament" (pp. 132–34), also argues that there is no saying by Jesus that proves his will to subordinate women or exclude them from ordination. The only participant in *Woman Priests: A Catholic Commentary* who

exegetes have called the "equality of discipleship," but the church soon began to compromise with pagan culture's subordination of women and thus came to exclude them from leadership roles.[28] This was intensified

---

speaks favorably of *Inter Insigniores* is Thomas P. Rausch, (pp. 123–31), who argues: the declaration is correct in building its case on Jesus' call of the Twelve to special authority among his disciples; this was "ordination" in the sense that it was investment with apostolic authority and empowerment to celebrate the Eucharist and forgive sins; the issue of whether there was a "laying on hands" is secondary, but it is mentioned in the case of the Seven (Acts 6:6); the Pontifical Biblical Commission did say that the New Testament does not conclusively settle the question on critical-historical grounds, but *Inter Insigniores* also took into consideration theological principles; and *Inter Insigniores* was not a definitive decision. In my opinion Rausch correctly pointed out that questions of tradition in the strong sense are ultimately questions of the succession of apostolic authority, not of historic reconstructions.

28. Rosemary Radford Ruether, "Women Priests and Church Tradition," *Women Priests: A Catholic Commentary*, 234–38, argues against the claim of *Inter Insigniores* to an "unbroken tradition," on the grounds that Jesus was not a priest, that there have in fact been women in leadership positions in the church, that the Protestant churches ordain women, and that the church can and has changed its position on important issues such as slavery. In the same volume, Madeleine Boucher, "Women and the Apostolic Community," (pp. 152–55), argues that Jesus was bound by customs of his time, and only broke with them to stress ethical values against cultic values, while Paul never claims that his anti-feminist views were Jesus' teaching. Christians should break the "constraints of tradition," which are merely human, and follow principles of inclusive love and liberation. Adela Yarbro Collins, "The Ministry of Women in the Apostolic Generation" (pp. 159–66), asks whether we can even speak of "ordination" in the apostolic generation. There is no proof that Jesus or Paul ever ordained anyone, or that the exclusion of women was "the will of Christ," rather than the cultural subordination of women. Similarly J. Massyngberde Ford, "Women Leaders in the New Testament" (pp. 132–34), finds no evidence that Jesus taught the subordination or exclusion of women. She argues in a second article, "The Permanent Value of Jesus and the Apostles," that no matter what the apostles actually did about appointing church leaders, we can depart from their precedent, since they evangelized only Jews and attended the synagogue and the temple though later Christians gave up all these practices. She also thinks we ought to ordain the handicapped because they are better images of the Crucified Christ (p. 184). She suggests that it remarkable that the New Testament never forbids priestesses in a culture that was very familiar with them; and argues (p. 188 n. 12) that since the church permits hermaphrodites to be ordained, why not women? (Actually the text she quotes says that persons who are *certo viri*, i.e., certainly males, even if somewhat physically deformed, can be validly ordained). She also concludes that if we follow Hebrews, an authentic New Testament priesthood "according to the priesthood of Melchizedech" should be marked, not by masculinity, but by the "indwelling of indestructible life, the Holy Spirit," based on a better covenant, i.e., human equality, and by holiness, fidelity, compassion, and obedience in suffering.

in the patristic period.[29] Similarly, in his "Representation or Self-Efface-ment," Ferrara tried to show that this subordination theory continued to be defended by the scholastics—since St. Bonaventure and St. Thomas Aquinas[30] relied solely on it to exclude women from ordination—and that it was only the later scholastics who tried to bolster this dubious argument by an appeal to an alleged *traditio divina*.[31] Legrand and Ferrara (writing

29. In *Women Priests: A Catholic Commentary*, Bernard P. Prusak, "Use the Other Door: Stand at the End of the Line" (pp. 81–84), charges the Church Fathers with sexism, and Carolyn S. Osiek, "The Church Fathers and the Ministry of Women" (pp. 75–80), points out that we know of women priests in the patristic period only through the attacks on them as heretics by "orthodox" Church Fathers who may have disapproved of the ordination of women more because it was as-sociated with "heresy" than on principle. The Church Fathers supported their po-sition by theories of feminine subordination and New Testament texts that leaned in this direction.

30. Christopher Kiesling, O.P. (now deceased), "Aquinas on Persons' Repre-sentation in Sacraments," *Women Priests: A Catholic Commentary*, says, "We must not overly emphasize natural resemblance for our understanding of sacra-mental signs. We could miss what is truly the divine choice of what is to be signified. The choice is constitutive of the sacraments and natural resemblances subordinated to it. This choice must be discerned by divine revelation" (pp. 256–57). He also argues that for Aquinas an "image" requires not only a resemblance, but derivation from what is represented (*ST* II, q. 83, a. 1, ad 3). Since a priest does not derive his maleness from Christ, he is not an "image" of Christ by reason of his maleness but by the sacramental character. As for Aquinas's argument that since a woman is in the "state of subjection" she cannot occupy an office of "eminence," it must be said that since a woman can be superior to man in soul, she *can* signify eminence, as she evidently does in performing a baptism. I loved and admired Chris as a brother in religion and a dear friend, and I agree with this interesting article that the act of divine institution is primary in the sacraments and is known only by revelation, while the natural symbolism is secondary. Nevertheless, since all the other sacraments have a natural symbolism, why would ordination be an excep-tion? Again, since the baptized are sons and daughters of Christ through baptismal regeneration, do they not truly "derive" their very persons from Christ, including their gender? Therefore, they can be said to be recreated in his image. Finally, the fact that a woman can be "eminent" in holiness but not a candidate for priesthood is evident from the case of the Blessed Virgin Mary.

31. For more in-depth studies on the views of the great scholastics on this matter see John Hilary Martin, O.P., "The Ordination of Women and the Theo-logians of the Middle Ages," *Escritos del Vedat* 16 (1986): 115–77, and "The Injustice of Not Ordaining Women: A Problem for Medieval Theologians," *Theo-logical Studies* 48 (1987): 303–16, especially note p. 303 n. 1 on the question of the certitude of the tradition. Also Jean Rezette, O.F.M., "La Sacerdoce et la Femme chez Saint Bonaventure," *Antonianum* 51 (1976): 520–27; and A. Bernal, "La Condicion de la mujer en Santo Tomás de Aquino," *Escritos del Vedat* 4 (1974): 285–335; and George H. Tavard, "The Scholastic Doctrine," *Women Priests: A Catholic Commentary*, 99–106. Tavard thinks the scholastics depended on canonical rather than truly theological arguments. A fine recent study is that of Philip Lyndon Reynolds, "Scholastic Theology and the Case Against Women's Or-

before *Ordinatio Sacerdotalis*) conclude that it is not very likely that the magisterium will change its position in the near future, but since it rests on such weak and inconsistent arguments and is put forward in documents that do not have final authoritative status, it is reformable, and indeed should be reformed in order to make the witness of the church more credible in our culture.[32] Legrand quotes a feminist theologian as saying that if the ancient church could change from promoting the equality of women to condoning their subordination in order to avoid the mockery of the pagans, why can it not now, since the times have changed, revive its original support of sexual equality for the same reason?

My response to these arguments can be reduced to three main points: First, have these authors stated correctly how the church verifies a *traditio divina*? If a tradition in the strong sense had to be proved *sola Scriptura*, then the definition of Trent reaffirmed by Vatican II, which said that divine revelation comes to us through "Scripture *and* Tradition" would be empty.[33] Again, if to be apostolic it had to be documented as such by critical-historical methods, then it would not be sacred tradition but scientific history. Were the bishops at Trent able to give biblical or historical proof for the tradition of the canon of the Bible, or the seven sacraments? Can we even establish by these criteria that there was a priesthood in the

---

dination," which I have read in manuscript. He concludes that "the most serious obstacle to women's ordination is a gendered, hierarchical and partly nuptial-system which provides a way of understanding what God is and how his people and his creation are related to him," but he says, "On the contrary, the symbol system is fundamentally hierarchical and assigns to men and to women roles that are respectively superior and inferior. To pretend otherwise is like pretending that royalism is egalitarian," and "There is a real and perhaps insoluble conflict between the archaic symbol system and modern Western beliefs and values." I would rather say that the Christian understanding of sexuality, which is indeed bound up with an "archaic symbol system" is the healing remedy for the profound sickness of our "modern Western beliefs and values."

32. Legrand wrote, "Every professional theologian must recognize the great care which went into writing *Inter Insigniores*. It certainly does not then merit the sometimes violent criticisms it has received." But he concluded that since it was only a document of a Roman congregation, approved by the pope merely *in forma communi*, it was "normative only with minor authority." *Ordinatio Sacerdotalis*, of course, corrects this deficiency (see note 7 above and Appendix 3). Legrand also expresses the opinion that, "the current theological and pastoral climate does not offer much hope for the possibility of change" (p. 507, italicized in the original).

33. Trent, DS no. 1501; Vatican II, *Dei Verbum*, no. 9. Vatican II says, "Hence there exists a close connection and communication between sacred tradition and sacred Scripture. For both of them, flowing from the same divine wellspring, in a certain way merge into a unity and tend toward the same end," but it does not retract Trent's teaching that distinguishes them as in some respects independent witnesses.

primitive church? Yet these dogmas have been infallibly defined, and practicing Catholics have no doubt that their priests administer valid sacraments.

Sacred tradition is not a critical reconstruction of the past, but the *depositum fidei* as it has been transmitted to us in the church and been verified as the church's unfailing witness to the gospel by the concurrence of various kinds of signs (some historical, but others liturgical, moral, and experiential), as well as by the *analogia fidei*. Ultimately such discernment of spirits has to be definitively verified by a magisterial definition.[34]

Second, the exegetical and historical difficulties brought forward by these authors are by no means conclusive.[35] Legrand rejects the magis-

---

34. See the Sacred Congregation for the Doctrine of the Faith, *The Ecclesial Vocation of the Theologian,* May 24, 1990, no. 23 (*Origins* 20 [July 5, 1990]: 117–27). See also Appendix 3.

35. Many of the articles in *Women Priests: A Catholic Commentary* struggle with the Pauline writings: John L. McKenzie, "St Paul's Attitude Toward Women," seems very angry with *Inter Insigniores* and says of it: "The Church is never served well by bad scholarship. I cannot think of any pontifical document which departs so far from the methods of sound learning as this document" (pp. 214–15). McKenzie thinks Paul contradicts himself on the subject, and that the early church was against all "sacralization": "Possibly I am arguing that women are not ordained and men should not be. Paul did fairly well with no consciousness of ordination but a great sense of mission" (p. 213). This view is stated, even more extremely by Harvey Nicolas, "Women's Ordination: A Sideways Look," *Month* 2nd n.s. 24 (1992): 232–34, for whom the very idea of "priesthood" is pagan and should be abandoned by Christians, since its only New Testament basis is Hebrews, which Nicolas understands to say that Christ's death put an end to all priesthood. Thomas L. Thompson, "The Divine Plan of Creation: 1 Cor 11:7 and Gen 2:18–24" (pp. 209–11), thinks that Paul's teaching on women does not rest on the doctrine of creation with its emphasis on gender equality, but on the culturally determined notion of the inferiority of women and on Paul's own personality. Even the creation narratives, he admits, are also culturally conditioned. Juliana Casey, "'Transitory Character' . . . Only in 'Disciplinary Cases of Minor Importance?'" (pp. 202–4), makes the point (with which I would agree) that *Inter Insigniores* too easily dismisses some of Paul's statements that seem to imply feminine inferiority, without trying to explain them. The foregoing authors, it seems to me, reduce Paul's teaching to historical conditioning without first trying to penetrate his *inspired* thought. Mary Ann Getty, "God's Fellow Worker and Apostleship," (pp. 176–82), complains that *Inter Insigniores* (no. 17, as well as the official commentary, note 23) cites the opinion of "exegetes of authority" who think that Paul uses the expression "God's fellow workers" of Apollos, Timothy, and himself as "apostles" (1 Cor 3:9; cf. 1 Thes 3:2), but speaks of other helpers simply as "my fellow workers" (Rom 16:3; Phil 4:2–3). Getty tries to refute this argument, which would imply that women helpers were not apostles. Pheme Perkins "Peter's Pentecost Sermon: A Limitation on Who May Minister . . . ?" (pp. 156–58), also complains about the "lax methodology" of *Inter Insigniores* in citing (no. 15) Acts 2:14 and saying "the proclamation of the fulfillment of the prophecies in Jesus was made only by Peter and the Eleven" with implication that Luke was saying that this re-

terial argument that Jesus' choosing of only the male Twelve as priests and not his own holy Mother is evident of Christ's will for his church. But is he relying for his biblical data on the views of those many historical-critical exegetes who contend that the earthly Jesus did not even found the church? Certainly the contrary is part of the *traditio divina* in the light of which the choice of the male Twelve may very well take on the significance *Inter Insigniores* finds in it. Similarly, the significance of the fact that Mary was not a priest only becomes apparent when her role is seen in the light of the Marian dogmas, which reveal her as the supreme member of the church.

Legrand also explains the New Testament texts that seem to support a certain type of woman's subordination by adopting the views of some feminist exegetes and those who hold the "early catholicism" theory. Such exegetes reconstruct a New Testament church which under the pressures of the pagan milieu quickly deserted an "equal discipleship" supposedly taught by Jesus and adopted an oppressive attitude toward women, allegedly reflected in the "domestic codes" of the deuteropauline epistles. Can this notion of a "canon within a canon" be squared with Vatican II's teaching on the divine inspiration of the whole canon?[36]

Third, we must ask whether it is really established that the magisterium has contradicted itself in rejecting theories of female inferiority while appealing to a tradition based on these very theories. Is it not possible that the tradition rests on an element of truth contained in these theories, which when freed of mistaken inferences of female inferiority, is consistent with the magisterial position? In other words, does the subordination of women to men in certain functional respects logically imply their personal inferiority? Certainly one can quote embarrassing statements of the

---

stricted priesthood to men, when in fact that intention is nowhere expressed in the text. In my view, these exegetical points are highly debatable and to accuse the Vatican documents of "lax methodology" is to suppose that they are proposed as works of biblical scholarship. In fact these documents draw their arguments from current scholarship (Getty does recognize, p. 180 n. 4, that the argument she faults may derive from the noted exegete I. de la Potterie), and such arguments are proposed as merely confirmatory and secondary.

36. I do not mean to say, of course, that historical-critical research is not theologically relevant. It certainly has very important uses, both apologetic and exegetical. The apologetic task is to ask in an objective and honest way whether the teaching of the Bible, tradition, and the church is *certainly* contradicted by historic fact. If that is the case we have a moral obligation to admit that Christianity is a lie, while if it is not, then its claims need to be taken seriously. The exegetical task is to avoid interpretations of the Bible, tradition, and church dogma that lack historical contextuality, e.g. "creationism" or a historical reconstruction of the activity of Jesus which would picture him as writing a ready-made canonical constitution for his church.

Church Fathers and the scholastic theologians that draw that implication of personal inferiority, and today the magisterium distances itself from them.[37] But this is not the whole story.

Ferrara, since the issuance of *Ordinatio Sacerdotalis,* has declared in an article entitled, "Note: The Ordination of Women: Tradition and Meaning,"[38] that unless the Holy See can make it intelligible why Christ would have willed to exclude women it is guilty of "voluntarism" in resting its position on Christ's "will" and of "fideism" in demanding the faithful's assent to its teaching.

The critically tenable conclusion is that unless the magisterium wishes to inculcate a form of fideism on this question, it will have to explain its position, and the mind of Christ himself, with reasons other than have appeared in the tradition of the Church thus far. Any such rationale, as has been noted, will have to address the central theological issue: the alleged link between the sexual difference and the nature of priesthood.[39]

In the foregoing chapters, I have tried to meet that challenge by showing the following: that the Bible and tradition were not mistaken in teach-

37. Since in this book I have already discussed the anthropological and ethical issues entailed in the exclusion of women from priesthood I will not deal with them further here, but I note some examples of those who criticize the magisterial position on such grounds. M. Nadine Foley, O.P., "Woman, Human and Ecclesial?" *Women Priests: A Catholic Commentary,* 53–60, notes: that the expansion of women's role characterizes our times; that sexual discrimination, social or cultural, must be overcome as against God's intentions; and that "Equality of rights must aim at the effective complementarity between men and women which will build an harmonious and unified world according to the designs of the creator." But in fact, she charges, the church unjustly restricts women's roles by a definition of woman's "nature" that is contrary to today's experience. Similarly, Elizabeth Carroll, "Women in the Life of the Church", *Women Priest: A Catholic Commentary,* 61–64, notes that women actually do most of the things Jesus did in his ministry, and thus, "People see a natural resemblance to Jesus in the love conveyed, the service rendered, the self shared, much more than they look to a physical characteristic like sex." Margaret A. Farley, R.S.M., "Discrimination or Equality? The Old Order or the New?" *Women Priests: A Catholic Commentary,* 310–15, claims this exclusion implies an "inequality that is not justified by morally relevant factors" (p. 314). Ida Raming, "'Equal but Other' and the Ordination of Women," *Theology Digest* 29 (1981): 19–27, also argues that the refusal of ordination is based on a wrong notion of the "nature of woman." Dominic O'Laoghaire, "The Dignity of Women," *Doctrine and Life* 39 (1989): 72–79, makes a similar case. Daniel C. Maguire, "The Exclusion of Women from Orders: a Moral Evaluation," *Cross Currents* 34 (1984): 141–52, develops this moral argument at length, and gives an exhortation to humility that is itself perhaps a little short on this quality: "Any position so beset by bad arguments, poor exegesis, uninformed scholarship, and strident appeals to undefined authority, is in need of humble reassessment" (p. 147).

38. *Theological Studies* 55 (1994): 706–19.
39. Ibid., 718.

ing a natural subordination of the wife to her husband as head of the family, but this in no way contradicts their equality as persons;[40] that God has used this complementary relation of the sexes as an analogy to reveal himself in terms of our basic human experiences as Father of the Incarnate Son who is Bridegroom of the church; and that freed from any implication of woman's personal inferiority,[41] this analogy may very well be the basis of a *traditio divina* that only a male priest fittingly acts *in persona Christi*.

In summary, it seems to me that these criticisms of *Inter Insigniores* and *Ordinatio Sacerdotalis* rest on three theologically unsupported, and in fact untenable, assumptions: (1) that the true equality of woman and man as persons excludes any inequality or complementarity of their roles in the family or in the church; (2) that the priest acts principally *in persona ecclesiae* and only secondarily or not at all *in persona Christi*; and (3) that a *traditio divina* needs to verified by exclusively historical-critical methods, rather than by a process of discernment in the ongoing life of the church, the definitive act of which is the authoritative judgment of the magisterium.

40. Legrand, "Traditio perpetuo servata," says, "Theology enjoys no particular competence to decide typically masculine or feminine qualities; this is better determined by social life and by the human sciences" (p. 498). But is it really credible that revelation fails to give us any guidance at all on our sexuality and what the proper relation of the sexes is to be, and leaves us to the guidance of the "social life" of today and the likes of Freud and Kinsey? Legrand also rejects as arbitrary and unprovable the efforts of Louis Bouyer and Hans Urs van Balthasar to define feminine and masculine roles, since our modern experience of the competency of women to exercise representation and authority shows that they can act *in persona Christi* representing "the faith of the Church and its communion" just as men do. But again he passes over the truth that the ordained priest represents not only the community to Christ but Christ to the community.

41. I believe that what *Inter Insigniores* intended by speaking of no longer tenable reasons for excluding women from ordination was not the principle of the "headship of the family" of the husband, which is grounded in the teaching of St. Paul, but the way this was frequently expressed by the Church Fathers and the scholastics as if it implied feminine inferiority in person, intelligence, or virtue, which it need not.

APPENDIX 2

She Who Is

One of the most remarkable "signs of the times" in the Catholic church is the emergence of women theologians of distinguished scholarship and originality. Surely through this sign God is saying something to the church to which all Christians need to listen and on which they ought to reflect critically, yet as learners more than mere critics.

Elizabeth A. Johnson's, *She Who Is: The Mystery of God in Feminist Discourse*[1] has recently received a prestigious award, as well as excellent reviews.[2] Schooled in classical theology and with a broad control of feminist literature, it synthesizes the major themes of feminist theology in a well-crafted, dialectical, and scholarly manner. Although it only alludes to the question of women's ordination (which not surprisingly it favors), it proposes a theology of God-language that, along with its implications for justice in the church and the world, stands in a dialogic relation to the position of *Inter Insigniores* and *Ordinatio Sacerdotalis* which I have defended and attempted to develop in the foregoing chapters. In them I cited Johnson's important article on "The Incomprehensibility of God," in which she first proposed the basic thesis that *She Who Is* expands and deepens. Rather than include detailed references to that book in my re-

1. Elizabeth A. Johnson, *She Who Is: The Mystery of God in Feminist Discourse* (New York: Crossroad, 1993).

2. For example, Robert P. Imbelli of Boston College writes in his review (*Church*, fall 1993), "So extraordinary is the achievement of Sister Elizabeth Johnson, C.S.J., in this book that it calls forth both deep gratitude and discriminating discernment from its readers. To neglect either is to pay this remarkable book less than its due, for it bears radical implications for every aspect of theology and church, for pastoral practice as well as academic reflection" (p. 51). Luke Timothy Johnson of Chandler School of Theology, Emory University, writes (*Commonweal*, Jan. 29, 1993), "Johnson's *She Who Is,* so far as I can tell, is the most substantial and sophisticated effort yet undertaken to connect 'feminist and classical wisdom' in a synthesis at once bold and discerning, critical and doxological, at once engaged with the sources of Christian theology and committed to a vision of Christianity pervasively and profoundly marked by feminist values" (p. 19). He marvels that the author "has survived within a communion which is still the most patriarchal in its structures and systematically repressive of women" of any of the Christian churches (ibid.).

vision of these lectures, I have chosen to provide my response to it in this appendix.

The principal thesis of *She Who Is* (afterwards *SWI*) is well stated in the following paragraph.

The mystery of God transcends all images but can be spoken about equally well and poorly in concepts taken from male or female reality. The approach advocated here proceeds with the insight that only if God is so named, only if the full reality of women as well as men enters into the symbolization of God along with symbols from the natural world, can the idolatrous fixation on one image be broken and the truth of the mystery of God, in tandem with the liberation of all human beings and of the whole earth, emerge for our time. (p. 56)

This thesis is developed through four parts, which I will summarize and criticize in order.

Part 1 of *SWI,* "Background: Speech About God at the Intersection of Mighty Concerns," shows that God is an "Incomprehensible Mystery," and can be spoken of only in analogical terms. If the range of analogues is too limited, an idolatrous image of God results. Furthermore, these terms shift with historical change so that if we remain too attached to one image of God we become blinded to new developments in our theological understanding. *SWI* argues that this problem of naming God is of special concern to feminist theologians because the androcentric, patriarchal images of classical theology seem to have been a major factor in the marginalization and oppression of women. Hence feminist theology must conduct a critique of classical theology, and to do this "one criterion recurs as a touchstone for testing the truth and falsity, the adequacy and inadequacy, the coherence and incoherence of theological statements and religious structures. This criterion, variously enunciated, is the emancipation of women toward human flourishing" (p. 31).[3]

3. Johnson refers approvingly to the feminist hermeneutical theories of Rosemary Radford Ruether, who writes, "The critical principle of feminist theology is the promotion of the full humanity of women. Whatever denies, diminishes, or distorts the full humanity of women is, therefore, appraised as not redemptive. Theologically speaking, whatever diminishes or denies the full humanity of women must be presumed not to reflect the divine or an authentic relation to the divine, or reflect the authentic nature of things, or to be the message or work of an authentic redeemer or a community of redemption. This negative principle also implies the positive principle: what does promote the full humanity of women is of the Holy, it does reflect true relation to the divine, it is the true nature of things, the authentic message of redemption and the mission of redemptive community" (*Sexism and God-Talk,* 18–19). This feminist hermeneutics is presented even more starkly by Elisabeth Schüssler Fiorenza, "I would therefore suggest that the revelatory canon for theological evaluation of biblical androcentric traditions and their subsequent interpretations cannot be derived from the Bible itself but can only be

Given this criterion, *SWI* opts for the name "God" in preference to "Goddess" or other possibilities, but seeks to understand it by feminine analogies that name not mere descriptive "traits" but the Godhead in its totality. Since the gender of "Spirit" in the Bible is not clear, it is necessary to seek other clearly feminine names of God equivalent to the biblical male names.

In reflection on part 1, I ask myself, Can this touchstone provide a sound theological foundation on which to build a theory of divine naming?[4] Certainly, one of the great achievements of contemporary theology is to elucidate the role of human experience in our efforts to understand divine revelation. Nevertheless, in our fallen human condition human experience remains ambiguous, a confused mixture of true contact with reality and of illusion and prejudice. "Faith is the evidence of things not seen" (Heb 11:1). It transcends human experience and passes judgment

---

formulated in and through women's struggle for liberation from all patriarchal oppression. It cannot be universal but must be specific since it is extrapolated from a particular experience of oppression and liberation. The 'advocacy stance for the oppressed' must be sustained at the point of feminine critical evaluation of biblical texts and traditions and their authority claims. The personally and political reflected experience of oppression and liberation must become the criterion of appropriateness for biblical interpretation and evaluation of biblical authority claims" (*In Memory of Her*, 32). See also her "Toward a Feminist Biblical Hermeneutics: Biblical Interpretation and Liberation Theology," in *The Use of Scripture in Moral Theology*, ed. C. E. Curran and R. A. McCormick, Readings in Moral Theology no. 4 (Ramsey, NJ: Paulist Press, 1984). On the relation of feminist theology to liberation theology see also Regina A. Coll, *Christianity and Feminism in Conversation* (Mystic, CT: Twenty-Third Publications, 1994). Of course, God's Word cannot be oppressive of God's creatures, but must promote their flourishing. Yet who knows what promotes their flourishing better than God? Therefore, is not the true criterion of theological truth God's Word and not our human notions or our post-lapsarian "experience" of what is good for us? How then can we use our human notions of our good or our unredeemed experience as the hermeneutic principle by which we decide what is and what is not God's Word? For a critical analysis of this feminist hermeneutic, see Francis Martin, *The Feminist Question* (cited above in Chapter III note 64 above).

4. For a collection of essays mainly by Protestant authors most of whom are critical of "inclusive language" see Alvin V. Kimel, Jr., ed., *Speaking the Christian God* (Grand Rapids, MI: Eerdmans, 1992). See also Donald D. Hook and Alvin V. Kimel, Jr., "The Pronouns of Deity: A Theo-Linguistic Critique of Feminist Proposals," *The Scottish Journal of Theology* 46 (1993): 297–393; and see "Forum: Is God a 'He'?" *Worship* 68 (1994): 145–56. For Catholic authors of the same opinion see Helen Hull Hitchcock, ed., *The Politics of Prayer* (San Francisco: Ignatius Press, 1992). Gail Ramshaw, *Worship* 56 (1982): 117–31, proposes the avoidance of gender language in liturgy. For a discussion of the problem from a Jewish perspective, see Rita Gross, "Female Language in Jewish Context," in *Womanspirit Rising*, ed. Carol P. Christ and Judith Plaskow (San Francisco: Harper Collins, 1979), 167–73.

on it; the Word of God breaks through the limits of our experience.[5] The real question that needs to be asked is not How should we name God? but How has God has been named for us *by God?*

The distinguished Protestant exegete and biblical theologian Bevard S. Childs asks, "How do we know that God is masculine? We know it from the very Bible which speaks of God as 'he'."[6] According to the Old Testament the foundational event of salvation history took place when God revealed to the chosen people who God is by giving them the name of "Yahweh" in order to initiate the Covenant with them (Ex 3:13–15). In the New Testament we read that the historic Jesus is the very Name of God (Phil 2:9–11), and that it is the Spirit who enables us to call on God as "Abba, Father!" (Rm 8:15).[7] Of course historic change permits the church to use new language to express ancient truths, yet we have to be sure that in fact that language we use *does* express these same truths.

In seeking feminine analogies for God, has *SWI* sufficiently explored the question of why God chose masculine rather than feminine names in the original, biblical, divine self-revelation? *SWI* attributes the Bible's use of such names to the patriarchal culture of the human authors, yet these authors typically claimed to speak in God's name (e.g., Is 1:2, "For the Lord says . . .") not in their own. Thus it would seem that somehow their inspired message in its fullness transcends their culture and their personal biases.

5. For the feminist view of the role of "woman's experience" in theology see an author commended by SWI: Anne Carr, *Transforming Grace: Christian Tradition and Woman's Experience* (San Francisco: Harper and Row, 1990).

6. The complete passage reads: "It is generally assumed by defenders of 'inclusive language' respecting God that the imagery of the Bible is arbitrary and merely a reflection of cultural metaphors projected on the deity. The form of language is a human attempt to symbolize an entity which is not identical with the imagery. However, it is precisely this assumption which is called into question by the biblical understanding of revelation. Biblical images refer to God without being mimetically related to what they signify. . . . The witness of the Bible is that God has entered into history and taken human form. Nevertheless, God has revealed his true identity even in historical acts. God is indeed truly as he has revealed himself to be. God is not some hidden entity, veiled in human symbolism, a deity behind the revealed God. Although the Bible continues to use the convention of the masculine pronoun in reference to God, it leans over backwards to supply the true content to its witness of god. How do we know that god is not masculine? We know it from the very Bible which speaks of God as 'he'?" (*Biblical Theology of the Old and New Testament* [Minneapolis: Fortress, 1993], 377).

7. SWI (pp. 79–82) even doubts that "Abba" should be translated "Father," and quotes Paul Santmire, "Retranslating 'Our Father': The Urgency and the Possibility," *Dialog* 16 (1977): 102–4. SWI also refers to Schüssler Fiorenza for the view that, "It is debatable whether fatherhood or the feminine *basileia* (reign of God) is the key image co-ordinating all others in Jesus' speech."

I cannot help but suspect in reading part 1 that its formulation of the problem is somewhat prejudiced by an unspoken philosophical assumption derived from Kant, which debilitated liberal Protestant theology and which is making inroads on current Catholic thinking, namely, that since God is "Incomprehensible Mystery," therefore God is an unknowable *Ding an sich,* a blank screen onto which we are free to project whatever images are serviceable to our ethical purposes. This imperils the very notion of *revelation,* which is that the unknown God is able to make God's inner life truly known to us in ways we can understand, ways that tell us that God is quite different from what we could ever have imagined.

In part 2, "Foreground Resources for Emancipatory Speech About God," *SWI* seems to acknowledge the risks I have already mentioned of using human experience as the criterion of theological truth when it recognizes that even "women's experience" requires to be transformed by a Lonerganian "conversion." This needed conversion, however, according to *SWI* is not repentance of sin in the traditional sense. Rather it is a raising of consciousness through which a woman discovers her female body, her dignity as woman, and her connectedness to others, especially her sisters in womanhood. Hence, she becomes fully able to realize that she is indeed an *imago Dei* and also an *imago Christi,* not, of course, as Jesus is male, but by "pneumatological participation" in Jesus as human (pp. 71–75). As Rahner and Metz have argued, this conversion can be validated by the principle that in discovering our true self we discover God. While by no means denying this principle, I ask myself at this point, But how can I know my true self unless my Creator shows me what I was intended to be?

Drawing on this "experience [of woman's true self] feminist ethics argues that the self is rightly structured not in dualistic opposition to the other but in relationship to the other" (p. 67). Thus "relationality" becomes, for *SWI,* a fundamental notion, which as we shall see, tends to function as a primary value defining authentic womanhood and hence as the primary analogue derived from woman's experience to be used to name the "Incomprehensible Mystery." To name God "She Who Is" amounts to naming God as "Relationality." In truth, this seems to me odd, because while "woman" or "mother" signifies "relationality," so too does "man" or "father." In fact they are *co-relative* terms, which cannot be defined except in relation to each other, just as one cannot define "up" except in relation to "down." Therefore, in order to use the term "woman" or "she" meaningfully as an analogue in naming God, is it not necessary somehow to specify the mutual, dyadic *relation* between "man" and "woman" that defines both terms? *SWI* seems to deal with this prob-

lem of saying what it means to call God "She" rather than "He" only by
contrasting positive aspects of womanhood with merely negative aspects
of manhood. Women typically are marked by "relationality," "inclusivity," "bodiliness," etc., and men are typically characterized by deficiency
in these qualities. But does not our inquiry really demand some kind of
definitions of "woman" and "man"? (The pronouncements of recent
popes, including *Inter Insigniores,* have at least attempted to do this.) And
must not these definitions take the form of a relation of *positive* complementarity?

Is it not inadequate to formulate such definitions of gender in terms of
a positive-negative dichotomy or even of a facile "mutuality" that signifies
the equality of the persons in a relationship but not their different positive
contributions to that relation?[8] I know that some feminists will be quick
to say that women have too long submitted to being defined negatively
by men, and now insist on defining themselves. Well and good, but that
still demands that any definition of womanhood be correlative to some
positive definition oí manhood and vice versa.

I am glad to see that *SWI* is not content simply to develop a feminist
theology based on women's uncriticized "experience," although this experience, transformed by conversion, remains its ultimate criterion of
truth. *SWI* also aims to *correlate* (pp. 8–12) this reflection of women's
experience with "classical theology," which tended androcentrically to
ignore that experience when interpreting the Scriptures. Since Scripture
always requires some interpretation, *SWI* argues that a feminist interpre-

8. SWI rejects "complementarity" in favor of "mutuality" to describe the ideal
relation of the sexes. "What is needed is not the notion of gender 'complementarity'
but the 'egalitarian gestalt'" (p. 154), which is then explained as "one human nature celebrated in an interdependence of mutual differences" (p. 155). "Mutual
differences" is an odd expression, since "mutual" usually refers to what persons
have in common. Does it mean that men and women have in common that they
are different from each other? Feminists reject "complementarity" as implying that
women are incomplete persons without men; yet surely "complementarity" also
implies men are incomplete persons without women. Feminists, however, assert
that customary usage always ignores the latter half of the equation. Instead, feminists favor "mutuality" as indicating a relation between equals. Certainly, the relation between women and men ought to be one of "mutuality" as human persons
who are complete as persons, but "mutuality" does not express their relation as
gendered persons, each of whom contributes something different but positive to
the relationship. If "relationality" is the mark of womanhood, and indeed (as SWI
admits) of the very notion of "person," then how does a woman being related to
men and men to women in a special, sexual manner render either an "incomplete
person"? It would seem to me much more helpful if feminists would speak of the
ideal woman-man relation as one which is "mutual *and* complementary" or as
"equal complementarity" than to try to simply use the generic, and evasive term
"mutuality."

tation is legitimate provided it is not literalistic. Of course it should accord also with the statement of Vatican II *(Dei Verbum)* that biblical inspiration was "for the sake of our salvation," a term which for *SWI* first of all means "liberation." Thus, the problem becomes a search for names of God in the Scripture that are "liberating" for women. *SWI* seems to think that it is obvious what "liberation" consists in, but for me at least, it is not an easy problem to say what it is to be truly "free," for woman, for man, or for humanity.

In summary there are Jewish and Christian biblical terms that, with their trajectories, bear potent female images of the living God present and active throughout the world. When within a feminist perspective the clearly personified figure of Sophia is linked with the hints half-guessed in spirit and *shekinah* and the power of the mother symbol, both the aptness of speaking in female terms of the mystery of God and a modicum of material content for doing so come to light. Discourse about holy mystery in the symbols of spirit, *sophia*, and mother provides glimpses of an alternative to dominant patriarchal language. (p. 103)

Since *SWI* has assumed that it is we, not God, who name God (provided our consciousness has been raised to share women's valid aspirations), one might wonder why the names we choose need to be found in the Scriptures at all. Happily, *SWI* does not accept the position of the more radical feminists, like Mary Daly, for whom the Scriptures are hopelessly patriarchal, but seeks to remain within what Rosemary Radford Ruether calls "the foundational memory"[9] of the Christian community.

9. Rosemary Radford Ruether writes, in "Feminism the End of Christianity? A Critique of Daphne Hampson's *Theology and Feminism*," *Scottish Journal of Theology* 43 (1990): 390–400, "I would see scripture as normative, not in the sense of infallible truths disclosed from beyond normal experience, or as a unique experience incomparable with other experiences, but rather as a foundational memory, in much the same way that any community develops its identity through foundational collections of stories, laws, and ethical norms" (p. 397). In another context, she writes, "But this relation of redeeming Christ and redeemed women should not be made into ultimate theological gender symbols. Christ is not necessarily male, nor is the redeemed community only women, but a new humanity, female and male. We need think in terms of a dynamic, rather than a static, relationship between redeemer and redeemed. The redeemer is one who has been redeemed, just as Jesus himself accepted the baptism of John. Those who have been liberated can, in turn, become paradigmatic, liberating persons for others. Christ as redemptive person and Word of God, is not to be encapsulated "once-for-all" in the historical Jesus" *(Sexism in God Talk,* 137–38). And, also: "If the interiority of our organism is a personal center, how much more so is the great organism of the universe itself? That great matrix supports the energy-matter of our individuated beings is itself the ground of all personhood as well. That great collective personhood is the Holy Being in which our achievements and failures are gathered up, assimilated into the fabric of being, and carried forward into new possibilities. We do not know what this [future life] means. It is beyond our power and our imagination. It is not then our direct responsibility. We can do nothing about the

The reasons given in this section for selecting "Spirit," "Sophia/Wisdom," and "Mother" to name "holy mystery" are further developed in part 3, and I will summarize them later.

Tradition as a source is treated mainly under the heading of "Classical Theology" (pp. 104–23), especially as represented by the thought of St. Thomas Aquinas on divine naming. Patristic thought on the subject is treated only incidentally and the recent attempts at less androcentric language in papal and conciliar documents largely ignored. *SWI* has a well-informed treatment of the three ways of knowing the "Incomprehensible Mystery" through causality, eminence, and negation, and also of the need to use a variety of names for God so as to avoid idolatry. Yet *SWI* always emphasizes that in the end we remain free to name God as we choose, since all our names only point to God while leaving us in the dark. Thus *SWI*, in concluding its presentation of the classical theology on divine naming says,

> Now it becomes clear that we [Catholic theologians] have not yet sufficiently articulated that the critical negation of analogy must be stringently applied to male images and conceptualizations of God no less than to other aspects of divine predication. The designation "he" is subject to all the limitations found in any other positive naming of God, and *in the end does not really tell us anything about the divine*. (p. 117, italics added).

Here one might ask whether *SWI* has really probed what the naming of God by masculine names in the Bible means "positively," not only negatively in terms of its abuse in supporting masculine pride and domination. But how can we find feminine equivalents for these male names unless we have first examined the positive meanings of these male names? Moreover, if we are to take *SWI* literally when it says that even any positive name for God "in the end does not really tell us anything about the di-

---

'immortal' dimension of our lives. It is not our calling to be concerned about the eternal meaning of our lives, and religion should make this the focus of its message. Our responsibility is to use our temporal life span to create a just and good community for our generation and for our children. It is in the hands of Holy Wisdom to forge out of our finite struggle truth and being for everlasting life. Our agnosticism about what this means is then the expression of our faith, our trust that Holy Wisdom will give transcendent meaning to our work, which is bounded by space and time" (*Sexism in God Talk*, 258). While this lyrical language no doubt suggests benign interpretation, it seems to empty biblical inspiration, the Incarnation, Redemption and Resurrection of anything more than a mythological significance. Ruether's stance seems to be that she has chosen to continue to work as a scholar within the Christian tradition, but that she feels free on principle to dissent from any particular item of that tradition, or to reinterpret it to fit her political concerns. Johnson does not commit herself to so radical a position, but she does not reject it either. Although SWI draws heavily from the work of Ruether and Schüssler Fiorenza, it does not subject them to serious criticism.

vine," then does it not follow that calling God "She" does not really tells us anything about God either, and therefore can hardly contribute theologically to woman's liberation, except in the way that meaningless political slogans win votes?

I also wonder why so little attention is given in the book as a whole to the classical distinction, which is mentioned only in passing (p. 114), between *metaphor* (improper analogy) and *proper analogy*. (*SWI* speaks of it as analogy in "formal substantive terms.") When Jesus says "I am the Gate" (Jn 10:9), he uses metaphor. When he says "I am the Truth" (Jn 14:6), he uses proper analogy, that is, an analogical term based on an essential similarity and freed of any imperfections inherent in its analogue in human experience. As Aquinas makes clear in the questions of the *Summa Theologiae* to which *SWI* refers in treating of analogy, this distinction is essential for theology if it is to avoid the very abuses of which *SWI* complains when it says that to speak of God in male terms draws along with it all sorts of connotations offensive to women.

Is this not to overlook the fact that it is precisely the business of theology to free biblical metaphors from such literalism and to convert them into proper analogies? For Aquinas as a theologian, to call God "Father" meant not that He had a male body, but that God is the "Principle" of all creation. This is what *SWI* also seems to do implicitly when it interprets "She" to mean "Relationality." The question remains unexamined in *SWI*, however, whether it is arbitrary to say that "Father" not "Mother" better signifies "Principle," and "Mother" not "Father" better signifies "Relationality."

Part 3, "Speaking About God from the World's History," seeks to show that "Spirit/Sophia," "Jesus/Sophia," and "Mother/Sophia" are neglected names for "Incomprehensible Mystery" in Scripture and classical theology, which properly understood in analogical and dialectical fashion can serve the cause of woman's liberation. Proceeding in customary fashion from the economic to the ontological Trinity, *SWI* prefers to begin not by considering an alternative name for the "Father" but rather with a treatment of the name "Spirit," since that Person is too much neglected in Latin theology or—Johnson suggests—its attributes are displaced into Mariology. Also the vagueness of the term tends to make "Spirit" gender-neutral. More importantly, women experience the mystery not as a dominating "Father" or "Son" but more as the presencing and absenting of the Spirit in the ecology of creation, in establishing relationships, and in the Spirit's speaking to our own inner spirits as a Friend, Sister, Mother, Grandmother, vivifying, renewing, and gracing us.

We must, however, says *SWI*, avoid the notion that the Spirit is

"Third" since this encourages the subordination and marginalization of women as self-effacing. We should instead emphasize the way the Spirit empowers women for action. Such carefully chosen feminist analogues deepen our understanding of God's *immanence, liberating empowerment, relational autonomy,* and the *wholeness* of reality.

The manifestation in history of "Jesus/Sophia" requires us to purify Christology of the patriarchal stress on Jesus' maleness. According to patristic thought, "What is not assumed, is not redeemed." Hence, to see any special theological significance in Jesus' maleness marginalizes women. Instead we should underline Jesus' *inclusive* humanity. On this point *SWI* pronounces an *anathema sit!* "The trivialization introduced into the doctrine of the incarnation by androcentric stress on the maleness of Christ fully warrants the charge of heresy and even blasphemy currently being leveled against it" (p. 167).[10] Since the term "Logos" or "Word became flesh" (Jn 1:14) is tainted by its "long connectedness in Greek philosophy with the male principle" (p. 152), it is better to say that Jesus is Sophia Incarnate who is manifested in the action, preaching, ingathering, confronting, dying, and rising of the historic Jesus. "Whoever espouses a wisdom Christology is asserting that Jesus is the human being Sophia became; that Sophia in all her fullness was in him so that he manifests the depth of divine mystery in creative and graciously saving involvement in the world" (p. 99).

If Jesus' historic maleness has any theological significance other than a merely historical one, it is that of *kenosis,* the suffering servant in whom male pride is humiliated. "It is not Jesus' maleness that is doctrinally important but his humanity in solidarity with the whole human race" (p. 165). This is even more evident in the Risen Christ, the "Whole Christ" (p. 161) who includes all redeemed humanity in the unity of the Spirit. "Maleness is not constitutive of the essence of Christ but, in the Spirit redeemed and redeeming humanity is" (p. 164). Such a Sophia Christology has the advantages of promoting the ecological, ecumenical, and liberation movements. It also deepens our understanding of God by the notion of the compassionate involvement of God in the cosmos (pp. 165–66).

Finally, the equivalent image for the Person of the Trinity to whom the concept of creation is commonly appropriated, is "Mother/Sophia," instead of the notion, based on Aquinas's "faulty biology raised to a metaphysical level" (p. 174), that the male is active, the female passive in generation.[11] Jesus' use of "Abba" was to signify not that God "the Fa-

10. Is this a discrete reference to criticism of *Inter Insigniores,* in which SWI seems to concur?

11. SWI is curiously mistaken in supposing that modern biology has in this

ther" is analogically "the Father," "after whom all paternity *(patria)*[12] in heaven and earth are named" (Eph 3:15), but rather to emphasize God's tender care (pp. 81–82) which for *SWI* is characteristically maternal. In the Hebrew Scriptures "Spirit," "Shekinah," and "Wisdom"[13] are images that often have a feminine character (as a substitute perhaps for Hellenistic Isis worship, pp. 90–91). As for "Mother," this term is very fitting for God, but only if it is purified of all suggestions of "complementarity" which might seem to require a male god as partner (p. 103).

SWI again asserts that the term "Mother" (although there is more to being a woman than being a mother) essentially signifies "relationality." Sophia as creator is active in forming the universe and in justice defending it from evil and in mercy caring for it. "The maternal source and compassionate matrix of the universe is also its goal, the point of homecoming at the end of the journey" (p. 181). For *SWI* this way of speaking about God emphasizes God's connectedness and intimacy with Her creation, but on reading that God is "matrix of the universe," I began to wonder if *SWI* understands this "connectedness" with the universe in a pantheistic sense. This doubt was not wholly resolved by the decision for *panentheism* made later in part 4.

The ingenuity of this resolution of all the Trinitarian terms into the single Divine Name of "Wisdom" conceived as a "Spirit," which is feminine because of its absolute relationality is brilliant. But what has this ingenuity accomplished? If the significance of naming God by a feminine name is to indicate God's "relationality," we have to ask once more, Why does "Woman" signify relationality any more than "Man," since they are correlative terms? Moreover, if we say that Jesus redeemed both women and men, because he assumed humanity to which his maleness was only accidental, what of St. Paul's teaching that Jesus is the New Adam who redeems both his daughters and his sons (Rm 5:12–21; 1 Cor 15:20–28)?

---

respect overturned "Aristotelian biology." In fact what is at issue is not *scientific* biology, ancient or modern, but commonsense perceptions in ordinary experience, which are the analogical symbols on which theological language needs to be based. See Chapter III note 84.

12. Or "From whom every *family* in heaven and on earth is named." For the author of Ephesians, however, the father is head of the family (Eph 5:23); see Chapter III note 77.

13. SWI opts for the view that the personified "Wisdom" of the Hebrew Scriptures is simply a name of God (p. 91 n. 28), as against the views that it is a divine attribute, or that it is a semi-independent hypothesis, or Gerhard von Rad's view in *Wisdom in Israel* (Nashville, TN: Abingdon Press, 1972) that this Wisdom is not a name of God, but "the personification of cosmic order, that is, of the meaning that God has implanted in creation," which seems to me exegetically to fit the range of texts best.

Thus we are left with a "Spirit Christology" in which the revelatory significance of Our Lord's historical humanity in its earthly and resurrected states is so spiritualized[14] that the incarnation, passion, and resurrection have, in spite of sincere denials (pp. 151–54), dissolved, almost docetically, into "mystery." Again, the failure to make clear in concrete terms what the analogues "man" and "woman" mean other than simply "human" nullifies their value as revelatory names of God.

Part 4, "Dense Symbols and Their Dark Light," discusses first the doctrine of the Trinity. Classical theology presented a patriarchal understanding of the Trinity with the names "Father" and "Son" and a hierarchy of "First, Second, Third Persons," which inevitably tends to inequality and subordinationism. Hence this symbol must be freed from over-literalness by emphasis on the economic Trinity and the human experience of hope. I am glad to say, that although the term "person" was rejected by Barth and Rahner, *SWI* somewhat grudgingly retains it: "In speaking of the triune mystery, person is perhaps the least inconvenient of labels, but it is highly inadequate, in fact, improper" (p. 203). *SWI* hastens to empty this term of any meaning except "relationality," which *SWI* has so often used as the defining notion of womanhood.

We emerge with the strong realization that the symbol of the Trinity is not a blueprint of the inner workings of the Godhead, nor an offering of esoteric information about God. In no sense is it a literal description of God's being *in se*. As the outcome of theological reflection on the Christian experience of relationship to God, it is a symbol that indirectly points to God's relationality, at first with reference to the world, and then with reference to God's own mystery. (pp. 204–5)

This claim to ignorance about everything except relationality is emphatically restated a little later:

Speaking about the Trinity expresses belief in one God who is not a solitary God but a communion in love marked by overflowing life. In no way is it a picture model that signifies secret information about the inner life of God, but a genuine symbol arising from divine-human relation in this ambiguous world and pointing to dimensions of this relation that we trust are grounded in no less a reality than the very mystery of God. (p. 222)

SWI insists that the "metaphors" applied to this mystery in Scripture are fluid (p. 211) and that the names of "Father," "Son," and "Third

14. It is true St. Paul speaks of the resurrected body as "spiritual" (1 Cor 15:44) but this primarily means "deathless" not immaterial, and what would a human body be that was not sexual and of a determined gender? Certainly the nature of the resurrected body is not easily imagined, but we should not reduce it to a ghost, an error that the Bible (Lk 24:39) explicitly rejects.

Person" say little to our age, especially to women. Rather we should begin with our own religious experience, find appropriate feminine metaphors to express that experience, and then correlate these feminine metaphors with the creeds of the church and classical theology. We will then see that God is relationality and that these relations constitutive of Godhead are necessarily those of absolute equality and mutuality (pp. 218–29). The Trinity is a community in diversity, in which "There is no subordination, no before or after, no first, second, third, no dominant and marginalized" (p. 219). Since the classical theology which distinguished the Persons by the hierarchical *order of processions* among the Persons can be misunderstood as subordinationism, the emphasis should be put on the *perichoresis* or mutual indwelling of the Persons in an eternal interchange after the analogue of human friendship and thus as the model of human *communio*.

The image of a woman being herself, expressing herself, and befriending herself in an inclusive movement that issues in care for the world forms one remote human analogue [of the Trinity]. So too does the image of three women friends circling around together in the bonds of unbreakable friendship. In threefold "personal" distinctiveness Holy Wisdom embraces the world with befriending power as unreachable Abyss, as self-expressive Word that joins history in the flesh, as overflowing Spirit that seeks out the darkest, deadest places to quicken them to new life. (p. 218)

In chapter 11, "One Living God: She Who Is," we learn that since a feminine name for God indicates a God whose essence is relationality, the classical saying that "The world is really related to God but not God to the world," found in St. Thomas Aquinas, is unacceptable. Yet the truth it contains is that God retains autonomy within relationality, i.e., the Divine Persons retain autonomous freedom in mutuality, which "converted" women also seek to retain in relationships.

SWI is well aware that Aquinas has been misunderstood on this question because "real relation" meant something different to him than it does in post-Cartesian talk, yet *SWI* insists that, since God creates freely while the world necessarily depends on God, the relations between God and world are "asymmetric" (p. 228), Aquinas said much too little about God's involvement with the world. Hence *SWI* opts for *panentheism* (or "dialectical theism") as middle ground between theism's uninvolved God and pantheism's God identified with the world. *SWI* even finds support in the kabbalistic theory of God's "contraction" or *kenosis* to make room for the world to be itself in relation to God, as a mother makes room in her body for her child (pp. 233–36).

Finally, God can be imaged as "Sheer Liveliness" (pp. 236–37), as an equivalent of the biblical "I am" and the classical *Esse Subsistens,* by which "Being" is understood not as a genus, but as a verb in the expression "She-Who-Is." This expression spiritually

discloses women's human nature as *imago Dei*, and reveals divine nature to be the relational mystery of life who desires the liberated human existence of all women made in Her image. In promoting the flourishing of women SHE WHO IS attends to an essential element for the well-being of all creation, human beings, and the earth inclusively. Politically, this symbol challenges every structure and attitude that assigns superiority to ruling men on the basis of their supposed greater godlikeness. If the mystery of God is no longer spoken about exclusively or primarily in terms of the dominating male, a forceful linchpin holding up structures of patriarchal rule is removed. (p. 243)

The last chapter of the book, "Suffering God: Compassion Poured Out," seeks to explain the ethical meaning of the involvement of this panentheistic God in a world full of evil, injustice, and death. After discussing the contemporary criticisms of an "apathic, omnipotent" God, *SWI* rejects the notion of a God of limited power as favored by some process theologians in order to explain evil in the world, since this would be harmful to woman's empowerment (p. 253). Instead, *SWI* speaks with deep feeling of metaphors taken from woman's experience such as pregnancy and giving birth, outrage at the suffering of women worldwide, grief over violence and war, and exploitation and abuse, and asks how a loving God can be involved in such tragedy.

Since all love involves suffering, and God is love, *SWI* argues, God must somehow suffer with all human suffering. Yet She should not be imagined as a self-sacrificing masochist, lest this lead women to accept the passive role patriarchalism has imposed on them. Rather She-Who-Is should be imagined as a woman activist engaged in the struggle against all manner of evil and injustice. She-Who-Is, therefore, out of love, freely suffers in the sense that She is committed to total solidarity (relationship with, care for) all the oppressed. Hence She is to be named as a liberating God from the analogy of women's own enduring *hope* grounded in their own experience of the power of love and of sisterhood to overcome evil.

The brief epilogue summarizes the argument of the book and reiterates that "Ideas of God are cultural creatures related to the time and place in which they were conceived. . . . No language about God will ever be fully adequate to the burning mystery which it signifies. But a more inclusive way of speaking can come about that bears the ancient wisdom with a new justice" (p. 273).

After reading part 3, I was afraid that *SWI* had dissolved all three Persons of the Trinity into the single concept of "Sophia" with various modes of existence, but this impression was corrected in part 4 where the book defends the orthodox conception of the Trinity as a *communio* of autonomous and equal Persons mutually sharing one being and life.

Nevertheless, it is here that we finally see what the term "equality" of persons really means for *SWI,* a term which, as noted in my comments on part 1, is essential to its whole argument. For *SWI* "equality" in a community excludes all hierarchy of office or authority. Hence, for *SWI* there cannot be within the Trinity, which is the perfect community, any order that implies asymmetrical relations of giving and receiving in processional order, no First, Second, or Third Person. All persons equally give and receive, hence there can be no "hierarchy" ("sacred order") in the relations within the Trinity or in any just human relationships because this necessarily implies a morally wrong domination of superior persons over inferior persons.

It would seem that this rejection of the classical explanation of how the Persons can be distinct and yet absolutely equal, namely, that they are equal in the Divine Nature but distinct by their *relations of origin* would leave us with no coherent metaphysical answer to modalism or unitarianism, but *SWI* once again confidently invokes the "Divine Incomprehensibility."[15] "The triune God is not simply unknown, but positively known to be unknown and unknowable—which is a dear and profound kind of knowledge" (p. 205).

This extremely obscure model of the Trinity, does, however, make daylight-clear the fundamental *political theory* on which the entire project of *SWI* rests, a theory which I believe political scientists would classify as "anarchism." Christian anarchism is not a new system, but in recent

15. Perhaps the model of the Trinity that SWI proposes can be better correlated with classical models if we note the ambiguity of its use of "Relationality" as a key concept. In classical theology, the Divine Persons are distinguished from each other by *relations of origin* and, as SWI itself notes, can be spoken of as *subsistent relations.* The analogue of such relations is the relation of cause to effect, with the proviso that the First Person does not "cause" the Second and Third Persons as if their Being were causally dependent on the First, since all three Persons have but one and the same Being. Thus, though Greek theology calls the First Person a "cause," Latin theology prefers to speak of that Person as a "principle" of the other two. But when SWI speaks of "relationality" it uses "relation" in the modern sense of "interpersonal relationships," i.e., the knowledge and love between persons, not their origin. Hence, SWI can speak about the "mutual" relationships between the Persons, because the Father, Son, and Spirit know and love each other symmetrically, no one being first, second, or third in knowledge or love, since they communicate in One Being which is One Act of knowledge and love. Classical theology of course affirmed this, but was concerned first about the *origin* of the Persons, which is asymmetric since the First Person generates the Second, and spirates the Third, while neither the Second nor the Third generates the First which is the "Unbegotten." SWI, however, leaves the impression that the model it substitutes for the classical model is somehow equivalent to the model embodied in the creeds of the church, which were intended to answer a quite different question, not about love and knowledge among the Persons, but about their being.

years it has surfaced as one of the strands within liberation theology. According to this theory the ideal human community is one in which there is no order of authority or obedience. Every member is autonomous, but all cooperate by consensus in the interest of the common welfare, without any member having to submit her or his autonomy of decision to any other member or even to the majority or the whole.

It seems that it was this kind of understanding of Christian freedom that St. Paul confronted pastorally in the Corinthian community, and which he tried to moderate by teaching them (1 Cor 12) that a distinction must be made between the *personal equality* of all members of the Christian community, by which all have a right to share in the common good, and the *functional inequality* which results from a diversity of gifts in the service of the common good. Functional inequality necessarily results in a certain *hierarchical inequality* within the community, for which the metaphor of "head" and various "members," superior and inferior in one body, is appropriate.

In this teaching St. Paul was basing himself on the teachings of his Master, who always supported the hierarchical order of society and established it among his own disciples, while insisting that those in authority must make themselves servants of the common good in even its least members, as he himself had given an example (Mt 20:25–28; Jn 13:1–20).

Thus *SWI* is certainly right in holding that the Trinity is the model of human society, but also certainly wrong in supposing that in the church and society there ought to be simply friendship without hierarchical order. In the Trinity there is perfect equality of Persons yet only one God, not because there is no First, Second, and Third, but precisely because there is among the Persons a determinant order. This processional order is realized so completely that the Father is the *arche* (principle, source) from whom the Son receives the Godhead, and from whom the Spirit also receives the Godhead, but through the Son. This is not simply one of many possible theological models (as *SWI* seems to think), it is embodied in the creeds that are fundamental data of any orthodox Christian theology.

The total receptivity of the Son and Spirit with respect to the Father in no way makes them inferior to the Father, and the obedience of a member of a human community to its legitimate authorities in no way makes them personally inferior to those authorities, but is a means for each member to contribute to and to share in the common good. The Catholic church in its social doctrine has consistently opposed both individualism and totalitarianism, capitalism and socialism, precisely because they alike lead to anarchism, and thence to the original sin of both angels and humans, the demand for the absolute autonomy of individuals.

Thus, *SWI*, if I have understood its argument, rests its case on two basic assumptions which it never thematizes or subjects to a thorough critical examination but which are philosophically highly debatable and whose influence on theology has not always been positive: First, it makes the *political* assumption that social justice requires not only personal but also anarchic equality. Hence it fails to examine the fact that the defining relation between woman and man is not only one of mutuality, but also of complementarity, so that not every social differentiation based on gender is unjust, but is in some cases (e.g., in family relations) for the common good of all. Second, it makes the *epistemological* assumption, derived from the Kantian tradition, that God is the Unknown on which we project our human concepts and values derived only from human experience and selected for their ethical and political advantages.

In my opinion until these assumptions are exposed and criticized, the hypothesis proposed by *SWI* remains so ambiguous and difficult to test either in authentic human experience or in the data of revelation, that it cannot do much for the great cause of a just human society to which it sincerely seeks to contribute. My hope is that Elizabeth Johnson and other women theologians will continue to examine the foregoing assumptions in the light of God's self-revealment in the Bible and living tradition, as well as their own most profound experiences. We are all obliged to free our thinking from the false notion of human freedom that the supremely androcentric, patriarchalist, and agnostic tradition of the Enlightenment has imposed on our culture and on us.

Infallibility and
Ordinatio Sacerdotalis

After the foregoing lectures had been written and revised for publication, a concise "Reply to a *Dubium* Concerning the Teaching Contained in the Apostolic Letter *Ordinatio Sacerdotalis*" was issued by the Congregation for the Doctrine of the Faith, with the approval of John Paul II, on October 28, 1995. It reads:[1]

Dubium: Whether the teaching that the Church has no authority whatsoever to confer priestly ordination on women, which is presented in the Apostolic Letter *Ordinatio Sacerdotalis* to be held definitively, is to be understood as belonging to the *depositum fidei.*

Responsum: In the affirmative. This teaching requires definitive assent, since, founded on the written Word of God, and from the beginning constantly preserved and applied in the Tradition of the Church, it has been set forth infallibly by the ordinary and universal Magisterium (cf. Vatican II, *Lumen Gentium* 25, 2). Thus, in the present circumstances, the Roman Pontiff, exercising his proper office of confirming the brethren (cf. Lk 22:32), has handed on this same teaching by a formal declaration, explicitly stating what is to be held always, everywhere, and by all, as belonging to the *depositum fidei.*

What is the significance and authority of this document which has troubled many, but gratified others?

First, it is unjust to see in it a regressive tendency of John Paul II or Cardinal Ratzinger to "retrench" or to defend or extend Vatican authority or to engage in "creeping infallibility." Developments such as the attempted ordination of women in Czechoslovakia, the schism in the Anglican church, problems with the religious sisterhoods, the drastic theological revisionism of some feminist theologians, and the continuing,

---

1. Translated as "Inadmissibility of Women to Ministerial Priesthood," with a cover letter by Cardinal Joseph Ratzinger to Bishop Conference Presidents and "Vatican Reflections on the Teaching of *Ordinatio Sacerdotalis*," followed by commentaries of Bishop Anthony Pilla, President of National Conference of Catholic Bishops and Father Augustine DiNoia, O.P., Secretary for Doctrinal and Pastoral Practices of the Conference, *Origins* 25 (Nov. 30, 1995): 401–9.

divisive agitation within the church after previous attempts at reconciliation, have made this problem one of deep pastoral concern. The Response
is an attempt to settle the matter in as moderate a manner as possible.

Second, the Response of a Vatican Congregation approved by the pope
in forma communi and not in *forma speciali* is not itself an infallible teaching of the magisterium, nor was *Ordinatio Sacerdotalis*. Rather, as the
"Reflections" published with the document states (referring to *Ordinatio
Sacerdotalis*), "In this case, an act of the ordinary papal magisterium, in
itself not infallible, witnesses to the infallibility of the teaching of a doctrine already possessed by the church."[2]

Third, the Response is, however, an authentic interpretation of *Ordinatio Sacerdotalis*. It is absurd to think that John Paul II would in any
form have approved a misinterpretation of what he himself had intended
to do in issuing *Ordinatio Sacerdotalis*. The question, therefore, is what
is the authority to be attributed to *Ordinatio Sacerdotalis* as thus authentically interpreted.[3]

Fourth, *Ordinatio Sacerdotalis* is not merely a disciplinary decree but
a doctrinal declaration by the successor of St. Peter that the teaching that
only men can be validly ordained to priesthood pertains to the *depositum fidei* as "taught infallibly by the universal and ordinary magisterium"
as "founded on the written Word of God, and from the beginning constantly preserved and applied in the Tradition of the Church," and hence
he and future popes and bishops lack the authority to validly ordain
women.

What authority then should be attributed to *Ordinatio Sacerdotalis*?
Some have reacted to this declaration as a shocking novelty that will surely
have to be reversed in the future.[4] But it should be noted that *Ordinatio*

2. See the commentaries of the canonist Ladislas Orsy, S.J., and a theologian
who is a specialist on such questions, Francis A. Sullivan, S.J., "Infallibility and
Women's Ordination," *America*, Dec. 9, 1995, pp. 4–6. The same point as Orsy's
was made in the commentary of DiNoia cited in note 1 above.

3. When Orsy, "Inadmissibility of Women," concludes (p. 5) that "the doctrinal message of the apostolic letter," i.e., *Ordinatio Sacerdotalis*, "remains the
same as it was on the day of its publication," he is correct as to the authority of
Ordinatio Sacerdotalis, but he fails to point out the great significance of the Response as an authentic interpretation of *Ordinatio Sacerdotalis*.

4. Thus Thomas C. Fox, editor of the *National Catholic Reporter* says, "For
now, this marks a defeat for reform-minded Catholics. But in the long term it may
have the opposite effect; if there is a schism in the church in the next century, its
source may well turn out to be the unyielding right. Influence by a Pope who is
conditioning people to believe that the church cannot and will not change, the
church's conservatives may make it impossible for their intellectual heirs to continue to exist under a papacy that will change."

Sacerdotalis is a declaration with regard to the requirements for *sacramental* validity. From the time of Stephen I (c. 256),[5] who declared in face of the formidable opposition of St. Cyprian of Carthage that the baptism of heretics is valid, such decisions by popes have been received in the church as definitive. To cite only a recent example, in 1947 Pius XII in the Apostolic Constitution *Sacramentum Ordinis* decided that the essential "matter" of ordination to the priesthood was not the *traditio instrumentorum* (the handing by the bishop of the chalice and patent to the ordinand) as taught by St. Thomas Aquinas and other great medieval theologians, but the laying on of hands. As far as I am informed, Pius XII did not consult the episcopacy before making this declaration, nor can we prove that the popes in similar cases in the past had done so. Note that if these papal definitions of sacramental validity made to the universal church could have been erroneous, we would have no certainty of the validity of the sacraments today. But that we do have such certainty is guaranteed by the indefectibility and infallibility of the church, which is surely *de fide*.

Thus the continuing doubts that are being expressed about whether the matter has been definitively settled appear to be without probable grounds. Francis A. Sullivan, S.J., in the *America* commentary already quoted says, "a long standing tradition of the past might not suffice as proof that a doctrine has been taught by the ordinary and universal magisterium." To demonstrate this one would need evidence, Sullivan says, that the pope had consulted all the bishops, or that it was "held by the universal and constant consensus of Catholic theologians to pertain to the faith," or that it was "manifested by the common adherence of Christ's faithful." He is not sure such criteria have been met.

What John Paul II is saying in *Ordinatio Sacerdotalis*, however, is that it is his definitive judgment as head of the church that this tradition is not just "long standing" but that it meets the criteria Sullivan lists, i.e., it has always been taught by the universal, ordinary magisterium as a truth of faith rooted in Scripture and tradition, has been supported by the common opinion of theologians, and has been accepted by the faithful. This is why it could be incorporated in the *Catechism of the Catholic Church*, after consultation with the bishops.[6]

6. *Catechism of the Catholic Church* no. 1577–78. I do not imply that everything in the *Catechism* is infallible! But it must be presumed that when the bishops have concurred with the pope on fundamental doctrines, such as the essential requirements of the sacraments, that this qualifies as ordinary, universal, and therefore infallible teaching. Their approval of teaching on many matters, such as discipline, liturgy, devotions, and historical questions (all of which are in the *Catechism*), do not necessarily so qualify.

Hence the burden of proof is not on those who think these criteria have not been met, but on those who think they are justified in disagreeing with John Paul II's authoritative decision. They are obliged to receive it with "submission of intellect and will" unless they are *certain* that it is mistaken, and then their difficulty is to be expressed with great prudence so as not to further injure Christian unity.[7] As Avery Dulles has commented on the Response,

> The presumption must be on the side of tradition. Even if it were shown to be probable that the whole tradition had erred, that probability would not clear the way to ordaining women, for the sacrament of holy orders could not be properly conferred unless its validity were certain. . . . I conclude therefore that the Pope and the Congregation for the Doctrine of the Faith seem to be on good ground in holding that the Church has no power to ordain women to the priesthood. The constancy of the tradition, based as it is on the practice of Jesus and the teaching of Scripture, supports the idea of infallibility.[8]

It remains, of course, for theologians to assist the teaching of the magisterium by showing more clearly on the basis of Scripture and tradition, as well as the human study of religion, the certain or probable reasons that Christ instituted the sacrament of holy orders in the way he did, as well as the pastoral purposes of the Holy See in making this judgment at the present time. I have attempted in this book to contribute to that task, and I am profoundly grateful to Christ and his Vicar John Paul II for bringing the present controversy to a definitive close, even if it for a time "brings not peace but a sword" (Mt 10:34). John Paul II's words have evoked among some a great deal of talk about "equality," but not much about "discipleship"—which after all means "docility to one's teacher." That one teacher is Jesus himself, who continues to guide us through our shepherds.

I pray also that those for whom this decision is painful, often because they have heard little but one side of the debate, will accept it in the spirit of faith and with confidence that in the long run it will benefit all members of the church and the women disciples of Jesus most of all. I believe it will do this by showing the men of the church that true manhood must image that of Jesus himself whose attitude toward women, raised as he was by Mary, mother, contemplative, and prophetess, was supremely liberating.

7. Congregation for the Doctrine of the Faith, *Ecclesial Vocation*, no. 28.
8. "Tradition Says No," *The Tablet* 249 (Dec. 6, 1995), 1572–73.

Bibliography

Church Documents

Denzinger, Henricus, S.J., and A. Schönmetzer, S.J. *Enchiridion Symbolorum*. 33d ed. revised. Barcelona: Herder, 1965.

Acta Apostolicae Sedis. Rome: Libreria Editrice Vaticana, 1904–.

Code of Canon Law, The. Latin-English edition: translation prepared under the auspices of the Canon Law Society of America. Washington, DC: Canon Law Society of America, 1983.

Catechism of the Catholic Church. Libreria Editrice Vaticana, 1994.

Pius XII. Encyclical, *Sacra virginitas*, March 15, 1954. N. 32, Claudia Carlen, *The Papal Encyclicals, 1939–1958*, p. 244. New York: McGrath Publishing Co., 1981.

Abbott, Walter M., S.J., ed. *The Documents of Vatican II*. Baltimore: Geoffrey Chapman, 1966.

Flannery, Austin, O.P., ed. *Vatican Collection*. Vol. 2, *Vatican Council II: More Postconciliar Documents*. Northport, NY: Costello Publishing Co., 1982.

Vatican II. "Constitution on the Sacred Liturgy" *(Sacrosanctum Concilium)*, 1963; Abbott, 137–78.

———. "Dogmatic Constitution on the Church" *(Lumen Gentium)*, 1964; Abbott, 14–101.

———. "Dogmatic Constitution on Divine Revelation" *(Dei Verbum)*, Nov. 18, 1965; Abbott, 111–28.

———. "Pastoral Constitution on the Church in the Modern World" *(Gaudium et Spes)*, 1965; Abbott, 199–308.

———. "Decree on the Bishops' Pastoral Office in the Church" *(Christus Dominus)*, 1965; Abbott, 396–429.

———. "Decree on Priestly Formation" *(Optatam Totius)*, 1965; Abbott, 437–57.

———. "Decree on the Appropriate Renewal of the Religious Life" *(Perfectae Caritatis)*, 1965; Abbott, 466–82.

———. "Decree on the Apostolate of the Laity" *(Apostlicam Actuositatem)*, 1965; Abbott, 489–521.

———. "Decree on the Ministry and Life of Priests *(Presbyterorum Ordinis)*, 1965; Abbott, 532–76.

———. "Declaration on the Relationship of the Church to Non-Christian Religions" *(Nostra Aetate)*, 1965, Abbott, 660–68.

———. "Declaration on Religious Freedom" *(Dignitatis Humanae)*, 1965; Abbott, 675–96.

Paul VI. Encyclical "On Priestly Celibacy" *(Sacerdotalis caelibatus)*, June 24, 1967. In Flannery, *Vatican Council II, More Conciliar Documents*, n. 95, 285–317.

———. Declaration as Doctor of the Church of St. Teresa of Jesus, Sept. 27, 1970; AAS 62, 1970): 590–96.

———. Declaration as Doctor of the Church of St. Catherine of Siena, Oct. 4, 1970 (AAS 62, 1970): 673–78.

———. *Motu Proprio Ministeria Quaedam*, Aug. 15, 1972.

John Paul II. Encyclical "The Christian Family in the Modern World" *(Familaris Consortio)*, November 22, 1981. AAS 74 (1982): 81–191; Flannery, *Vatican II: More Postconciliar Documents*, 815–98).

———. Encyclical "The Mother of the Redeemer" *(Redemptoris Mater)*, March 25, 1987, n. 6. Washington, DC: United States Catholic Conference, 1987.

———. Encyclical "On The Dignity and Vocation of Woman" *(Mulieris Dignitatem)*, August 15, 1988; Origins 18, 17 (Oct. 6, 1988): 261–83.

———. "Apostolic Letter on Ordination and Women" *(Ordinatio Sacerdotalis)*, May 22, 1994; Origins 24, 4 (June 9, 1994): 50–52.

Holy Office, Decree of. March 29 (April 8), 1916, DS 3632.2

Congregation for the Doctrine of the Faith, "Declaration on the Question of the Admission of Women to the Ministerial Priesthood" *(Inter Insigniores)*, October 15, 1976, AAS 69 (1977); Origins 6, 33 (Feb. 3, 1977): 518–31.

———. "Instruction on Certain Aspects of 'The Theology of Liberation'" *(Libertatis nuntius)*, AAS 76 (1984), 867–77. Also, Boston: St. Paul Editions, 1984.

———. "Letter to Fr. Schillebeeckx regarding His Book *Ministry*," Origins 14 (January 24, 1985): 523, and "Note on Response of Fr. Schillebeeckx," Origins 14 (April 4, 1985): 683.

———. *"Instruction on Christian Freedom and Liberation*, 1986. Boston: St. Paul Editions.

———. "Letter to the Bishops of the Catholic Church on the Pastoral Care of Homosexual Persons," 1986. In Jeannine Grammick and Pat Furey, eds., *The Vatican and Homosexuality*, pp. 1–12. New York: Crossroads, 1988.

———. "Instruction on the Ecclesial Role of the Theologian." Vatican City: Libreria Editrice Vaticana, 1990.

———. "Reply to a *Dubium.*" October 28, 1995. *Origins* 25, 24 (November 30, 1995): 401–3.

Congregation for Religious and Secular Institutes. *"Instructio de vita contemplativa et de monialium clausura."* November 10, 1969. *AAS* 61 (1969): 674–90.

———. "The Contemplative Dimension of Religious Life." Feb. 12, 1981. *Origins* 10 (35): 550–60.

Synod of Bishops. "The Ministerial Priesthood" *(Ultimis temporibus),* November 30, 1967. *AAS* 63 (1971), 898–942. Flannery, *Vatican II: More Postconciliar Documents,* n. 118, 672–94.

Synod of Bishops, 1980. "The Christian Family in the Modern World," 1980. n. 25., Flannery, *Vatican II: More Postconciliar Documents,* pp. 815–898.

Synod of Bishops, Rome 1995. "The Consecrated Life" *(Vita Consecrata).* Washington, DC: United States Catholic Conference, nos. 7–8, 32, 34, 59.

National Conference of Catholic Bishops. "Principles to Guide Confessors in Questions of Homosexuality." Washington, DC, 1973.

———. *Theological Reflections on the Ordination of Women.* Washington DC: National Conference of Catholic Bishops, 1973.

———. "Campaign for a Retirement Fund for Religious." December 1988; see *Origins* 19, 17 (Sept. 28, 1989): 274.

Books

Allen, Prudence. *The Concept of Woman. The Aristotelian Revolution 750 BC–1250 AD.* Montreal: Eden Press, 1985.

Aristotle. *The Basic Works of Aristotle.* Ed. Richard McKeon. *Physics, De Generatione, Nicomachean Ethics, Politics.* New York: Random House, 1941.

Ashley, Benedict M., O.P. *The Dominicans.* Collegeville, MN: The Liturgical Press, 1990.

Ashley, Benedict M., O.P., and Kevin O'Rourke, O.P. *Healthcare Ethics: A Theological Analysis.* 3d ed. St. Louis: Catholic Health Association, 1989.

———. *Theologies of the Body: Humanist and Christian.* Braintree, MA: Pope John Center, 1985.

Aubert, M.-J. *Des Femmes Diacres: Un nouveau chemin pour l'Eglise.* Paris: Beauchesne, 1986.

Audet, Paul Audet. *Structures of Christian Priesthood,* pp. 77–92. New York: Macmillan, 1968.

Augustine of Hippo, St., *The City of God (De Civitate Dei).* Trans. and ed. G. E. McCracken et al. Loeb Library, 7 vols. Cambridge: Harvard University Press, 1963–72.

Austin, Gerard, O.P. *Anointing with the Spirit: The Rite of Confirmation: The Use of Oil and Chrism.* New York: Pueblo Publishing Co., 1985.

Bailey, Derrick S. *Homosexuality and the Western Christian Tradition.* Hamden, CT: Shoe String Press, 1975.

Balinsky, B. I., with the assistance of B. C. Fabian. *An Introduction to Embryology.* 5th ed. Philadelphia: Saunders College Publishing, 1981.

Ballacchino, Salvatore M. *The Household Order Texts: Colossians 3:18–4:1; 1 Peter 2:17–3:9; 1 Timothy 2:8–15 (5:1–2) and Titus 2:1–10) Present State of the Question and Assessment.* Unpublished dissertation, Washington, DC: John Paul II Institute for Studies in Marriage and Family, 1992.

Ballou, Patricia K. *Women: A Bibliography of Bibliographies.* 2d ed. Boston: G. K. Hall, 1986.

Balz, Horst, and Gerhard Schneider *Exegetical Dictionary of the New Testament.* Grand Rapids, MI: W. B. Eerdmans, 1993.

Barbeau, Clayton. *The Head of the Family.* Chicago: Regnery, 1961.

Barnett, James Monroe. *The Diaconate: A Full and Equal Order.* New York: Seabury, 1981.

Barnhouse, Ruth Tiffany. *Homosexuality: A Symbolic Confusion.* New York: Seabury, 1977.

Batchelor, Edward, Jr., ed. *Homosexuality and Ethics.* New York: The Pilgrim Press, 1980.

Beauvoir, Simone. *The Second Sex.* Trans. and ed. H. M. Parshley. New York: Bantam Books, 1953; original 1949.

Behr-Siegel, Elisabeth. *Le ministère de la femme dans l'Église.* Paris: Ed. du Cerf, 1987.

Belensky, Mary Field, Blythe McVicker Clinchy, Nancy Rule Goldberger, and Jill Mattuck Tarule. *Women's Ways of Knowing: The Development of Self, Voice, and Mind.* New York: Basic Books, 1986.

Bell, Alan P., and Martin S. Weinberg. *Homosexualities: A Study of Diversity among Men and Women.* New York: Simon and Schuster, 1978.

Benson, Leonard G. *Fatherhood: A Sociological Perspective.* New York: Random House, 1968.

Bianchi, Eugene C. *From Machismo to Mutuality: Essays on Sexism and Woman-Man Liberation.* New York: Paulist, 1976.

Biller, Henry B. *Paternal Deprivation.* Lexington, MA: Lexington Books, 1974.

Bloesch, Donald G. *Is the Bible Sexist? Beyond Feminism and Patriarchalism.* Westchester, IL: Crossway Books: Good News Publishers, 1982.

———. *The Battle for the Trinity: The Debate over Inclusive God-Language.* Ann Arbor: Servant Publications: Vine Books, 1985.

Boerrensen, Kari Elisabeth. *Subordination and Equivalence: The Nature and Role of Woman in Augustine and Thomas Aquinas.* Washington, DC: University Press of America, 1981.

Bohr, David. *Catholic Moral Tradition: In Christ, A New Creation.* Huntington, IN: Our Sunday Visitor Publishing Division, 1989.

Bouyer, Louis. *Woman in the Church.* Trans. Marilyn Techert. Epilogue by Hans Urs von Balthasar. Essay by C. S. Lewis, "Priestesses in the Church." San Francisco: Ignatius Press, 1979.

Bronstein, Phyllis, and Carolyn Pape Cowan, eds. *Fatherhood Today: Men's Changing Role in the Family*. New York: John Wiley, 1988.

Brown, Peter. *The Body and Society: Men, Women, and Sexual Renunciation in Early Christianity*. New York: Columbia University Press, 1988.

Brown, Raymond E., S.S. *Priest and Bishop: Biblical Reflections*. Paramus, NJ/New York, 1970.

Brown, Raymond E., S.S., Joseph A. Fitzmyer, S.J., and Roland E. Murphy, O.Carm., eds. *The New Jerome Biblical Commentary*. Englewood Cliffs, NJ: Prentice-Hall, 1990.

Brown, Raymond E., S.S., et al., eds. *Peter in the New Testament: A Collaborative Assessment by Protestant and Roman Catholic Scholars*. Minneapolis: Augsburg Publishing House, 1973.

Caplan, Arthur L., ed. *The Sociobiology Debate*. New York: Colophon Books, 1978.

Carmody, Denise Lardner. *Femininity and Christianity: Two Way Reflection*. Nashville, Abingdon Press, 1982.

Carr, Anne. *Transforming Grace: Christian Tradition and Woman's Experience*. San Francisco: Harper and Row, 1990.

Cath, Stanley M., Alan Gurwitt, and Linda Gunsberg, eds. *Fathers and Their Families*. Hillsdale: NJ: Analytic Press, 1989.

Catherine of Siena, St. *The Dialogue*. Trans. and intro. by Suzanne Noffke, O.P. The Classics of Western Spirituality. New York: Paulist Press, 1980.

Catholic Theological Society of America. *Research Report: Women in Church and Society*. Mahwah, NJ: Darlington Seminary, 1978.

Chervin, Ronda. *Feminine, Free, and Faithful*. San Francisco: Ignatius Press, 1986.

Cholij, Roman. *Clerical Celibacy in East and West*. Herefordshire, England: Fowler Wright Books, 1989.

Chomsky, Noam. *Cartesian Linguistics: A Chapter in the History of Rationalist Thought*. New York: Harper and Row, 1966.

———. *Language and Mind*. Enlarged ed. New York: Harcourt Brace Jovanovich, 1972.

Clark, Stephen B. *Man and Woman in Christ: An Examination of Man and Woman in the Light of the Scriptures and the Social Sciences*. Ann Arbor: Servant Books, 1980.

Cochini, Christian, S.J. *Origines apostoliques du celibat sacerdotal*. Paris: P. Lethielleux, Le Sycomore, 1980.

Cohen, Ronald, and Elman R. Service, eds. *Origins of the State: The Anthropology of Political Evolution*. Philadelphia: Institute for the Study of Human Issues, 1978.

Colson, Jean. *Ministre de Jésus Christ ou Le Sacerdoce de l'Évangile*. Paris: Beauchesne, 1966.

Conn, Joann Wolski, ed. *Women's Spirituality: Resources for Christian Development*. New York: Paulist Press, 1986.

Conzelmann, Hans. *1 Corinthians*. Hermeneia Biblical Commentaries. Philadelphia: Fortress Press, 1975.

Corea, Gena. *The Mother Machine*. New York: Harper and Row, 1985. Chapters 15 and 16, pp. 283–317, abridged in Kenneth D. Alpern, ed., *The Ethics of Reproductive Technology*, pp. 220–31. New York: Oxford University Press, 1992.

De Koninck, Charles. *De la primauté du bien commun contre les personalistes*. Laval: University of Laval, 1943.

Deely, John N., and Ralph A. Powell. *Tractatus De Signis: The Semiotic of John Poinsot*. Berkeley: University of California Press, 1985.

Detroit Ordination Conference, 1975. *Women and the Catholic Priesthood*. New York: Paulist Press, 1976.

Downing, Christine. *The Goddess: Mythological Images of the Feminine*. New York: Crossroads, 1981.

Doyle, James A. *The Male Experience*. Dubuque, IA: W. C. Brown Co., 1983.

Dulles, Avery, S.J. *Models of the Church*. Expanded ed. Garden City, NY: Doubleday Image Books, 1987.

———. *The Craft of Theology* (New York: Crossroad, 1992).

Dunn, Patrick. *Priesthood: A Re-Examination of the Roman Catholic Theology of the Presbyterate*. Staten Island, NY: Alba House, 1990.

Dunne, Joseph. *Back to the Rough Ground: 'Phronesis' and 'Techne' Modern Philosophy and in Aristotle*. Notre Dame, IN: University of Notre Dame Press, 1993.

Dupont, Jacques. *Nouvelles Études sur les Actes des Apôtre*. Lectio Divina 118. Paris: Cerf, 1984.

Elia, Irene. *The Female Animal*. Intro. by Ashley Montagu. New York, Henry Holt, 1988.

Elshtain, Jean Bethke. *Public Man, Private Woman: Woman in Social and Political Thought*. Princeton, NJ: Princeton University Press, 1981.

Encyclopedia of Philosophy, The. Ed. Paul Edwards. Reprint ed. 6 vols. in 3. Macmillan/Free Press, 1972.

Epstein, Cynthia Fuchs. *Deceptive Distinctions: Sex, Gender, and the Social Order*. New Haven: Yale University Press for the Russell Sage Foundation, 1988.

Ferder, Sister Fran, C.F.S.P.A. *Called to Break Bread?* Mt. Rainier, MD: Quixote Center, 1978.

Ferguson, Ann. *Blood at the Root: Motherhood, Sexuality and Male Domination*. London: Pandora, 1989.

Fiorenza, Elisabeth Schüssler. *In Memory of Her: A Feminist Theological Reconstruction of Christian Origins*. New York: Crossroad, 1984.

Flood, Sister Marie Walter, O.P. *The Place of Women in the Ministerial Offices of the Church as Witnessed by Ecclesiastical Tradition and Rites of Ordination*. Dissertation. University of Toronto, 1976.

Freedman, David Noel, ed. *The Anchor Bible Dictionary.* New York: Doubleday, 1990.

French, Marilyn. *Beyond Power: On Women, Men, and Morals.* New York: Ballantine Books, 1985.

Freud, Sigmund. *Three Essays on the Theory of Sexuality.* Trans. and rev. James Strachey. New York: Basic Books.

Gallup, George, Jr. *Religion in America: 50 years: 1935–1985.* Princeton, NJ: The Gallup Report, No. 236, May, 1985.

Galot, Jean. *Theology of the Priesthood.* San Francisco: Ignatius Press, 1984.

Garber-Talmon, Yonina. *Family and Community in the Kibbutz.* Cambridge: Harvard University Press, 1972.

Gay, Peter. *The Enlightenment.* 2 vols. New York: Alfred Knopf, 1967.

Gilbert, Scott F. *Developmental Biology.* 3d ed. Sunderland, MA: Sinauer Associates, 1991.

Gilder, George F. *Sexual Suicide.* New York: Quadrangle, 1971.

———. *Men and Marriage.* Gretna: Pelican Publishing Co., 1986.

Gilligan, Carol. *In a Different Voice: Psychological Theory and Women's Development.* Cambridge: Harvard University, 1982.

Gimbutas, Marija. *The Gods and Goddesses of Old Europe.* Berkeley: University of California Press, 1974.

Ginsburg, Benjamin, and Alan Stone, eds. *Do Elections Matter?* 2d ed. Armonk, NY: M. E. Sharpe, 1991.

Glendon, Mary Ann. *Rights Talk: The Impoverishment of Political Discourse,* pp.42–43. New York: The Free Press/ Macmillan, 1991.

Goldberg, Steven. *The Inevitability of Patriarchy.* New York: Morrow, 1974.

Gray, Elizabeth Dodson. *Patriarchy as a Conceptual Trap.* Wellesley, MA: Roundtable Press, 1982).

Görres, Ida Frederike. *Is Celibacy Outdated?* Trans. Barbara Waldstein-Wartenberg in collaboration with the author. Westminister, MD: Newman Press, 1965.

Grammick, Jeannine, and Pat Furey, eds. *The Vatican and Homosexuality: Reactions to the "Letter to the Bishops of the Catholic Church on the Pastoral Care of Homosexual Persons."* New York: Crossroads, 1988. The *Letter* is translated on pp. 1–12.

Greeley, Andrew, and William McManus. *Catholic Contributions: Sociology and Polity.* Chicago: St. Thomas More Press, 1987.

Green, David G. *The New Conservatism: The Counter-revolution in Political, Economic, and Social Thought.* New York: St. Martin's Press, 1987.

Gregory the Great, St. *Homilies on Ezekiel* (Lib. 1, 11: CCL 142, 170–72) from *The Liturgy of the Hours According to the Roman Rite.* IV, p. 1366. New York: Catholic Book Publishing Co., 1975.

Grelot, Pierre. *Église et ministères: pour un dialogue critique avec Edward Schillebeeckx.* Paris, Éditions du Cerf, 1983.

Grisez, Germain, with the help of Joseph Boyle, Jeanette Grisez, Russell Shaw, et al. *The Way of the Lord Jesus.* Vol. 2. *Living a Christian Life.* Quincy, IL: Franciscan Press, 1993.

Groeschel, Benedict J., O.F.M.Cap. *The Courage to Be Chaste.* Mahwah, NJ: Paulist Press, 1985.

Gryson, Roger. *Les origines du célibat ecclésiastiques du premier au septieme siècle.* Gembloux: 1970.

———. *Le ministère des femmes dans l'Église ancienne.* Gembloux, 1972.

Hammerton-Kelly, Robert. *God the Father: Theology and Patriarchy in the Teaching of Jesus.* Philadelphia: Fortress, 1979.

Harris, Marvin. *Cultural Materialism: The Struggle for a Science of Culture.* New York: Random House, 1979.

Harvey, John F., O.S.F.S. *The Homosexual Person: New Thinking in Pastoral Care.* San Francisco: Ignatius Press, 1987.

Hathaway, Ronald F. *Hierarchy and the Definition of Order in the Letters of Pseudo-Dionysius.* The Hague: Martinus Nijhoff, 1969.

Hauke, Manfred. *Women in the Priesthood? A Systematic Analysis in the Light of the Order of Creation and Redemption.* Trans. David Kipp. San Francisco: Ignatius Press, 1988.

Hayes, Zachary, O.F.M. *The Hidden Center.* New York: Paulist Press, 1981.

Heine, Susanne. *Women in Early Christianity: A Reappraisal.* Minneapolis: Augsburg Publishing House, 1987.

———. *Matriarchs, Goddesses and Images of God: A Critique of a Feminist Theology.* Minneapolis, MN: Augsburg, 1989.

Hildebrand, Dietrich Von. *Man and Woman.* Chicago: Francisco Herald Press, 1966.

Hopko, Thomas, ed. *Woman and the Priesthood.* Introduction by Alexander Schmemann. Crestwood, NY: St. Vladimir's Seminary Press, 1983.

Hourcade, Janine. *La Femme dans l'Église.* Paris: Téqui, 1986.

Johnson, Paul. *The Birth of the Modern: World Society, 1815–1830.* Chapter 12. New York: Harper Collins, 1991.

Johnson, Elizabeth A., C.S.J. *Consider Jesus: Waves of Renewal in Christology.* New York: Crossroad, 1990.

———. *She Who Is: The Mystery of God in Feminist Discourse.* New York, Crossroad, 1993.

Jordan of Saxony, Bl. *The Origins of the Order of Friars Preachers.* From *Early Dominicans: Selected Writings.* Trans. and ed. Simon Tugwell. The Classics of Western Spirituality. New York: Paulist Press, 1982.

Jugie, Martin, S.J. *Theologia dogmatica christianorum orientalium ab ecclesia catholica dissidentium.* Vol. 3. Paris: Letouzey et Ane, 1926–35).

Jung, Carl Gustav, with M. L. Franz, J. L. Henderson, J. Jacobi, and A. Jaffé. *Man and His Symbols.* Garden City, New York: Doubleday, 1964.

Kant, Immanuel. *Religion within the Limits of Reason Alone.* Trans. T. M. Greene and H. H. Hudson. Essay by John R. Silber, "The Ethical Significance of Kant's Religion." New York: Harper Torchbooks, 1960.

Kaus, Mickey. *The End of Equality.* New York: A New Republic Book/ Basic Books, 1992.

Keen, Sam. *Fire in the Belly: On Being a Man.* New York: Bantam Books, 1991.

Kilpatrick, Clifford. *The Family: Its Process and Institution.* New York: Ronald Press, 1963.

Koch, Adolf G. *Religion of the American Enlightenment.* New York: Thomas Y. Crowell, 1968; originally 1933.

Kolmer, Elizabeth, A.S.C. *Religious Women in the United States: A Survey of the Influential Literature from 1950–1983.* Preface by Marie Augusta Neal, SND de Namur. Consecrated Life Series, No. 4 Wilmington, DE: Michael Glazier, 1984.

Küng, Hans. *Infallible? An Inquiry.* Rev. ed. Trans. Edward Quinn. Garden City, New York: Doubleday, 1983.

Lamb, Michael E., ed. *The Role of the Father in Child Development.* New York: John Wiley & Sons, 1976.

———. *The Father's Role: Cross-cultural Perspectives.* Hillsdale, NJ: L. Erlbaum Associates, 1987.

Lawler, Michael G. *Symbol and Sacrament: A Contemporary Sacramental Theology.* New York: Paulist Press, 1987.

Lécuyer, Joseph. *Le Sacrament de l'Ordination: Recherche historique et théologique.* Paris: Beauchesne, 1983.

Legrand, Lucien. *The Biblical Doctrine of Celibacy.* New York: Sheed and Ward, 1963.

Lerner, Gerda. *The Creation of Patriarchy.* New York: Oxford University Press, 1986.

Lo Bello, Nino. *The Vatican Empire.* New York: Trident, 1968.

Lubac, Henri de, S.J. *Exégèse mediéval: Les quatre sens de l'écriture.* 2 (4) vols. Paris: Aubier, 1960.

Lynn, David B.Lynn. *The Father: His Role in Child Development.* Monterey, CA: Brooks/Co. Publishing Co., 1974.

Machan, Tibor R., ed. *The Libertarian Reader.* Totowa, NJ: Rowman and Littlefield, 1982.

MacIntyre, Alasdair. *After Virtue: A Study in Moral Theory.* Notre Dame, IN: University of Notre Dame Press, 1982.

Maritain, Jacques. *Christianity and Democracy.* French original in 1943. Trans. Doris C. Anson, republished with *The Rights of Man and Natural Law* and an introduction by Donald A. Gallagher. San Francisco: Ignatius Press, 1986.

———. *The Person and the Common Good.* New York: Charles Scribner's Sons, 1947.

Martimort, Aimé Georges. *The Signs of the New Covenant.* Rev. 2d ed. Collegeville, MN: The Liturgical Press, 1968.

————. *Deaconesses: An Historical Study.* San Francisco: Ignatius Press, 1986.

Martin, Malachy. *Rich Church, Poor Church.* New York, Putnam, 1984.

Martin, Francis. *The Feminist Question: Feminist Theology in the Light of Christian Tradition.* Grand Rapids, MI: Eerdmans, 1994.

McCormick, Richard A., S.J. *The Critical Calling: Reflections on Moral Dilemmas since Vatican II.* Washington, DC: Georgetown University Press, 1989.

McFague, Sallie. *Models of God: Theology for an Ecological, Nuclear Age.* Philadelphia: Fortress Press, 1987.

McKee, L., and M. O'Brien, eds. *The Father Figure.* London/New York: Tavistock Publications, 1983.

McKenna, Sister Mary Lawrence, S.C.M.M. *Women of the Church: Role and Renewal.* Foreword by Jean Daniélou, S.J. New York: P. J. Kenedy & Sons, 1967.

McKenzie, John L., S.J. *Dictionary of the Bible.* Milwaukee, WI: 1965.

McNeill, J. *The Church and the Homosexual.* Kansas City: Sheed, Andres and McMeel, 1976.

Meer, Haye van der. *Women Priests in the Catholic Church: A Theological-Historical Investigation.* Trans. Arlene and Leonard Swidler. Philadelphia: Temple University Press, 1973.

Melzer, Arthur M. *The Natural Goodness of Man: On the System of Rousseau's Thought.* Chicago: University of Chicago Press, 1990.

Ware, Kallistos. *The Orthodox Way.* Crestwood, NY: St. Vladimir's Seminary, 1979.

Miguens, Manuel, O.F.M. *Church Ministries in New Testament Times.* Arlington, VA: Westminster Press, 1976.

Miletic, Stephen F. *"One Flesh" (Eph 5:22–24; 5:31): Marriage and the New Creation.* Analecta Biblica. Rome: Biblical Institute Press, 1988.

Miller, John W. *Biblical Faith and Fathering: Why We Call God "Father."* New York: Paulist, 1989.

Miller, J. Michael, C.S.B. *What Are They Saying about Papal Primacy.* New York: Paulist Press, 1983.

Moberly, Elizabeth R. *Psychogenesis: The Early Development of Gender Identity.* London: Routledge and Kegan Paul, 1983.

————. *Homosexuality: A New Christian Ethic.* Greenwood, S.C.: Attic Press, 1987.

Moll, Willi. *Father and Fatherhood.* Trans. E. Reinecke and P. C. Bailey. Notre Dame, IN: Fides, 1966.

Mollenkott, Virginia Ramey. *The Divine Feminine: The Biblical Imagery of God as Female.* New York: Crossroad, 1983.

Moltmann-Wendel, Elizabeth. *A Land Flowing with Milk and Honey: A Perspective on Feminist Theology.* New York: Crossroad, 1986.

Moore, Robert L., and Douglas Gillette. *King, Warrior, Magician, Lover: Rediscovering the Archetypes of the Mature Masculine.* San Francisco: Harper, 1990.

Nicolosi, Joseph. *Reparative Therapy of Male Homosexuality: A New Clinical Approach.* Northvale, NJ: Jason Aronson, 1991.

Nolan, Richard T., ed. *The Diaconate Now.* Washington/Cleveland: Corpus Books, 1968.

Notman, Malkah T., and Carol C. Nadelson, eds. *Women and Men: New Perspectives on Gender Differences.* Washington, DC: American Psychiatric Press, 1991.

Nozick, Robert. *Anarchy, State, and Utopia.* New York: Basic Books, 1974.

Ohlig, Karl-Heinz. *Why We Need the Pope: The Necessity and Limits of Papal Primacy.* Trans. Dr. Robert C. Ware. St. Meinrad, IN: Abbey Press, 1975.

Olsen, Carol. *The Book of the Goddess and Present.* New York: Crossroads, 1983.

Orsy, Ladislas M., S.J. *The Church: Learning and Teaching: Magisterium, Assent, Dissent, Academic Freedom.* Wilmington, DE: Michael Glazier, 1987.

Osborne, Kenan B., O.F.M. *Priesthood: A History of the Ordained Ministry in the Roman Catholic Church.* New York: Paulist, 1988.

Pallenberg, Corrado. *Vatican Finances.* Peter Owen, 1971.

Patai, Raphael. *The Hebrew Goddess.* New York: KTAV Publishing House, 1967.

Phipps, William. *Was Jesus Married?* New York: Harper and Row, 1970.

Pieper, Josef. *Happiness and Contemplation.* Trans. Richard and Clara Winston. New York: Pantheon, 1958.

———. *Leisure, the Basis of Culture.* Trans. Alexander Dru. Intro. by T. S. Eliot. New York: New American Library, 1963.

Plato. *Republic.* Trans. with Introduction by H. D. P. Lee. Harmondsworth, England: Penguin Classics, 1955.

Pleck, Joseph H., and Jack Sawyer, eds. *Men and Masculinity.* Englewood Cliffs, NJ: Prentice-Hall, 1974.

Powell, Ralph A. *Freely Chosen Reality.* Washington, DC: University Press of America, 1983.

Prickett, Stephen. *Words and the Word: Language, Poetics and Biblical Interpretation.* Cambridge: Cambridge University Press, 1986.

Quay, Paul M., S.J. *The Christian Meaning of Human Sexuality,* pp. 85–109. Evanston, IL: Credo House, 1985.

Rad, Gerhard von. *Wisdom in Israel.* Nashville, TN: Abingdon Press, 1972.

Ramey, Virginia. *The Divine Feminine: The Biblical Imagery of God as Female.* York: Crossroad, 1983.

Raming, Ida. *The Exclusion of Women from Priesthood: Divine Law or Sex Discrimination?* Trans. Norman R. Adams. Meutchen, NJ: Scarecrow Press, 1976.

Rawls, John. *A Theory of Justice.* Cambridge: Harvard University Press, 1971.

Reardon, Bernard M. G., ed. *Roman Catholic Modernism*. Introduction, pp. 9–67. Stanford: Stanford University Press, 1970.

Rockmore, Tom, William J. Gavin, James G. Colbert, Jr., and Thomas J. Blakeley. *Marxism and Alternatives: Towards the Conceptual Interaction Among Soviet Philosophy, Neo-Thomism, Pragmatism, and Phenomenology*. Sovietica Series. Boston/Dordrecht: D. Reidel, 1981.

Roof, Wade Clark, and William McKinney. *American Mainline Religion*. New Brunswick, NJ: Rutgers University Press, 1987.

Rousseau, Jacques. *Lettres Morale* in *Oeuvres completes*, vol. IV, 1109; *Emile* I, 42; cf. IV: 290.

Royo, Antonio, O.P., and Jordan Aumann, O.P. *The Theology of Christian Perfection*. Dubuque, IA: Priory Press, 1962.

Ruether, Rosemary Radford. *Sexism and God-Talk: Toward a Feminist Theology*. New York, 1983.

———. *Women-Church: Theology and Practice of Feminist Liturgical Communities*. San Francisco: Harper & Row, 1985.

Russell, Letty M., ed. *Feminist Interpretations of the Bible*. Philadelphia: Westminister Press, 1985.

Schillebeeckx, Edward, O.P. *Celibacy*. New York: Sheed and Ward, 1967.

———. *Ministry: Leadership in the Community of Jesus Christ*. New York: Crossroad, 1981.

———. *The Church with a Human Face: A New and Expanded Theology of Ministry*. New York: Crossroad, 1985.

Schnackenburg, Rudolf. *The Moral Teaching of the New Testament*. New York: Seabury Press, 1973.

Schneiders, Sandra. *New Wineskins: Re-Imagining Religious Life Today*. New York: Paulist Press, 1986.

Otto, Rudolf. *The Idea of the Holy*. 2d ed. London: Oxford, 1950).

Schrage, Wolfgang. *The Ethics of the New Testament*. Philadelphia: Fortress Press, 1988.

Stewart, Lea P., Pamela J. Cooper, and Sheryl A. Friedley. *Communication between the Sexes: Sex Differences and Sex-Role Stereotypes*. Scottsdale, AZ: Gorsuch Scarisbrick Publishers, 1986.

Senft, Christophe. *La première épître de Saint Paul aux Corinthiens*. Delachaux and Nestlé, 1979.

Sherman, Lynn C. *The Diaconate in the Church*. Staten Island, NY: Alba House, 1991.

Simon, Yves. *A General Theory of Authority*. Notre Dame, IN: University of Notre Dame Press, 1962.

Sipe, A. W. Richard. *A Secret World: Sexuality and the Search for Celibacy*. Foreword by Robert Coles, M.D. New York: Brunner/Mazel, 1990.

Stadelmann, Luis. *Love and Politics: A New Commentary on the Song of Songs*. New York: Paulist, 1992.

Starhawk. *The Spiral Dance: A Rebirth of the Ancient Religion of the Great Goddess*. San Francisco: Harper Row, 1979.

Stephens, William N. *The Family in Cross-Cultural Perspective.* New York: Holt, Rinehart and Winston, 1963.

Stuhlmueller, Carroll, C.P., ed. *Women and Priesthood: Future Directions.* Collegeville, MN: Liturgical Press, 1978.

Sullivan, Francis, S.J., *Magisterium: Teaching Authority in the Catholic Church.* Ramsey, NJ: Paulist, 1984.

Sunday, Peggy Reeves. *Female Power and Male Dominance: On the Origins of Sexual Inequality.* Cambridge: Cambridge University Press, 1981.

Sussman, Marvin B., and Suzanne K. Steinmetz, eds. *Handbook of Marriage and the Family.* New York: Plenum Press, 1987.

Swidler, Arlene and Leonard, eds. *Women Priests: A Commentary on the Vatican Declaration.* New York: Paulist Press, 1977.

Tavard, George. *Woman in Christian Tradition.* Notre Dame: University of Notre Dame, 1973.

Thérèse of Lisieux, St. *Manuscripts autobiographique,* Lisieux, 170–72 from *The Liturgy of the Hours According to the Roman Rite* (New York: Catholic Book Publishing Co., 1975), IV, p. 1451.

Thomas Aquinas, St., O.P. *Summa Theologiae.* Turin: Marietti, 1952.

——. *Librum Beati Dionysii De divinis nominibus Expositio.* Ceslaus Pera, O.P., ed. Turin/Rome: Marietti, 1950.

——. *In X libros Ethicorum Aristotelis ad Nicomachum.* R. M. Spiazzi, O.P., ed. Turin/Rome: Marietti, 1949.

——. *Super Epistolas S. Pauli.* R. P. Cai, O.P., ed. Turin: Marietti, 1953.

Thurian, Max. *Marriage and Celibacy.* London: SCM Press, 1959.

Tiger, Lionel, and Robin Fox. *The Imperial Animal.* London: Secker and Warburg, 1977.

Tillard, J. M. R., O.P. *The Bishop of Rome.* Trans. John de Satge. Wilmington, DE: Michael Glazier, 1983.

Tournay, R. J., O.P. *Quand Dieu parle aux hommes le langage de l'amour.* Cahiers de la *Révue Biblique* 21. Paris: Gabalda, 1982.

Towner, Philip H. *The Goal of Our Instruction: The Structure of Theology and Ethics in the Pastoral Epistles.* Sheffield, ISOT Press, 1989.

Vanier, Jean. *Man and Woman He Made Them.* Foreword by Henri J. M. Nouwen. Mahwah, NJ: Paulist Press, 1985.

Virtue, William D. *Absence and Desire in Christian Married Love.* Unpublished S.T.L. dissertation. John Paul II Institute for Studies in Marriage and Family, Washington, DC, 1990.

Walby, Sylvia. *Theorizing Patriarchy.* Oxford: Basil Blackwell, 1990.

Walsh, E. A. *Priesthood in the Writings of the French School: Bérulle, de Condren, Olier.* Washington, DC: The Catholic Unviersity of America Press, 1949.

Wills, Gary. *Inventing America: Jefferson's Declaration of Independence.* Garden City, NY: Doubleday, 1981.

Wilson-Kastner, Patricia. *Faith, Feminism, and the Christ.* Philadelphia: Fortress, 1983.

Wire, Antoinette Clark. *The Corinthian Women Prophets: A Reconstruction through Paul's Rhetoric.* Philadelphia: Fortress Press, 1990.

Witherington, Ben, III. *Women in the Ministry of Jesus: A Study of Jesus' Attitudes to Women and Their Roles as Reflected in His Earthly Life* and *Women in the Earliest Churches.* Society for New Testament Studies Monograph Series, Nos. 51 and 59. Cambridge: Cambridge University Press, 1984 and 1988.

Woodcock, George. *Anarchism: A History of Libertarian Ideas and Movements.* Cleveland: Meridian Books, 1962.

Articles

Adler, Mortimer, and Walter Farrell, O.P. "The Theory of Democracy." *The Thomist* 3 (1941): 397–449, 588–652; 4 (1942): 121–81, 286–354, 446–522, 692–761; 6 (1943): 49–118, 251–77; 7 (1944): 80–131.

Adnés, Pierre. "Mariage spirituel." *Dictionnaire de Spiritualité,* vol. 10, 387–408.

Allen, Prudence. "Hildegard of Bingen's Philosophy of Sex Identity." *Thought* 64 (1989): 231–41.

Anderson, Gary. "Celibacy or Consummation in the Garden? Reflections on Early Jewish and Christian Interpretations of the Garden of Eden." *Harvard Theological Review* 82 (2, 1989): 124–48.

Annechino, Robert. "Song of the Groom: Spiritual Marriage and Masculinity." *Review for Religious* 50 (Nov./Dec. 1991): 822–38.

Ashley, Benedict M., O.P. "Compassion and Sexual Orientation." In Jeannine Grammick and Pat Furey, eds., *The Vatican and Homosexuality: Reactions to the "Letter to the Bishops of the Catholic Church on the Pastoral Care of Homosexual Persons,* pp. 105–11. New York: Crossroads, 1988.

———. "Contemporary Understandings of Personhood." *The Twenty-Fifth Anniversary of Vatican II: A Look Back and a Look Forward.* Proceedings of the Ninth Bishops' Workshop, Dallas, Texas. Russell E. Smith, ed. Braintree, MA: The Pope John Center, 1990.

Boazo, Emmanuele, O.Carm. "La Clasura: Origine e sviluppo storico-giuridico-spirituale." *Vita Consecrata* 29 (July-August 1993): 492–512.

Bradley, Sister Ritamary. "Patristic Background of the Motherhood Similitude in Julian of Norwich." *Christian Scholar's Review* 8 (1978): 101–13.

Briefs, Goetz A. "The Ethos Problem in the Present Pluralistic Society." In *The Solidarist Economics of Goetz A. Briefs,* special number of *Review of Social Economy* 41 (Dec. 1983): 271–99, pp. 275–76.

Brown, Raymond E., S.S. "Dead Sea Scrolls." *The New Jerome Biblical Commentary,* 67:113–117, pp. 1076–77.

———. "The Twelve and the Apostolate." Ibid., 81: 135–57, pp. 1377–81.

Buchanan, George Wesley. "Jesus and Other Monks of New Testament Times." *Religion in Life* 48 (1979): 136–42.

Buckley, Michael J., S.J. "Seventeenth Century French Spirituality." In Louis Dupré and Don E. Saliers, eds., *Christian Spirituality*. Vol. III, "Post Reformation and Modern Spirituality," vol. 18 of *An Encyclopedia of World Spirituality* (New York: Crossroad, 1989), 28–68.

Butler, Sister Sara, M.S.B.T. "The Findings of the Research Team of the Catholic Theological Society of America." *New Woman, New Church, New Ministry, New Women, New Church, New Ministry: Proceedings of the Second Conference on the Ordination of Roman Catholic Women, Nov. 10–12, 1978, Baltimore, Maryland*, pp. 117–25. Rochester, NY: Kirk-Wood Press, 1980.

Caludot, Michel Dortel. "Vie Consacrée." Part II, *Dictionnaire de Spiritualité*, fasc. 104, pp. 663–703.

Cardman, Francine. "The Medieval Question of Women and Orders." *The Thomist* 42 (Oct. 1978): 582–99.

Catholic Biblical Association Task Force. "The Role of Women in Early Christianity." *Catholic Biblical Quarterly* 41 (1979): 608–13.

Congar, Yves, O.P. "Collège, primauté . . . conférences épiscopales: quelque notes," *Esprit et Vie* 96 (10 serie), 27 (July 3, 1986): 385–90.

Cross, Nancy M. "The Bible's Use of Sexual Language." *Review for Religious* 50 (Nov./Dec. 1991): 839–48.

Crouzel, Henri, S.J. Review of Christian Cochini, S.J., *Origines apostoliques du celibat sacerdotal*, in *Nouvelle Revue Theologigue* (1971), 649–53.

———. "Dix ans de recherches sur les origines du célibat ecclésiastique: Reflexion sur les publications des annees 1970–1979." *Revue Theologique Louvain* (1980), 157–85.

Day, John. "Ashtoreth (Astarte)," vol. 1, 491–93, and "Asherah," vol. 1, 483–87. *The Anchor Bible Dictionary*.

De Koninck, Charles. "In Defense of St. Thomas." *Laval Théologique et Philosophique* 1 (2, 1945): 1–103.

Donfried, K. P. "The Allegory of the Ten Virgins as a Summary of Matthean Theology." *Journal of Biblical Literature* 93 (1974): 415–28.

Drucker, Peter. "Management as a Social Function and a Liberal Art." In his *The New Realities in Government and Politics, in Economics and Business, in Society and World View*. New York: Harper and Row, 1990.

Engelhardt, H. Tristram, Jr. "Some Persons Are Humans, Some Humans Are Persons, and the World Is What We Persons Make It." In Stuart C. Spiker and H. Tristram Engelhardt, Jr., eds., *Philosophical Medical Ethics*, pp. 183–94. Boston: Reidel, 1977.

Eschmann, I. Th., O.P. "In Defense of Jacques Maritain." *Modern Schoolman* 22 (May 1945): 182–208.

Finnis, John. "Natural Law and Legal Reasoning." In Robert P. George, ed., *Natural Law Theory: Contemporary Essays*, pp. 134–57. Oxford: Oxford University Press, 1992.

Fiorenza, Elizabeth Schüssler. "You are not to be called Father." *Cross-Currents* (Fall 1979): 356–58.

―――. "Toward a Feminist Biblical Hermeneutics: Biblical Interpretation and Liberation Theology." In C. E. Curran and R. A.McCormick, eds., *The Use of Scripture in Moral Theology*. Readings in Moral Theology, No. 4. New York: Paulist Press, 1984.

―――. "The Will to Choose or to Reject." In Letty M. Russell, ed., *Feminist Interpretations of the Bible*. Philadelphia: Westminister Press, 1985.

Fletcher, Joseph. "Four Indicators of Humanhood: The Enquiry Matures." *Hastings Center Report* 4 (1974): 4–7, with replies in "Correspondence" 5 (1975): 4, 43–45.

Florovsky, George. "The Problem of the Diaconate in the Orthodox Church." In Richard T. Nolan, ed., *The Diaconate Now*, pp. 81–99. Washington/Cleveland: Corpus Books, 1968.

Frank, Karl Suso. "Vie Consacrée." I, 4, "Le consecration des vierges." *Dictionnaire de Spiritualité*. Vol. 104, cols. 655–61.

Gaudemet, Jean. "Anointing." *New Catholic Encyclopedia* 1:565–68.

Gibbs, Nancy R. "Bringing Up Father." *Time*, June 28, 1990, 52–61.

Gill, James J., S.J. Review of A. W. Richard Sipe, *A Secret World*, in *Commonweal* 118 (Feb. 8, 1991): 108–10.

Goethals, Gregor T. "TV's Iconic Imagery in a Secular Society." *New Theology Review* 6 (Feb. 1993): 40–53. Excerpted from *The Electronic Golden Calf: Images, Religion, and the Making of Meaning*. Cambridge, MA: Cowley Publications, 1990.

Goldenberg, Naomi. "A Feminist Critique of Jung." In Joann Wolski Conn, ed., *Women's Spirituality: Resources for Christian Development*, pp. 150–58. New York: Paulist Press, 1986.

Gonbola, Patricia A., and Edward H. Thompson, Jr. "Single-Parent Families." In *Handbook of Marriage and the Family*, pp. 397–418.

Grant, Robert M. Reviews of Elisabeth Schüssler Fiorenza, *In Memory of Her: Journal of Biblical Literature* 104 (1985): 72; *Journal of Religion* 65 (1985): 83–88.

Gribomont, Jean. "Monachisme." *Dictionnaire de Spiritualité*, vol. 10, cols. 1524–1617.

Hardy, Edward D. "Deacons in History and Practice." In Philip Harner's *Understanding the Lord's Prayer*, pp. 37–56. Philadelphia: Fortress, 1975.

Harrison, Beverly Wildung. "Human Sexuality and Mutuality." In Judith L. Weidman, *Christian Feminism: Visions of a New Humanity*, pp. 158–80. San Francisco: Harper and Row, 1984.

Hegermann, H. "Sophia." *Exegetical Dictionary of the New Testament*, vol. 3, 258–61. Edited by Horst Balz and Gerhard Schneider. Grand Rapids, MI: W. B. Eerdmans, 1993.

Hein, David. "Women's Ordination Redivivus." *Liturgy* 23 (March 1978): 31.

Hill, William, O.P. "Does the World Make a Difference to God?" *The Thomist* 38 (1974): 146–64.

Hutter, U. *"Patría," Exegetical Dictionary of the New Testament,* vol. 3, p. 58. Edited by Horst Balz and Gerhard Schneider. Grand Rapids, MI: W. B. Eerdmans, 1993.

Johnson, Elizabeth, C.S.J. "The Incomprehensiblity of God and the Image of God Male and Female." *Theological Studies* 45 (1984): 441–65.

Kant, Immanuel. "An Answer to the Question: What Is Enlightenment?" Translated with introduction by Ted Humphrey, in *Perpetual Peace and Other Essays on Politics, History and Morals,* p. 41. Indianapolis, IN: Hackett, 1983.

Karlen, Arno. "Homosexuality as a Mental Illness." *International Journal of Psychiatry* 10 (March 1972): 108–13.

Kasper, Walter. "Ministry in the Church: Taking Issue with Edward Schillebeeckx." *Communio* (Summer 1983): 185–95.

———. "Theological Foundation of Human Rights." *The Jurist* 50 (1990): 148–66.

Keefe, Donald J., S.J. "Gender, History and Liturgy in the Catholic Church." *Review for Religious* 46 (6, Nov.–Dec. 1987): 866–81.

Kelly, Anthony. "God: How Near a Relation." *The Thomist* 34 (1970): 191–229.

Kobleski, Paul J. "The Letter to the Ephesians." *The New Jerome Biblical Commentary,* pp. 883–89.

Komonchak, Joseph. "Theological Questions on the Ordination of Women." *Catholic Mind* 75 (Jan. 1977): 13–28.

Kraemer, Ross S. Review of Elisabeth Schüssler Fiorenza, *In Memory of Her,* in *Journal of Biblical Literature* 104 (1985): 722–25.

Langley, Wendell E., S.J., and Rosemary Jermann. "Women and the Ministerial Priesthood: An Annotated Bibliography." *Theology Digest* 29 (Winter 1981): 329–42.

Legrand, Hervé, O.P. "The Presidency of the Eucharist According to the Ancient Tradition." *Worship* 53:5 (Sept. 1979): 413–38.

Lemaire, André. "The Ministries in the New Testament." *Biblical Theology Bulletin* III, 2 (June 1973): 133–66.

Leone, Bruno, and M. Teresa O'Neill. *Male/Female Roles: Opposing Viewpoints.* St. Paul, MN: Greenhaven Press, 1983.

Ligier, L. "Women and the Ministerial Priesthood." *Origins* 7 (April 20, 1978): 694–702.

Maier, Walter A., III "Anath." *The Anchor Bible Dictionary,* vol. 1, 225–27.

Maly, Eugene H. "Celibacy." *The Bible Today* 34 (Feb. 1968): 2392–2400.

Martin, Charles, S. J., Review of Christian Cochini, S. J., *Origines apos-*

toliques du celibat sacerdotal, 1980, *Nouvelle Revue Theologique,* 105 (1983): 437–438.

Martin, Francis. "Feminist Hermeneutics: An Overview." *Communio* 18 (1991): 144–63; 398–424.

McDonough, Elizabeth, O.P. "Beyond the Liberal Model: Quo Vadis?" *Review for Religious* 50 (March/April 1991): 866–81.

McKenzie, John L., S.J. "Virgin." *Dictionary of the Bible,* p. 914. Milwaukee, WI: Bruce, 1965.

May, William E. "Marriage and the Complementarity of Male and Female." *Antropotes* 8 (1, June 1992): 41–60.

Meier, John. "On the Veiling of Hermeneutics (1 Cor 11:2–16)." *Catholic Biblical Quarterly* 40 (26 Apr. 1978): 212.

Moberly, Dr. Elizabeth R. "Counseling the Homosexual." *The Expository Times* (June 1985), pp. 261–66.

Murphy, Roland E., O.Carm. "The Canticle of Canticles." *The New Jerome Biblical Commentary,* pp. 462–65.

Murphy-O'Connor, Jerome, O.P. "1 Corinthians." *The New Jerome Biblical Commentary,* pp. 715–813.

Oberti, Armando. "I fondamenti della 'consacrazione' negli istituti secolari: La Secolaritá consecrata nel Magistero pontificio." *Vita Consecrata* 29 (July–August 1993): 457–67.

Podles, Mary, and Leon J. "The Emasculation of God." *America* 25 (Nov. 1889): 373.

Purvis, Sally P. "Christian Feminist Spirituality." In Louis Dupré and Don E. Saliers, eds., *Christian Spirituality.* Vol. III, "Post Reformation and Modern Spirituality," pp. 500–519. Vol. 18 of *An Encyclopedia of World Spirituality.* New York: Crossroad, 1989.

Quinn, Jerome D. "Celibacy and the Ministry in Scripture." *The Bible Today* 46 (Feb. 1970): 3163–75.

Rahner, Karl, S.J. "The Celibacy of the Secular Priest Today." *The Furrow* (Feb. 1968), pp. 59–72, included in his book *Servants of the Lord,* pp. 149–72. New York: Herder and Herder, 1968.

———. "Priestertum der Frau." *Stimmen der Zeit* 195 (May 1977): 291–301.

Ruether, Rosemary Radford. "Feminism the End of Christianity? A Critique of Daphne Hampson's *Theology and Feminism.*" *Scottish Journal of Theology* 43 (1990): 390–400.

———. "The Way of Wicca." A review of Starhawk, *The Spiral Dance,* in *The Christian Century* 97, 6 (Feb. 20, 1980): 208–9.

Santmire, Paul. "Retranslating 'Our Father': The Urgency and the Possibility." *Dialog* 16 (1977): 102–4.

Sattler, H. Vernon. "An Agenda to Reject Celibacy." *Homiletic and Pastoral Review* 91 (June 1191): 72–77.

Settles, Barbara H. "A Perspective on Tomorrow's Families." In *Handbook of Marriage and the Family,* pp. 3–36, 157–81.

Steinfels, Peter. "Churches Are Caught in Economy's Grip." *The New York Times,* June 20, 1991, Final Ed. Sec. A, p. 1, col. 1.

Sweig, Arnulf. "Krause, Carl C.F." *The Encyclopedia of Philosophy,* vol. 4, p. 363.

Teachman, Jay D., Karen A. Polenko, and John Scanzoni. "Demography of the Family." In *Handbook of Marriage and the Family,* pp. 3–36.

Thiering, Barbara. "The Biblical Source of Qumran Asceticism." *Journal of Biblical Literature* 93 (3 Sept. 1974): 429–44.

Thomson, Judith Jarvis. "A Defense of Abortion." *Philosophy and Public Affairs.* Fall 1971.

Tribe, Laurence H. " 'Natural Law' and the Nominee." *The New York Times,* Monday, July 15, 1992.

Van Eijk, T. H. C. "Marriage and Virginity, Death and Immortality." In Jacques Fontaine and Charles Kannengiesser, eds., *Epektasis: Mélanges patristiques offerts au Cardinal Jean Daniélou,* pp. 209–35. Paris: Beauchesne, 1972.

Vanhoye, Albert, S.J., and Henri Crouzel, S.J. "The Ministry in the Church: Reflections on a Recent Publication." *The Clergy Review* 5, 68 (May 1983): 156–74.

Verkamp, Bernard. "Cultic Purity and the Law of Celibacy." *Review for Religious* 30 (1971): 199–217.

Viviano, Benedict T., O.P. "The Gospel According to St. Matthew." *The New Jerome Biblical Commentary,* pp. 630–74.

Wehr, Demaris. "A Feminist Perspective on Jung's Concept of the Archetype." In Joann Wolski Conn, ed., *Women's Spirituality: Resources for Christian Development,* pp. 158–73. New York: Paulist Press, 1986.

Weissleder, Wolfgang. "Aristotle's Concept of Political Structure and the State." In Ronald Cohen and Elman R. Service, eds., *Origins of the State: The Anthropology of Political Evolution,* pp. 187–203. Philadelphia: Institute for the Study of Human Issues, 1978.

Williams, Bruce, O.P. "Homosexuality: The New Vatican Statement." *Theological Studies* 48 (1987): 259–77.

Winandy, J., O.S.B. "Une curieux *casus pendens:* 1 Corinthians 11:10 et son interpretation." *New Testament Studies* 38 (Oct. 1992): 621–29.

Index

Justice in the Church: Gender and Participation was composed in Sabon by Brevis Press, Bethany, Connecticut; printed on 60-pound Natural Smooth and bound by Braun-Brumfield, Inc., Ann Arbor, Michigan; and designed and produced by Kachergis Book Design, Pittsboro, North Carolina.

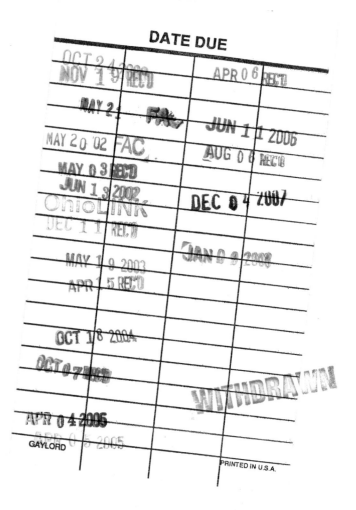